The Big Smallness

This book is the first full-length critical study to explore the rapidly growing cadre of amateur-authored, independently published, and niche market picture books that have been released during the opening decades of the twenty-first century. Emerging from a powerful combination of the ease and affordability of desktop publishing software; the promotional, marketing, and distribution possibilities allowed by the Internet; and the tremendous national divisiveness over contentious socio-political issues, these texts embody a shift in how narratives for young people are being creatively conceived, materially constructed, and socially consumed in the United States. Abate explores how titles such as *My Parents Open Carry* (about gun laws), *It's Just a Plant* (about marijuana policy), and *My Beautiful Mommy* (about the plastic surgery industry) occupy important battle stations in ongoing partisan conflicts, while they are simultaneously changing the landscape of American children's literature. The book demonstrates how texts like *Little Zizi* and *Me Tarzan, You Jane* mark the advent of not simply a new commercial strategy in texts for young readers; they embody a paradigm shift in the way that narratives are being conceived, constructed, and consumed. Niche market picture books can be seen as a telling barometer about public perceptions concerning children and the social construction of childhood, as well as the function of narratives for young readers in the twenty-first century. At the same time, these texts reveal compelling new insights about the complex interaction among American print culture, children's reading practices, and consumer capitalism. Amateur-authored, self-published, and specialty-subject titles reveal the way in which children, childhood, and children's literature are both highly political and heavily politicized in the United States. This book will be of interest to scholars and students in the fields of American studies, children's literature, childhood studies, popular culture, political science, microeconomics, psychology, advertising, book history, education, and gender studies.

Michelle Ann Abate is Associate Professor of Literature for Children and Young Adults at The Ohio State University, USA.

Children's Literature and Culture

For a full list of titles in this series, please visit www.routledge.com.
Jack Zipes, *Founding Series Editor*
Philip Nel, *Current Series Editor*

The Big Smallness

Niche Marketing,
the American Culture Wars,
and the New Children's Literature

Michelle Ann Abate

Routledge
Taylor & Francis Group

NEW YORK AND LONDON

First published 2016
by Routledge
711 Third Avenue, New York, NY 10017

and by Routledge
2 Park Square, Milton Park, Abingdon, Oxon OX14 4RN

Routledge is an imprint of the Taylor & Francis Group, an informa business

Library of Congress Cataloging-in-Publication Data

Names: Abate, Michelle Ann, 1975– author.
Title: The big smallness: niche marketing, the American culture wars,
and the new children's literature / by Michelle Ann Abate.
Description: New York; London: Routledge, 2016. | Series: Children's
literature and culture | Includes bibliographical references and index.
Identifiers: LCCN 2015041945
Subjects: LCSH: Children's literature—Publishing—United States—
History—21st century. | Children's books—United States—History—
21st century. | Children—Books and reading—United States—History—
21st century. | Publishers and publishing—United States—History—
21st century. (2016)
Classification: LCC Z480.C48 A23 2010 | DDC 070.5083—dc23LC
record available at http://lccn.loc.gov/2015041945

ISBN: 978-1-138-95001-6 (hbk)
ISBN: 978-1-315-66887-1 (ebk)

Typeset in Sabon
by codeMantra

Printed and bound in the United States of America by Publishers Graphics,
LLC on sustainably sourced paper.

Contents

Acknowledgments

Seth Godin, in *Small Is the New Big*, made the following observation about the business strategy necessitated by niche products: "The new marketing requires less planning and more interaction, more now and less later" (123). While a great deal of planning certainly went into the pages that follow, so too did much interaction. Accordingly, I'd like to begin by thanking the many people who supported, encouraged, and—when necessary—nudged me. Echoing Seth Godin's observation about niche marketing, their reminders of "more now and less later" helped to keep my work on this project moving forward.

I am very grateful for the intellectual support along with convivial friendship of my colleagues in the Literature for Children and Young Adults Program at The Ohio State University: Patricia Enciso, Mollie Blackburn, Caroline Clark, Linda Parsons, and Barbara Kiefer. A finished book can seem like a monologue, but it is really a dialogue, and I have enjoyed many stimulating conversations with these individuals.

I am equally appreciative of the men and women who comprise my fellow cohort of new faculty members at OSU: Mileidis Gort, Francis Troyan, Tim San Pedro, Sarah Gallo, Youngjoo Yi, Marc Johnson, and Erin Fletcher. Your kindness, your friendship, and your good cheer have made the often-abstract notion of a campus community a wonderful concrete reality.

I also owe a long-overdue thanks to Kate Mertes, who produced the fantastic index that appears in this book along with all of my previous ones. It has been a delight to work with her over the years, and I look forward to a long, continued affiliation.

I would like to extend my thanks to several colleagues who provided invaluable assistance with the project: Francis Troyan, who offered timely and expert input on Chapter 3; Annette Wannamaker, who had many helpful comments that improved Chapter 2; Rhonda Brock-Servais and Karly Marie Grice, whose sharp editorial eyes and equally astute critical comments were tremendous assets to the manuscript; Jodi Pilatowski, the departmental coordinator in Ramseyer Hall, who provided wonderful administrative support; Philip Nel and Elizabeth J. Levine, my excellent editors at Routledge, as well as the anonymous outside readers, for their encouragement and insight; and, finally, the members of both the International Board on Books for Young People (IBBY) and the Children's Literature Association (ChLA), who formed the audience for conference paper versions of some of this material and offered many thought-provoking comments.

I am likewise indebted to Ricardo Cortés, Dr. Michael Salzhauer, and Cinco Puntos Press for allowing me to reproduce images from their picture books in this project. The photograph that appears on the cover to *The Big Smallness* was taken by Yann Chemineau of Florentijn Hofman's art. I am very grateful to both of these individuals for their kind permission to use this material, as well as to Susan Strayer for her skilled and very timely assistance preparing these images for press.

A version of Chapter 2, titled "Plastic Makes Perfect: My Beautiful Mommy, Cosmetic Surgery, and the Medicalization of Motherhood," appeared in *Women's Studies: An Interdisciplinary Journal* (39.7, October/November 2010: 715–46). Likewise, an edition of Chapter 5, "'Learning How to Be the Boy or Girl that You Are': *Me Tarzan, You Jane* the Crusade to 'Cure' Pre-Homosexual Children, and the New Face of the Ex-Gay Movement in the United States," was previously published in the *Journal of the History of Childhood and Youth* (7.3, Fall 2014: 534–55). I would like to thank the editors and publishers of these journals for their kind permission to reprint this material.

Finally, I wish to offer a special thanks to a certain *petit chou*. Your humor, your love, and your generosity—whether in person or in virtual space—brought many delightful respites from the often lonely task of researching and writing. You will forever occupy a special niche in my life.

Introduction

It's a Small World After All: Micro Markets, Specialty Subjects, and Customized Culture

> Big used to matter. ... And then small happened.
> —Seth Godin, *Small Is the New Big* (2006)

In January 2011, coauthors Brian G. Jeffs and Nathan R. Nephew released their picture book, *My Parents Open Carry*. Illustrated by Lorna Bergman, the narrative follows thirteen-year-old Brenna Strong and her parents "as they spend a typical Saturday running errands and having fun together" ("My Parents Open Carry," par. 1). That said, one detail separates this experience from the commonplace: while out in public, Brenna's mother and father each have a handgun in a very visible holster at their hip, a legal practice in the United States known as "open carry."

As the title of *My Parents Open Carry* suggests, the public display of personal firearms for the purpose of self-defense is not simply included in the story; it forms the book's main focus. "The Strongs join a growing number of families that are standing up for their 2nd Amendment rights by open carrying and bringing gun ownership out of the closet and into the mainstream," the Preface explains. Accordingly, the narrative provides a positive portrayal both of the practice of open carrying and of gun ownership as a whole. As the promotional materials for the book explain, *My Parents Open Carry* teaches young readers "about the growing practice of open carry, the 2nd Amendment and the right and responsibility of self-defense" ("My Parents Open Carry"). In this way, Jeffs and Nephew correct what they felt was an oversight in existing literature for young readers. As they have said in numerous articles and interviews: "Before writing this, we looked for pro-gun children's books and couldn't find any" (qtd. in Petri, par. 2).

My Parents Open Carry was published by White Feather Press, a small, independent imprint that specializes, as its website states, in books dedicated to "Reaffirming Faith in God, Family, and Country!" (*White Feather Press*). Both Brian G. Jeffs and Nathan R. Nephew are first-time children's authors with no previous literary training. Indeed, the opening line to Jeffs's author profile page says that he is a "senior geologist" for the state of Michigan ("Brian Jeffs," par. 1). Meanwhile, Nephew identifies himself as a "software developer" ("About the Author: Nathan Nephew," par. 1). While the two coauthors did not have any experience writing for children, they did have a background in gun advocacy. As their biographies explain, Jeffs and Nephew are founding members of Michigan Open Carry, "a non-profit organization that promotes the open carry of a handgun and works to protect all firearm rights" ("Brian Jeffs," par. 1). Moreover, prior to penning *My Parents Open Carry*, the two men cohosted "a Gun Rights show called 'Saturday Afternoon Shootout' for the internet [*sic*] network Flint Talk Radio" ("A Conversation").

For the first few years of its release, *My Parents Open Carry* was for sale only through its publisher. But, in early 2014, the text became available through the massive online retailer Amazon.com (Schmidt, par. 4). This new commercial platform marked a significant expansion to the book's commercial accessibility and, as a result, to its public visibility. In August of that year, in fact, *My Parents Open Carry* caught the attention of the HBO cable program *Real Time with Bill Maher* which did a story about it. Given both the controversial nature of national gun laws and the fact that this issue was being discussed in a picture book for young readers, the segment received widespread attention: it was replayed by millions of people on YouTube, was discussed by commentators on news broadcasts, and was the subject of posts on social media sites like Twitter and Facebook. In the days and weeks that followed, numerous other print, television, radio, and Internet venues did profiles of *My Parents Open Carry*. This coverage emanated from both sides of the political aisle, with right-leaning entities like Bill O'Reilly, Glenn Beck, and Fox News praising the book for "standing up for the Second Amendment" (McKay, par. 1), and left-leaning ones such as *The Huffington Post*, *The Daily Kos*, and *The Daily Show with Jon Stewart* lamenting it for romanticizing guns and teaching kids to regard everyone they encounter as a potential threat.

Whether individuals were celebrating or condemning *My Parents Open Carry*, they were buying a copy. Throughout late summer and into fall 2014, the picture book experienced "a massive boost in sales" (McKay, par. 1). As Skip Coryell, founder of White Feather Press, revealed, prior to being featured on *Real Time with Bill Maher*, "Sales were very, very slow—we sold about one book per month" (qtd. in McKay, par. 3). By contrast, "over the six-day period since Bill [Maher] talked about it on his show, we have sold over 2,000 copies, and it's still selling very well" (qtd. in McKay, par. 3). Within weeks, CNN called *My Parents Open Carry* nothing less than "a sensation" (Schmidt).

While the specific subject matter of *My Parents Open Carry* was unique, this project reveals how the general type of text was not. *The Big Smallness* discusses how the release of an amateur-authored, independently published picture book about a highly specialized subject for an equally specialized audience was far from an anomaly by 2014. On the contrary, it was part of a growing trend in the United States. Emerging from a powerful combination of the ease and affordability of desktop publishing software; the promotional, marketing, and distribution possibilities made possible by the Internet; and the tremendous national divisiveness over contentious socio-political issues, narratives of this nature had been increasing in both number and notoriety. *My Parents Open Carry* was a product of these elements—and it was not alone. Whereas books, television shows, and news broadcasts had long sought to engage with broadly universal issues in order to appeal to the largest possible audience, a significant number now targeted a highly specific subject for an equally specialized demographic. As Patrick Goldstein asserted in a 2006 article from the *Los Angeles Times*: "We are now a nation of niches" (par. 7). He went on to explain: "There are still blockbuster movies, hit TV shows, and top-selling CDs, but fewer events that capture the communal pop culture spirit. The action is elsewhere, with the country watching cable shows or reading blogs that play to a specific audience" (Goldstein, par. 7).

Both during the time when Goldstein's article was first published and especially in the years since, this increasing specialization—or, what I refer to in the pages that follow, "nichification"—has permeated nearly every facet of popular, print, and material culture. Examples range from the steady splintering of subjects on cable television channels (History Channel, Military History Channel, History International Network, etc.), the increasingly minute distinctions between musical genres embodied by satellite radio stations (Classic Hard Rock, Deep Classic Rock, and Adult Album Rock on SIRIUS XM), and the seemingly endless specialty interests represented on the Internet. Nichification has become *de rigueur*.

This book charts the presence of an overlooked but important facet in the ongoing specialization of millennial American life. The chapters that follow examine the rapidly growing and highly influential cadre of niche market picture books that have been released during the opening decades of the twenty-first century. Akin to recent trends in cable television and radio broadcasting, these texts are not trying to appeal to the masses. Instead, reflecting the steady nichification of millennial life, they are about a very specific topic for an equally specific audience. Finally, echoing the fragmentation of the nation along partisan political lines, they address controversial subjects. Ricardo Cortés's *It's Just a Plant* (2005), for instance, questions the criminalization of marijuana. Michael Salzhauer's *My Beautiful Mommy* (2008) spotlights a mother's decision to get plastic surgery. Meanwhile, Paul M. Kramer's *Maggie Goes on a Diet* (2011) addresses the problem of pediatric obesity. By contrast, Janice Barrett Graham's *Me Tarzan, You Jane* (2011) spotlights what has come to be known, both with the conservative Christian and secular scientific communities, as "prehomosexual" children. Finally, Thierry Lenian's *Little Zizi* (2007) targets a child who is dealing with a very specific problem: the narrative tells the story of a preadolescent boy who is bullied by his classmates because he has a small penis.

As even this overview demonstrates, niche market picture books engage with a broad range of socio-cultural topics: silly as well as serious, topical along with timeless, personal, and political. The focus of these narratives on intentionally selective subjects for an equally selective readership, however, has not prevented them from enjoying big sales or, at least, big publicity. Akin to *My Parents Open Carry*, many of these books have received widespread media coverage. For instance, *My Beautiful Mommy* and its author Michael Salzhauer were featured on the nationally syndicated television program, the *TODAY* show. Meanwhile, Ricardo Cortés's *It's Just a Plant* was not only reviewed in newspapers and magazines around the country, but it was also mentioned during Congressional testimony on Capitol Hill. And finally, even before Paul M. Kramer's *Maggie Goes on a Diet* was released, it was the subject of mainstream media attention, from articles in *Time* magazine, *The Washington Post*, and the *Los Angeles Times* to profiles on Fox News, *Good Morning America*, and CNN. While some of this coverage can be attributed to the novelty appeal, along with shock value, of these texts, it also extends far beyond this realm, pointing to changing cultural attitudes and even aesthetic tastes in the new millennium.

Accordingly, this project explores the new big smallness in picture books and the way in which it is remaking children's literature in the United States. Filling a gap in ongoing critical conversations about transformations to "the book" in the twenty-first century, I reveal how Susan Friedmann's observation that there are "riches in niches" also applies to the realm of narratives for young readers. As my discussion in the following pages will demonstrate, texts like *My Beautiful Mommy*, *It's Just a Plant*, and *Little Zizi* mark the advent not simply of a new commercial strategy in texts for young readers; they embody a shift in the way that narratives are being conceived, constructed, and consumed in the United States during the twenty-first century. Both the growing number and the widespread public attention of niche market picture books reveal that the customization of American culture extends to narratives for young readers. Niche market picture books greatly expand the range of topics that are represented in texts for young readers, pushing them in daring and even radical socio-political directions. In so doing, these texts reveal compelling new insights about the complex interaction among American popular culture, the children's publishing industry, and consumer capitalism in the new millennium.

The significance of niche market picture books extends beyond merely economic concerns, however. Both the origins and the impact of these texts are also closely connected to ongoing national debates over a variety of divisive socio-cultural events. Because many of these books engage with controversial cultural topics and offer an equally specialized viewpoint about them, they offer a window onto the contentious nature of the American socio-political climate and a compelling commentary on some of its most polarizing issues. Texts like *It's Just a Plant*, *My Beautiful Mommy*, and *Me Tarzan, You Jane* reveal the way in which children, childhood, and children's literature are highly political as well as heavily politicized in the United States in the twenty-first century. In so doing, these books can be seen as a telling barometer about changing public perceptions concerning children and the social construction of childhood, along with the function or purpose of narratives for young readers. Accordingly, *The Big Smallness* does not look merely at the ascendency of niche marketing nor solely at the impact of the ongoing U.S. culture wars; rather, it examines the synergistic relationship that has emerged between these two entities.

In spite of both the growing commercial presence and rich social implications of niche market picture books, they have not been the subject of any sustained critical interest from a literary, economic, or cultural standpoint. To date, searches for the subject terms "children's literature" and "niche marketing" in major academic databases like the Project Muse, JSTOR, and Modern Language Association International Bibliography yield only a handful of relevant results, such as Anne Lundin's "Little 'Pilgrim's Progress': Literary Horizon's for Children's Literature," Charles Hatfield's "Comic Art, Children's Literature and the New Comics Studies," and Sanjay Sicar's "The Sense of the Nineties: Current Assumptions about Children's Literature." In spite of the many compelling insights contained in these essays, they mention niche marketing briefly and only in passing; none of these essays take this issue as their main focus. Moreover, even articles that embody seeming exceptions to this trend—such as Lissa Paul's "Niche Marketing and the (Shallow) World of Crabtree" or James Russell's "Narnia as a Site of National Struggle: Marketing, Christianity and National Purpose in *The Chronicles of Narnia: The Lion, The Witch and the Wardrobe*"—examine only one isolated fact of niche products and promotions. They do not situate these elements within a larger material, literary, or economic trend.

Discussions about niche market picture books are likewise absent from recent scholarship addressing transformations to the picture book. Teresa Colomer, Bettina Kümmerling-Meibauer, and Cecilia Silva-Díaz's illuminating essay collection *New Directions in Picturebook Research* (2010), for example, addresses a wide array of developments in picture books, including alterations to the genre's role as a means of literacy education, variations on its engagement with both past and present cultural context, innovations in its deployment of storytelling devices, and expansion of possible interpretive strategies used to examine them. In spite of both the range and the diversity of the subjects discussed, the recent growth of narratives about niche issues and for niche audiences is not mentioned.[1]

The new niche phenomenon in books for young people has also not received widespread attention from figures who track trends in publishing. John B. Thompson's fantastic *Merchants of Culture: The Publishing Business in the Twenty-First Century* (2012) touches only briefly on the topic. While his exploration of the millennial publishing landscape in the United States and Great Britain encompasses more than 400 pages, the question of niche audiences, as the index indicates, are analyzed on just a scant 3 pages. When the related issues of "small books" and "small independent publishers" are added to this footprint, several dozen more pages of discussion come into play. However, very little of this analysis addresses the realm of children's publishing.[2]

Even more astounding, the growing public visibility and increasing commercial success of niche market picture books has not been the subject of discussion among American political scientists, even though many of these narratives occupy a clear battle station in the nation's ongoing culture wars. Texts like *It's Just a Plant, My Beautiful Mommy,* and *Me Tarzan, You Jane* are a product of the intensely partisan political climate during the early twenty-first century while they simultaneously help to perpetuate this condition. These narratives reflect the intense divide—between liberals and conservatives, Democrats and Republicans, Christians and secular individuals—over issues like drug control, feminism, and LGBTQ (lesbian, gay, bisexual, transgender, and queer) rights.

Perhaps not surprisingly, when the growth of niche marketing in children's literature has been discussed, it has been in articles, blogs, and essays posted on the Web. Notable among these are Linda Stanek's "Corporate Publishing and the Need for the Niche Publisher" (2011), Sue Bradford Edwards's "Children's Nonfiction: A Niche Worth Pursuing" (2011), and the post "Creating a Book for a Niche" (2011). But, these discussions are brief, typically just a few paragraphs or, at most, a few pages. In addition, most are how-to pieces aimed at authors. They focus on the logistics of creating a niche market text—explaining what one is, the professional benefits of writing one, and some possible topics—rather than examining the larger social, cultural, aesthetic, economic, or political implications of this phenomenon.

This project offers a corrective to this trend. *The Big Smallness* makes a case that 'nichification' is a powerful but largely unexamined force in American children's literature in general and picture books in particular during the twenty-first century. This opening introduction provides an overview of the origins, history, and evolution of the niche mode of production in the United States. I begin by discussing how, during the 1960s and 1970s, a combination of growing dissatisfaction with the generic blandness of mass-produced goods, coupled with the increasing cultural and consumer power of heretofore ignored specialty markets like women, gays and lesbians, and racial and ethnic minorities precipitated a sea change in the way products were made and marketed. Next, I explore how the new publishing and marketing opportunities made possible first by the proliferation of the personal computer and then by the advent of the Internet greatly accelerated this trend. These powerful technological forces worked in tandem with equally potent socio-political ones during this same period, namely, the ascendency of the U.S. culture wars and the increasingly partisan national climate. This environment cultivated while it catered to viewpoints that existed on the margins rather than the center of the American political spectrum; that is, to issues, attitudes, and opinions that were niche. Placing these events in the context of larger socio-economic phenomena like the emergence of post-Fordism and the rise of small batch production, I map the process by which niche marketing was created and quickly conquered.

In each of the chapters that follow, I showcase a different contemporary picture book that is an aesthetic, material, and commercial product of the niche marketing approach and philosophy. In everything from the subject matters that these authors selected and the style in which they presented their material to the publishers who have released their work and the advertising campaigns that they or their editors have used for promotion, these narratives demonstrate how the next "big thing" in U.S. children's literature is smallness. As my discussion will address, this phenomenon is both a byproduct of and a significant force propelling the ongoing atomization of American cultural, social, and political life.

Joel Taxel, in an article discussing the state of books for young readers in the twenty-first century, lamented: "the impact of the business side of children's literature has not been given the sustained and systematic scrutiny it deserves by children's literature scholars and the education community in general" ("Children's" 146). *The Big Smallness* works to close this critical gap by examining one of the most influential recent developments in children's publishing as well as American capitalism. As Taxel notes, by the dawn of the twenty-first century, awareness of an author's racial, cultural, and socio-political circumstance was "no longer [considered] a novelty in discussions of children's literature and culture" ("Children's" 181). This project seeks to make the same point regarding current economic trends, prevailing business models, and extant modes of material production. Drawing on an eclectic mix of literary criticism, microeconomics, American cultural studies, consumer marketing, childhood studies, political science, the history of the book, popular culture, and new media technologies, *The Big Smallness* details how less became more, diminutive became dominant, and specialized became standardized.

The Death of One-Size-Fits-All: Niche Marketing Is Created—and Then Conquers

Given the growth and expansion of niche marketing over the past few decades, this phenomenon seems like a relatively recent development. However, the concept has a long and rich history. As the *Oxford English Dictionary* notes, the term "niche" dates back to the early seventeenth century when it was used to denote a "shallow ornamental recess or hollow set into a wall, usually for the purpose of containing a statue or other decorative object." Over the next 100 years, the word migrated from the decorative arts to the natural sciences. By the dawn of the eighteenth century, niche came to refer to the "hole, lair, etc., of an animal. More generally: a place of retreat or refuge."

Less than a decade later, in the 1730s, the meaning of "niche" shifted once again, this time acquiring the usage that is most common today: "A place or position suited to or intended for the character, capabilities, status, etc., of a person or thing. Freq. in (to find) one's niche: (to find) a comfortable or suitable position in life or employment." To be sure, Doris Barrell and Mark Nash provide an explanation of this concept that encapsulates its modern understanding:

> What exactly is a "niche" market? The dictionary defines niche as "a nook or special corner." When we are referring to people, we see the nook or special corner as a group of people who have something shared in common. This commonality may be a shared culture or nationality, or a matter of age, work experience, or lifestyle. (ix–x)

While the etymology of "niche" extends back several centuries, its application in business is far more recent, emerging during the consumer boom of the mid-twentieth century. As David A. Hounshell has discussed, the Industrial Revolution during the early nineteenth century marked the moment when businesses strove to appeal to the masses (309). Products were no longer custom-made by hand and tailored to fit each consumer's individual needs or unique specifications. On the contrary, they were now mass-produced by machines on assembly lines. As a result, consumers did not purchase different goods; rather, they all bought the same item. The uniformity of the product for the consumer meant ease of production for the manufacturer. Industrialization gave rise to mass production and a "one-size-fits-all" mentality. Advances in communication that allowed businesses to advertise their goods and services widely, along with improvements in transportation, which made it possible to distribute these items faster and to greater distances, fueled this phenomenon (Hounshell 303–8).

The early days of the Ford Motor Company provide an oft-cited example of this philosophy in action. In what has become a well-known comment, in 1909 Henry Ford quipped about his newly released Model T that a customer could "have a car painted any color that he wants so long as it is black" (72). Patrons were offered the exact same vehicle; the goal of mass production was mass consumption. Thus, the Ford Motor Company, akin to that of all big business during this era, did not try to cater to different consumers in different regions who may have different requirements.[3] The more that an item was customized, the smaller the range of individuals to which it would appeal. Instead, the objective was to reach the broadest possible clientele. The larger the base of potential consumers, the greater the sales and, by extension, the greater the earnings. As Seth Godin notes, "Big meant power and profit and growth. Big meant control over supply and control over markets" (*Small* 216). As a result, for generations, big was the golden rule of business, and companies in any field or industry desired nothing else than to grow large and take their goods and services national. In the words of Godin once again, "Big meant economies of scale. (You never hear about 'economies of tiny' do you?)" (*Small* 216).

After generations of operating under this one-size-fits-all mentality, the desirability of mass production for mass consumption began to wane during the 1960s and 1970s. While efforts to appeal to the biggest possible audience may have yielded big profits, it also resulted in a dull sameness: "Companies that are built around mass marketing develop their products accordingly. These companies round out the edges, smooth out the differentiating features, and try to make products that are bland enough to work for the masses" (Godin, *Purple* 66–67). This phenomenon was powerfully evident during the consumer boom that followed the Second World War. As Thomas Frank has written, "It was ... a time of intolerance for difference, for look-alike commuters clad in gray flannel and of identical prefabricated ranch houses in planned suburban Levittowns" (10).

Especially for children who were raised during this era, this culture of consumer conformity became tiresome. When these individuals came of age as shoppers, many of them longed for increased choice. Allison J. Pugh has written that, by the late 1960s, instead of buying items in an effort to "keep up with the Joneses" many Americans now sought out goods that would make them "different from the Joneses": that showcased their specific tastes, unique interests, and overall individuality (107–11). Anthony Bianco, in an article aptly called "The Vanishing Mass Market," explained this shift in the following way: "As levels of affluence rose markedly in the 1970s and 1980s, status was redefined. ... 'From the consumer point of view ... we've had a change from "I want to be normal" to "I want to be special"'" (par. 28). Contradicting nearly 100 years of consumer practice, the formula for success was no longer offering everyone the same exact product. Customers now looked for—and economically rewarded—businesses that provided more individualized goods.

Such shifts in consumer attitudes during the 1960s and 1970s were coupled with equally profound shifts in national demographics. The era of the Vietnam War witnessed the growing visibility of formerly marginalized segments of the population. From the feminist and black Civil Rights Movements to the disability rights and gay and lesbian liberation movements, these efforts shattered the former homogenization—or, at least, the perceived homogenization—of U.S. culture. They demonstrated that, contrary to previous perceptions, Americans were not all the same race, gender, class, physical constitution, or sexual orientation. Rather, they were distinct and unique—with equally distinct and unique needs.

From a business standpoint, these transformations of American social and cultural life translated into economic opportunity. The feminist, black civil rights, disability rights, and gay and lesbian liberation movements created not simply social change but new consumer markets. From single mothers and blended families to the disabled and members of racial and ethnic minority groups, companies discovered whole new pockets of potential profitability. By tailoring their products to one of these new specialized—or niche—groups, corporations could expand their base of operations and sell at least as much as, and maybe even more, than when they tried to target everyone. As business advice authors Robert E. Linneman and John L. Stanton have explained:

> Cutting up the market into small niches often leads to a sum greater than the original market. By splitting up traditional markets into

segments and devising separate marketing strategies for each niche, you will be selling products and services that more closely meet customer needs. Overall, your markets will grow. And since people will pay more for products and services that more closely meet their needs, you'll make more money. (2)

Niche marketing was born. The *Oxford English Dictionary* (*OED*) traces the first use of "niche" in the business world back to the United States in 1963. Although initially conceived as a "position from which an entrepreneur seeks to exploit a shortcoming or an opportunity in an economy, market, etc.," the term quickly came to denote "a specialized market for a product or service" (*OED*). The exact characteristic that constitutes the niche may vary—encompassing everything from such tangible traits as an individual's race, gender, and class to less tangible ones like their personal taste, leisure-time hobbies, or esoteric political opinions—but the end result was the same: a distinct cadre of consumers.

As the twentieth century drew to a close, niche marketing steadily increased. An article that appeared in *Marketing Week* in 1986, for instance, discussed the tremendous new niche opportunities in the consumables industry. The growing number of working mothers, it explained, prompted many companies to recognize the sales opportunities that emerged in the area of "convenience-type foods" (qtd. in "Niche," entry 1, def. 4c, *OED*). Offering prepared meals, ready-made snacks, and heat-and-eat entrees for "the busy mom on the go," these products catered to the needs of this specific market. Moreover, during the economic turndown that permeated the Carter and Reagan eras, these new niches constituted some of the few growth areas. As the Turner Corporation said about the key to its own success during this period: "The search for new and different types of markets was especially important during the recessionary years of the late 1980s and early 1990s" when the U.S. economy slumped ("Company History").

This shift toward increasing specialization in American commercial life dovetailed with a similar shift toward increasing specialization in the nation's socio-political one. In an event that embodied nothing less than a watershed moment in the nation's political history, in 1992, evangelical Christian minster Pat Buchanan delivered the opening speech at the Republican National Convention in Houston. As I have written elsewhere, "His address represented the culmination of the postwar conservative intellectual movement, the powerful influence of evangelical Christians, and the ongoing debates over changing morals" (Abate, *Raising* 17). In an oft-discussed comment, Buchanan announced near the end of the speech: "There is a religious war going on in our country for the soul of America. It is a cultural war, as critical to the kind of nation we will one day be as was the Cold War itself" (par. 37). Far from mere rhetorical grandstanding, these comments would prove prophetic. Throughout the decade, bitter national debates erupted over a variety of social issues, ranging from funding for the National Endowment for the Arts and "efforts to make the canon of Western literature, history and philosophy more diverse by including the voices of women, the working class, and racial and ethnic minority groups" to women's reproductive rights and the growing public visibility as well as political power of the LGBTQ community (Abate, *Raising* 17–18). These subjects quickly came to be known as "wedge issues" for the way that they divided the nation, separating liberal from conservative, secular from religious, Democrat from Republican. Moreover, discussions about these controversial socio-cultural issues in the United States are routinely marked by acrimony, enmity, and even vitriol. Indeed, the lack of respect that each side holds for the other is evident via the titles for some of the most popular and partisan-minded nonfiction books over the past few decades, such as Al Franken's *Rush Limbaugh is a Big Fat Idiot* (1996) and Ann Coulter's *If Democrats Had Any Brains, They'd Be Republicans* (2006). Bill Bishop has discussed how this antipathy has caused Americans to increasingly seek out likeminded intellectual, political, and even geographic communities. Wishing to live, work, and associate only with those who share their beliefs, the culture wars have given rise to what one individual characterized as "the ideological balkanization of America" (qtd. in B. Bishop 4).

The growing nichification of mass media during the late twentieth century and early twenty-first century has been fueled in large part by this phenomenon. Many of the new and more specialized cable shows, radio stations, and news blogs also have a more partisan focus. For example, the massively popular right-leaning cable program *The O'Reilly Factor* first aired in 1996; likewise, its counterpart, the left-leaning *The Daily Show* debuted that same year. Other equally partisan-minded media ventures— ranging from *The Huffington Post* and *The Drudge Report* to *Fox News* and *The Colbert Report*, to name just a few—possess a similar history and formula for success. The fragmented American political climate has given rise to an equally fragmented realm of entertainment media, with individuals increasingly wishing to see, hear, and read material that reflects their specific social, political, cultural, economic, and religious viewpoints. In this way, the culture wars may have signaled the death of civil debate, but they simultaneously gave birth to a vast array of new niches: shows, websites, radio broadcasts, and, of course, books with a specialized socio-political focus. Indeed, beginning in the late 1990s and extending into the opening decades of the twenty-first century, many of the nonfiction books by partisan political commentators such as Ann Coulter, Michael Moore, Sean Hannity and Al Franken were bestsellers. Likewise, some of the most popular cable news shows and radio programs possess a clear political viewpoint, ranging from the aforementioned *The Daily Show* and *The O'Reilly Factor* to *Glenn Beck* and *The Rush Limbaugh Show* (Abate, *Raising* 3, 154, 189).

When these socio-cultural forces fueling the nichification of American life are combined with the economic ones, niche marketing emerges as not simply a shift in the production and advertising of goods, but a whole-sale transformation in U.S. media entertainment, cultural materialism, and consumer capitalism. Specialty products for specialized customers formed part of a new economic system that became known as "post-Fordism" or, sometimes, "fast capitalism." As the name implies, "post-Fordism" refers to the move away from the "one-size fits all" ethos that had dominated Western, industrialized countries since the nineteenth century: "On the level of production, the move from Fordism to post-Fordism involved a shift from the mass production of homogenous goods to small batch customization. That is, economic production was transformed from a basic concern with uniformity and standardization to more flexible and variable manufacture for niche markets" ("Post-Fordism," par. 3).

By the closing years of the twentieth century, niche marketing had become the rule, not the exception. Rather than simply one of the strate-gies that businesses used to reach customers, it embodied *the* strategy—the primary way that everyone did business. As Godin asserts in the opening pages to one of his marketing manuals: "The traditional approaches are now obsolete ... One hundred years of marketing thought are gone. Alter-native approaches aren't a novelty—they are all we've got left" (*Purple* 4). He was not alone in such beliefs. Susan Friedmann, in her own business advice book, commented on this phenomenon from a slightly different per-spective. Rather than focusing on the supply side of it, she spotlighted the demand one, writing: "the consumer hankers after specialization ... They seek out providers of niche products and services" (Friedmann 9). For this reason, instead of thinking of themselves as entrepreneurs, businesses ought to regard themselves as "nichepreneurs" (Friedmann 15).

In a powerful index of the ascendency of the niche marketing model, this approach has even permeated a venue whose business strategy seems anti-thetical to this philosophy: massive online retailers like Amazon and Barnes & Noble. Given the growing trend toward customizing services for select markets, Amazon began tailoring its operations in 1997 with the launch of the first of what would eventually become many personalization features (Mahoney 13). Now, when customers return to Amazon.com, the site not only offers them a personal greeting—"Hello, Michelle Ann Abate"—but it also makes specific recommendations based on their previous purchases and search histories. As financial commentator Leslie Walker said about Jeff Bezos, the founder and CEO of Amazon, who implemented these new features: "He paints a rosy view of electronic retailing, likening it to the days before the Industrial Revolution ushered in mass production and mass merchandising, when all clothes were custom-made and small-town mer-chants knew what their customers liked" (H01). Bezos himself remarked, in comments that reflect a desire for Amazon.com to seem more like a niche boutique instead of a "big-box" store: "If we have 4.5 million customers, we shouldn't have one store ... We should have 4.5 million stores" (qtd. in Walker H01). In so doing, Amazon.com tries to make its big business look small. Susan Friedmann once remarked, "The days of one-size fits all are dead!" (9), and, by the opening decade of the twenty-first century, the veracity of this observation was widely apparent.

New Modes of Production for New Modes of Consumption: The Democratization of Distribution and the Ascendency of the Amateur

The concept of niche marketing long predates the proliferation of the personal home computer and certainly the advent of the Internet. However, these two forms of technology have played an instrumental role in the way that this business model has taken shape—as well as the fact that it has taken hold.

In many ways, niche markets and the World Wide Web were made for each other. The Internet provides an excellent tool for companies to reach specific customers, and vice versa. Through specialty websites, pop-up advertisements, and e-mail listservs, businesses can target the exact consumer who would be interested in their product. In turn, the Internet also allows individuals to find the specific business that offers the merchandise that best fits their needs. Chris Anderson calls this phenomenon "*connecting supply and demand*, introducing consumers to these new and newly available goods. ... This can take the form of anything from Google's wisdom-of-crowds search to iTunes' recommendations, along with word-of-mouth, from blogs to customer reviews" (55; italics in original).

At the same time, the Internet also creates new and emerging niche markets. For nearly any interest or activity that you can imagine, there is a community for it on the Web. From Frisbee golf and fire walking to cupcake decorating and Victorian parlor games, the Internet really does have it all. And if, by some chance event, an individual's interest is not already represented, he or she can create a site about it. In so doing, the Internet is a crucible for new niches. It gives rise to specialty markets that may not have formed otherwise—or, at least, would not have become as sizable. As Simon Pont remarked in *Digital State*, the Web is a space of "accelerating opposites, allowing new collectives to rally and [take] shape ... allowing micro-cliques and atomization to spark and run riot" (4–5).

Of course, the personal computer is more than simply the platform by which individuals can surf the Web; the home PC plays its own important role in what Chris Anderson has called "democratizing the tools of production" (54). Through the software available for home computers, individuals have the ability to create their own visual, audio, and print materials. As Anderson has written, "the personal computer ... has put everything from the printing press to the film and music studios in the hands of anyone" (54). This ability for individuals to generate their own original content, of course, is coupled with their ability to upload, advertise, and sell it worldwide via the Internet. As Anderson has pointed out, "The fact that anyone can make content is only meaningful if others can enjoy it. The PC made everyone a producer or publisher, but it was the Internet that made everyone a distributor" (55). In this way, while the PC has democratized the means of production, the Internet has done the same with distribution. The music industry provides the most vivid example of this transformation. As Anderson documents: "In music, for instance, the number of new albums released grew a phenomenal 36 percent in 2005, to 60,000 titles (up from 44,000 in 2004), largely due to the ease with which artists can now record and release their own music. At the same time, bands uploaded more than 300,000 free tracks to MySpace" (54).

This phenomenon has led to a massive expansion in both the number and the variety of choices available, along with an equally radical shift in the profile of those who produce them. No longer are consumers limited to the items offered by professionals; now, they can also choose from goods created by nonprofessionals: the teenager making music in his parent's basement; the hobbyist photographer offering sales of her prints online; and the film student uploading a rough cut of his latest movie. This development has eroded the formerly firm demarcation between producers and consumers as well as between professionals and amateurs. According to Chris Anderson, "we're starting to shift from being passive consumers to active producers" (63). Gone are the days when individuals were the mere receivers of content; they are now also often providers of it in some way, shape, or form. From selling their handicrafts on Etsy.com and posting their videos on YouTube to printing their own custom-designed t-shirt at CafePress and editing an entry on Wikipedia, they contribute to a commercial environment that was once reserved only for professionals. To be sure, most twenty-first century consumers move seamlessly between venues created by professionals and those generated by amateurs: they may purchase the latest bestselling novel at Barnes & Noble and then also read fan fiction online; they may subscribe to *The New York Times* but likewise follow various political blogs. In so doing, they blur the line or collapse the distinction between trained specialists and leisure-time hobbyists. Consequently, "a once-monolithic industry structure where professionals *produced* and amateurs *consumed* is now a two-way marketplace, where anyone can be in any camp at any time" (C. Anderson 84; italics in original). As John Lankford has said about this phenomenon: "There will always remain a division of labor between professionals and amateurs. But it may be more difficult to tell the two groups apart in the future" (qtd. in C. Anderson 62).

Lankford is not alone in this belief. According to Chris Anderson, "Today, millions of ordinary people have the tools and the role models to become amateur producers. ... Because the means of production have spread so widely and to so many people, the talented and visionary ones, even if they're just a small fraction of the total, are becoming a force to be reckoned with" (65). Blogs form a poignant example:

> So what if 99 percent of blogs will never attract an audience of more
> than a few dozen? The fraction of a percent that *do* emerge with

broader reach still number in the thousands. And collectively, that 1 percent can draw as much traffic as many mainstream media. The typical "viral video" sensation is seen by several million people, something that can only be said for the most popular TV shows.

(C. Anderson 82; italics in original)

For instance, *The Drudge Report*, which is a conservative-minded aggregate news site created by a solitary individual—Matt Drudge—competes for readership with professional and long-established news sources like *The Washington Post* and *The New York Times*. And this is only one example. As Chris Anderson asserts: "Don't be surprised if some of the most creative and influential work in the next few decades comes from this Pro-Am [Professional-Amateurs] class of inspired hobbyists, not from the traditional sources in the commercial world" (65).

Even in instances where the impact of niche items by nonprofessionals remains small, it is not negligible. "The point is simply that the product exists and it's taking audience share. It isn't a creation of the traditional commercial industry, but it competes with it," Chris Anderson asserts (82). Moreover, while some amateur products may lack the polish of professional ones, they have other advantages: "From filmmakers to bloggers, [hobbyist] producers of all sorts ... can afford to take chances. There's no need for permission, a business plan, or even capital" (C. Anderson 78). To be sure, most amateur producers "start ... with few expectations of commercial success" (C. Anderson 78). They create their videos, post their artwork, or maintain their political blog out of a passion for this activity, not a desire for financial remuneration. Moreover, because these amateur producers are not trying to appeal to the masses, they enjoy creative freedoms that are unavailable to their more commercial counterparts. Once again, recent trends in the music industry provide a representative example: "As the audience continues to move away from Top 40 music and blockbusters, the demand is spreading to vast numbers of smaller artists *who speak more authentically to their audience*" (C. Anderson 82; emphasis added). Because niche products are not attempting to please everyone, they are able to present material in ways that their mainstream-oriented counterparts cannot: they can take risks, defy current trends, and generally subvert convention. In so doing, this growing cadre of amateur-generated items embodies a "crucible of creativity, a place where ideas form and grow before evolving into commercial form" (C. Anderson 78).

Technology is instrumental not only in the creation and distribution of niche products, but also in their promotion. As Godin points out: "People are more connected than ever. Not only are we more aware that our friends have friends but we can connect with them faster and more frequently" (*Unleashing* 28). From e-mail and cell phones to Facebook and Twitter, information about what we are reading, watching, or listening to is more publicly visible or spreads more quickly. While word-of-mouth buzz has always been an important component to the success of a book, film, or television show, this phenomenon has become even more important given the changing rhythms of twenty-first century life. "We live in a world where consumers actively resist marketing. So it's imperative to stop marketing *at* people. The idea is to create an environment where consumers will market *to* each other," Godin stresses (*Unleashing* 20; italics in original). These modes of consumer-generated advertisement include traditional forms like talking about the product with their friends but also more recent ways of generating buzz such as posting about it on social media sites like Twitter and Facebook.

These developments have led to the wholesale reconsideration of long-standing conceptions about the consumer marketplace. In the words of Chris Anderson: "Niches operate by different economics than the mainstream" (116). He goes on to explain: "Our culture and economy are increasingly shifting away from a focus on a relatively small number of hits (mainstream products and markets) at the head of the demand curve, and moving toward a huge number of niches in the tail" (C. Anderson 52). Anderson calls this phenomenon "the long tail." The statistics for songs purchased at music-sharing sites like iTunes or the programming downloaded by customers of Netflix provide representative examples: "Hits are great, but niches are emerging as the big new market. ... Apple said that every one of the then 1 million tracks in iTunes had sold at least once (now its inventory is twice that). Netflix reckoned that 95% of its 25,000 DVDs (that's now 55,000) rented at least once a quarter" (C. Anderson 8). Because so many of these new niche products are available via the Internet—where shelf space is unlimited—such trends have only increased in the years that have followed. "More than 99 percent of music albums on the market today are not available at Wal-Mart," which is the largest retail seller of music in the United States (C. Anderson 26). Moreover, in an even more eye-opening statistic:

> the companies for which we have the most complete data—Netflix, Amazon, and Rhapsody—sales of products *not offered* by their bricks-and-mortar competitors amounted to between a quarter and nearly half of total revenues—and that percentage is rising each year. In other words, the *fastest-growing* part of their businesses is sales of products that aren't even available in traditional, physical retail stores at all.
>
> (C. Anderson 24; italics in original)

Such figures indicate that within this new highly specialized commercial environment, "narrowly targeted goods and services can be as economically attractive as mainstream fare" (C. Anderson 52).

The growing popularity of niche products is not only transforming the way in which companies do business, it is also altering the attitudes that consumers hold toward items that were not created by professionals. Previously, as Linda Stanek has discussed, "Those that usurped the powers that be through self-publishing, were looked down upon as 'not good enough,' 'not publishable,' and even 'vain.' In fact the term 'Vanity Press' emerged, suggesting that these were sub-par books. ... Now, all of that has changed" ("Organizations," pars. 3–4).

The democratization of the tools of production and distribution has eroded formerly entrenched views like "amateur equals amateurish," "self-published is a euphemism for bad," and "independent means they couldn't get a deal" (C. Anderson 167). As Daniel Pink has written, "Instead of clearly delineated lines of authority," these new products operate "on radical decentralized and self-organization; [they represent] open source in its purest form" (qtd. in C. Anderson 66). The growing success of niche market narratives has demonstrated that "not having a wide market doesn't mean that there's no market at all, or that the book is not well-written" (Stanek, "Organizations," par. 4). On the contrary, these texts affirm, as Linda Stanek reminds us, that "[n]ot everything has mass appeal" ("Corporate," par. 3).

Taken collectively, the ongoing nichification of the twenty-first century marketplace is nothing short of revolutionary. "For the first time in history," Chris Anderson writes, "hits and niches are on equal economic footing, both just entries in a database called up on demand, both equally worthy of being carried. Suddenly, popularity no longer has a monopoly on profit-ability" (24). Self-published books by hobbyist authors are for sale alongside those from Pulitzer Prize winners; songs by a local garage band are as easy to access as those by artists in the Top 40; and, finally, the downloadable file for an obscure movie by a first-time filmmaker is the same number of mouse-clicks away as the one for the latest Hollywood blockbuster. In this way, "The simple picture of the few hits that mattered and the everything else that didn't is now becoming a confusing mosaic of a million mini-markets and micro-stars" (C. Anderson 5).

N is for Niche: Specialty Subjects, Amateur Authors, and Independent Imprints Arrive in American Picture Books

For generations, children's picture books operated far afield from the philosophy of niche marketing. While these narratives have always focused on a particular topic or theme, they have tended to feature ones that are familiar and even universal. From the process of going to bed in Margaret Wise Brown's *Goodnight Moon* (1947) and the impulse to be mischievous in Beatrix Potter's *The Tale of Peter Rabbit* (1902) to the dangers of dawdling in Janette Sebring Lowrey's *The Poky Little Puppy* (1942) and the delight of imaginative play in Crockett Johnson's *Harold and the Purple Crayon*

(1955), writers of picture books selected subjects to which the vast majority of children could relate.[4]

Titles that are commonly considered classics of the genre offer further affirmation of this feature. Don Freeman's *Corduroy* (1968), for example, examines a child's love for a stuffed animal. Meanwhile, Gertrude Crampton's *Scuffy the Tugboat* (1946) taps into young people's desire to grow up faster, have more freedom, and experience, akin to the title character, "bigger things." Conversely, Dr. Seuss's *The Cat in the Hat* (1957) spotlights the mayhem that often erupts when adults are not around. Finally, H. A. Rey's Curious George series (1942–present) uses the simian title character as a stand-in for children's inquisitiveness, impulsiveness, and penchant for mischief. Ironically, even books that address being different or not fitting in—like Hans Christian Anderson's *The Ugly Duckling* (1843) or Kathryn Jackson's *The Saggy Baggy Elephant* (1947)—have found a mass audience because, as it turns out, such feelings are common.

Moreover, many picture books that have been released over the past few decades and become modern favorites also typify by this trait. Titles like Maurice Sendak's *Where the Wild Things Are* (1963), Judith Viorst's *Alexander and the Terrible, Horrible, No Good, Very Bad Day* (1972), Robert Munsch's *Love You Forever* (1986), and Marcus Pfister's *The Rainbow Fish* (1992) all spotlight common experiences: a child's temper tantrum in Sendak; bad luck and "off" days in Viost; parental love in Munsch; and the importance of sharing in Pfister. Finally, an array of picture books that have attained widespread commercial success in recent years spotlight subjects that have a similarly universal appeal. Mo Willems's *Knuffle Bunny* (2004), for example, chronicles a child's anxiety when a beloved toy is accidentally left behind. Similarly, Ian Falconer's Olivia books follow in the tradition of Dr. Seuss, H. A. Rey, and Maurice Sendak in many ways: they spotlight the adventures of the inquisitive, mischievous, and strong-willed eponymous character. Meanwhile, the wildly popular *Walter, the Farting Dog* (2001) along with *Everyone Poops* (1977 original; 1993 English translation), address similarly shared human experiences, albeit ones that are a tad more personal (and scatological) in nature.

Beginning in the era of the Vietnam War, however, this seemingly firm formula began to change. Fueled in part by civil rights efforts that called attention to long-neglected racial, ethnic, and gender minority groups, and in part by growing societal beliefs that adults ought to be more honest and open with children, narratives began appearing that featured topics not designed for the masses but for a selected audience. During the 1970s and 1980s, for instance, Judith Vigna made a career writing picture books about specialized subjects for specific readers. Her text, *Mommy and Me by Ourselves Again* (1987) addresses the loss that a little girl feels when her mother separates from a longtime boyfriend. Meanwhile, the narrative *I Wish Daddy Didn't Drink So Much* (1978) tackles the difficult subject of parental alcoholism.[5]

The breakout book to the phenomenon that I am discussing appeared in the years directly following Vigna's career. In 1989, Lesléa Newman released *Heather Has Two Mommies* and arguably inaugurated the new niche trend. Published by the specialty imprint Alyson Books, the narrative was the first picture book to address the subject of same-sex parenting. What differentiated *Heather Has Two Mommies* from previous efforts to spotlight a specialized subject was the level of public visibility and commercial success that it enjoyed. Newman's narrative received national media attention, with discussions appearing in newspapers like *The New York Times*, magazines such as *Newsweek*, and commentary pieces on television news shows such as *Larry King Live* on CNN. Not all of this coverage was positive. On the contrary, *Heather Has Two Mommies* was then and remains now on the front lines of the U.S. culture wars and the accompanying battles over LGBTQ rights, same-sex marriage, and so-called American family values. But, the publicity that Newman's picture book received propelled it into the national spotlight. In so doing, it dispelled lingering beliefs that only narratives that appealed to the broadest possible audience could be successful.

Picture books that give voice and visibility to other long-neglected literary themes, overlooked socio-cultural subject matters, and especially formerly marginalized demographic groups have likewise flourished. As Joel Taxel has written, "multicultural literature has become a paradigmatic instance of niche publishing within children's literature" ("Children's" 172). Beginning with the Civil Rights Movement during the 1950s and then accelerating rapidly after the passage of the Elementary and Secondary Education Act in 1965, which provided funds for school and public libraries to purchase reading materials, "industry insiders [came] to understand that 'minorities represent a huge and growing market, waiting to be tapped'" (Taxel, "Children's" 172). As a result, in examples ranging from Ezra Jack Keats' *The Snowy Day* (1962), which was one of the first picture books to feature an African-American child protagonists and to win the Caldecott Medal, to Carolivia Herron's *Nappy Hair* (1997), which spotlighted while it celebrated African-American hair types, these narratives embodied a new niche that was as critically acclaimed as it was commercially successful.[6] In the years since, the market for multicultural books has both expanded and become more specialized. In the words of Taxel once again, initially "multiculturalism meant 'black, pure and simple.' In time, Hispanic was added to Black" ("Children's" 172). By the dawn of the twenty-first century, however, new and increasingly customized combinations emerged. Taxel discusses characters in millennial-era books whose racial and ethnic heritages are "Cuban-Irish-Cherokee and Norwegian-African-Japanese" ("Children's" 172).

This book documents the next phase of this phenomenon. Unlike previous niche texts that spotlighted widely recognized vectors of identity—like race, ethnicity, or sexual orientation—this new crop of narratives encompasses a wide array of personal, political, familial, cultural, biological, and psychological issues. From a picture book offering advice for how to cope with having a small penis to another providing information on marijuana laws, these books take specialty subjects to places that previous niche market texts never dreamed—or even dared—to go. At the same time, and in an equally significant implication, niche market texts represent a splintering of popular conceptions about children and childhood. Narratives like *It's Just a Plant* and *My Beautiful Mommy* challenge formerly univocal notions of "the child" as well as longstanding perceptions that the needs, interests, and difficulties that young people experience are universal. Niche market picture books make a case for viewing millennial children in more multifaceted and multivalent ways. They dispel the notion of a monolithic American childhood and make a case for the presence of childhoods, in the plural. In this way, when niche market books are viewed from either side of the political spectrum, they represent the avant-garde of socio-cultural trends. Indeed, many subjects that were regarded as niche—race, ethnicity, sexuality, etc.—first began appearing in books being published by independent or, at least, by small presses. Later, however, these topics began to merge with the mainstream. As a result, niche market texts contribute to the current diversity of children's print culture while they can also be seen as a potential bellwether of its future landscape.

As even this brief discussion demonstrates, niche market picture books constitute an important facet of twenty-first century literature for young readers as well as a neglected aspect of postmodern consumerism and the economics of late capitalism. At the same time, these narratives take up a direct battle station in the U.S. culture wars and the ongoing national debates over controversial socio-political issues. Titles like *Maggie Goes on a Diet* and *It's Just a Plant* may be momentary media sensations, but they are part of a much larger social, artistic, and economic trend. While the books profiled in *The Big Smallness* address a diverse array of themes and topics, they are united by a powerful set of shared assumptions about how narratives for young readers may be created, marketed, and sold in the twenty-first century.

By the Book: From Methodology and Organization to Ideology and Theory

While niche marketing has exerted an influence on nearly every format of children's literature, picture books have arguably felt the greatest impact. The reason for this phenomenon is multifold, involving cultural interests, consumer tastes, and millennial publishing trends.

However, one powerful factor is the lingering societal perception that picture books are the least complicated genre of children's literature and therefore something that anyone—even an untrained novice—can create. Nathalie op de Beeck has articulated this assumption:

> Because of its limited written content, numerous illustrations, and liberal use of open or negative space, the picture book looks easy. With

its oversize print and diverting, often caricaturish imagery, it conjures the illusion of simplicity and the expectation of entertainment. Any semiliterate reader can skim a picture book's pages in a matter of moments, then recall the text's plot and give an opinion. (x)

This same attitude holds true for composing one. A number of websites that encourage aspiring authors to try their hand in the children's literature market make this claim. One how-to page, for example, matter-of-factly informs its audience: "Kids books and illustrated books are probably the easiest to create" ("Exploit"). It goes on to cite a variety of reasons for this condition, including "They don't need much research to get started" ("Exploit"). As a result, the site goes on to proclaim in large font further down on the page: "Anyone Can Create a Picture Book" ("Exploit").

Of course, as a bevy of past and present writers, reviewers, and scholars of children's literature have asserted, the reality of creating a picture book is far more complicated. As op de Beeck explains, the genre is predicated on the complex interaction of written and visual codes:

> The picture book is a constellation of textual and peritextual elements that carries a thick concentration of meaning, not exclusively related to plot, words, images, sequence, or materiality. Strict attention to written story, or even visual-verbal expression, fails to register the effects of the text's size, shape, and media—not to mention its referent, given that the child is both subject and object of the modern picture book. (xi)

For these reasons, composing an aesthetically inviting, intellectually stimulating, and psychologically engaging picture book is exceedingly difficult. In what has become an oft-repeated anecdote, Caldecott Award-winning author and illustrator Maurice Sendak made the following confession about his own experience working in this genre: "For me, it is a damned difficult thing to do, very much like a complicated poetic form that requires absolute concentration and control. You have to be on top of the situation all the time to finally achieve something that effortless" (186).

My discussion in the chapters that follow remains alert to this condition, even if all of the books that I am profiling do not. While each of the niche market narratives featured in *The Big Smallness* draw on innovative modes of production and marketing, this condition does not always mean that they employ equally pioneering aesthetic, literary, or creative principles. Akin to the larger corpus of picture books, the narratives exhibit a wide array of production values in areas ranging from the originality of their plots and the artistry of their illustrations to the quality of their writing and the nature of the interaction between their words and images. In so doing, these books demonstrate niche modes of production both at their groundbreaking best and at their contrived worst. As I address in the chapters that follow, some of these narratives challenge longstanding conceptions about how we commonly conceive of young people and the books intended for them, framing these entities as more sophisticated, more nuanced, and more capable of engagement with complex issues. Meanwhile, others affirm existing paradigms by trafficking in stereotypical conceptions of children as naïve, childhood as a time of innocence, and children's literature as simplistic.

In keeping with the nature of niches, *The Big Smallness* is itself equally and even appropriately specialized. Rather than attempting to address a wide variety of custom-audience narratives for young people, I spotlight a specific type. First, and perhaps most surprising, I am interested in texts that exist in print. Over the past decade, much attention has been given to the growing niche of narrative-based children's media, such as electronic books for devices like Kindles, interactive texts that can be downloaded onto personal computers, and storytelling apps that are available for smartphones or iPads. As an article that appeared in *The Washington Post* in 2010 flatly announced in its title: "Building Apps for Children [Is] a Profitable Niche" (Shinn). In what has become an oft-repeated—not to mention eye-popping—statistic, file downloads that offer educational, entertaining, or storytelling content for young people increased by more than 400% in 2011 (Harrop, par. 1).[7] For this reason, numerous newspapers, magazines, trade papers, and blogs discuss this rich and dynamic new niche in children's publishing. Indeed, even a quick search using a nonspecialty site like Google reveals that this issue is the subject of widespread attention by librarians, teachers, authors, journalists, publishers, and literary critics.

This project spotlights an equally important, but comparatively neglected, area in discussions about the future of the book in the twenty-first century. As the chapters that follow reveal, transformations in children's publishing are not limited merely to the advent of electronic texts and the rise of interactive storytelling media. They are also occurring in the realm of traditional printed texts. In the words of John B. Thompson: "the book has proven to be a most satisfying and resilient cultural form" (408–9). This project documents another previously overlooked facet to the ongoing cultural evolution and material agility of the printed text.

Given the synergy that I see between the increasing specialization of the American commercial market and the increasingly fragmented U.S. sociopolitical climate, I am also interested in niche market books that engage with controversial cultural issues. At this point in the history of children's literature criticism, it has become commonplace to acknowledge the inherently political nature of books for young readers. As Robert D. Sutherland aptly observed back in 1985 in one of the first essays to address this subject, "most of what children read is filled with ideology, whatever the source, purpose or mode of expression, whether consciously promulgated by the author or not" (157). For this reason, in fact, he characterized all books for young readers as "hidden persuaders" (143). Numerous subsequent critics have expanded on this observation. John Stephens's *Language and Ideology in Children's Fiction* (1992) noted: "the discourses of children's fiction are pervaded by ideological presuppositions, sometimes obtrusively and sometimes invisibly" (1–2). Finally and more recently, Julia Mickenberg and Philip Nel summarized many of these previous assertions via their remark: "All literary expressions inevitably embody an author's political sensibility" ("Introduction: What's Left?" 352). For this reason, they went on to contend, "The useful question is not whether children's literature *should* be political, but rather how children's literature should engage with political issues because, after all, children cannot be separated from growing up in the world" ("Introduction: What's Left?" 352).

The books that I examine in the chapters that follow are acutely aware of this condition. Instead of merely consigning themselves to being the inherently political products of inherently political authors working in inherently political time periods, narratives like *It's Just a Plant* and *Me Tarzan, You Jane* have chosen to directly engage with politically charged subject matter. In so doing, these books invite us to consider children's literature—along with the young people for whom these books are intended—as not merely intrinsically political but highly politicized. As Henry Jenkins remarked, the "dominant conception of childhood innocence presumes that children exist in a space beyond, above, outside the political" (2). Yet, as he goes on to point out:

> Every major political and social dispute of the twentieth century has been fought on the backs of our children, from the economic reforms of the Progressive Era (which sought to protect immigrant children from the sweatshop owners) and the social readjustments of civil rights era (which often circulated around the images of black and white children playing together) to contemporary anxieties about the digital revolution (which often depict the wide-eyed child as subject to the corruptions of cybersex and porn websites). (Jenkins 2)

For this reason, Jenkins continues, "Far from noncombatants whom we seek to protect from the contamination posed by adult knowledge, children form the very basis on which we fight over the nature and values of our society, and over our hopes and fears for the future" (2).

The niche market picture books discussed in *The Big Smallness* make vivid the continued veracity of this claim. While each of these narratives purports to break a silence in literature for young readers about a specialty subject—the legalization of marijuana, the ethics of plastic surgery, etc.—they join a large and already existing chorus of voices engaging in another conversation: the American culture wars. Viewing texts like *It's Just a Plant* or *Me Tarzan, You Jane* from this perspective adds another dimension to the cultural work that these books are performing, while it simultaneous quells the temptation to dismiss these narratives as mere comedic parodies, faddish novelties, or even outright jokes. These texts are potent sites of contemporaneous debate about contentious socio-political issues and, as such, they embody rich artifacts about a particular historical moment. Consequently, *The Big Smallness* can be seen as a continuation of the work that I did in one of my previous books, *Raising Your Kids Right: Children's Literature and American Political Conservatism* (2010). While the texts profiled in this project do not all present conservative social views nor are they all aligned with left-leaning ideology, they engage with topics that are equal-parts political and politicizing. Indeed, it is precisely this wide range of socio-political perspectives—from the progressive politics of *It's Just a Plant* to the reactionary position of *Me Tarzan, You Jane*—that gives these books their ideological as well as material import. Niche market books are not the product of one isolated movement, faction, or group; they embody a powerful point of collection for an array of millennial American social, political, and economic developments.

The engagement of niche market picture books with the American culture wars does more than simply situate these texts within a broader socio-cultural context; it also complicates our understanding of their intended aim and alleged readership. While all of these narratives were ostensibly created for young people who are grappling with a unique social challenge or struggling with a specific personal problem, the real audience with which many of these books engage is adults. In examples ranging from the choices that adults make that they then need to explain to their children (like smoking marijuana or getting plastic surgery) to the problems that adults believe children possess (such as exhibiting pro-to-queer behavior), these books can be seen as arising from and appealing to adult needs and desires at least as much as those of young people. Far from a new phenomenon that is specific to niche market picture books, this tendency has a longstanding presence in narratives for young readers. Jacqueline Rose, in a now-classic book, famously asserted that there is an "impossibility" to children's literature. In spite of the longstanding belief that a book for young people "represents the child, speaks to and for children, addresses them as a group which is knowable and exists for the book, much as the book (so the claim runs) exists for them," this claim "is a fraud" (Rose 1). Narratives for young people can more accurately be seen as serving adult needs, goals, and purposes. "Children's fiction is impossible," Rose contends, "not in the sense that it cannot be written (that would be nonsense), but in that it hangs on an impossibility, one which it rarely ventures to speak. ... Children's fiction sets up a world in which the adult comes first (author, maker, giver) and the child comes after (reader, product, receiver)" (1–2).

More than three decades later, Perry Nodelman echoed while he expanded on this observation: "The issue here is not what children do actually like or do need. It is how adult perceptions of what children like or need shape the literature that adults provide for children" (*Hidden* 188). For Nodelman, like for Rose, children's literature is a construction that arises from adult conceptions about children and childhood. As a result, books for young readers say far more about adult beliefs regarding children's literary tastes, cultural interests, and personal needs—either what adults believe they are or what they think these elements should be—than those of any actual children. Consequently, in his book by the same name, Nodelman discusses "the hidden adult" lurking in the background of all narratives for young readers. Rather than seeing this adult-centric facet of the text obfuscating the one intended for children, he frames the two as existing in tandem and offering differing and often even competing messages, morals, and information. As Nodelman asserts: "The simple text implies an unspoken and more complex repertoire that amounts to a second, hidden text—what I call a 'shadow text'" (8).

The arguments by Nodelman and Rose about the adult presence that permeates all narratives for young readers are arguably even more apparent when considering picture books. As Maria Nikolajeva and Carole Scott point out, "picturebooks provide a special occasion for a collaborative relationship between children and adults" (261). Because these narratives are often read together by children and adults—be it in the form of a parent reading aloud to a child before bedtime or a teacher sharing a book with the students in her classroom—they provide particularly rich and compelling examples of the role that adults play in the construction, selection, and dissemination of children's literature.

The Big Smallness, given its focus on picture books coupled with the fact that these texts all spotlight politically charged subject matter, remains particularly mindful of the influence that adults have over children's literature. As my discussion in the following chapters will demonstrate, even though all of these narratives present themselves as texts that a child would *want* to read and even *needs* to read, they were largely created in response to—and, consequently, largely minister to—adult agendas, interests, and anxieties.[8] Moreover, the appeal that niche market picture books have for adults places them in dialogue with the phenomenon of "crossover" children's literature that Sandra L. Beckett has recently discussed. As she explains in *Crossover Picturebooks: A Genre for All Ages*, these texts "cross from child to adult or adult to child audiences" (Beckett 1). While J. K. Rowling's *Harry Potter* series embodies perhaps the most well-known example of crossover fiction, picture books constitute "an important and largely unexplored cultural phenomenon" (Beckett 1). In the words of Beckett: "The almost complete lack of attention paid to picturebooks within the discussion of crossover literature in most countries is particularly surprising since, more than any other genre, they can genuinely be books for all ages" (1). In this way, *The Big Smallness* gives much-needed critical attention to a growing subgenre within American children's literature—the niche market picture book— while it also helps to correct the widespread critical neglect of narratives that appeal to both adult and child audiences.

One final remark about methodology: the niche market picture books profiled in the subsequent chapters are equal-parts illuminating and emblematic examples of this growing genre. However, they do not embody a comprehensive survey of them. While I selected these texts as a telling cross-section, there are many additional titles that participate in this phenomenon. Of course, *My Parents Open Carry*—which received widespread media attention as I was finishing this project and with which I began my discussion—belongs in this category. So, too, does Stephanie Messenger's *Melanie's Marvelous Measles* (2012), which is geared for families who subscribe to the anti-vaccination movement and which also spent some time in the national spotlight as I was completing this manuscript. Meanwhile, Phil Padwe's *Mommy Has a Tattoo* (2006), which targets the growing number of parents who have some form of body adornment and the fact that some children can find tattoos and piercings frightening, embodies another niche market picture book. Padwe's text was so popular when it was initially released that it sparked a sequel, *Daddy Has a Tattoo* (2012). Similarly, Carlton Mellick III's *The Faggiest Vampire: A Children's Story* (2008) could also have been profiled in these pages. Issued by a new specialty imprint dedicated to offbeat books for young readers, the narrative brings a camp sensibility and cult fiction style to children's literature. Finally, and perhaps most famously of all, is Adam Mansbach's *Go the F**k to Sleep* (2011). Geared to an adult audience and addressing the frustration that many parents experience trying to get their young children to go to bed, this picture book points to the possible limit of both specialty subjects and the generic boundaries of children's literature. Mansbach's funny, irreverent, and profanity-laced text became not merely a media sensation but a national bestseller.

As even this brief survey suggests, by the start of the second decade of the twenty-first century, a new picture book written by a first-time children's author, issued by a small independent press, addressing a contentious topic, intended for an equally specialized audience, and receiving national coverage appeared with increasing frequency in the United States. Indeed, Robert Beveridge, in his customer review of *My Beautiful Mommy* on Amazon, commented: "It seems that every couple of months there's another hugely controversial children's book coming down the pike" (par. 1). The regularity of these episodes, along with the volume of attention that they generate, attests to the material growth, cultural power, and political significance of niche market narratives.

Chapter 1 examines Ricardo Cortés's *It's Just a Plant* (2005). As the subtitle of the narrative—"A Children's Story about Marijuana"—indicates, the book is designed for a particular subset of parents: those who smoke cannabis occasionally and wish to discuss this decision with their children. Breaking from previous assessments of Cortés's book, I argue that *It's Just a Plant* is controversial not merely because it calls into question the legalization of marijuana. Rather, the tumult surrounding the narrative also emanates from a second equally powerful, but as-yet unspoken, source: its advocacy for child agency. In stark contrast to the steadfast prohibition against marijuana use, *It's Just a Plant* makes a case that individuals—including children—have the right to investigate, learn, and decide about this issue for themselves. While *It's Just a Plant* does not condone marijuana use among youngsters, it also does not condemn it among adults. Even more radically, *It's Just a Plant* urges young people who disagree with current public policy about cannabis to work toward social change. For all of the lip service paid in the United States to empowering children, valuing their opinions, and encouraging their ambitions, it is ultimately this message about child activism and even youth civil disobedience that makes Cortés's book threatening, at least as much as its focus on marijuana—and perhaps even more so.

Chapter 2 spotlights *My Beautiful Mommy* (2008). Written by board-certified plastic surgeon Michael Salzhauer and illustrated by Victor Guiza, the narrative is billed as the first picture book to address the subject of cosmetic surgery. While Salzhauer presents his text as an altruistic one designed to fill an overlooked but important need, my discussion makes the case that *My Beautiful Mommy* is as at least as much of an advertising campaign intended to promote the cosmetic surgery industry as a children's book designed to educate and enlighten. That said, the problematic messages contained in *My Beautiful Mommy* can be seen as more than merely the unsurprising product of Salzhauer's status as a plastic surgeon. The perspective that the narrative offers is also heavily influenced by a second, less-visible but arguably even more powerful force: the author's conceptions of children and childhood. Salzhauer's desire to inform young people about the experience of cosmetic surgery is overshadowed by his competing and even stronger belief that young people ought to be shielded from upsetting information, unpleasant events, and unsavory details. As a result, while *My Beautiful Mommy* offers an explicit commentary on Western standards of female beauty, it also embeds another revealing message: the impossibility or, at least, incompatibility of writing about a daring new subject for children while still maintaining traditional and highly romanticized views about them.

Chapter 3 concerns the 2008 picture book *Little Zizi*, by French author-illustrator Thierry Lenain. Translated by Daniel Zolinsky and published by the independent imprint Cinco Punto Press, the narrative offers a very specialized take on the now-ubiquitous issue of peer harassment. *Little Zizi* spotlights a prepubescent boy who is being ridiculed by his classmates for having a small penis. Akin to all of the other specialty texts presented in this project, however, *Little Zizi* has significance that extends far beyond either its specific subject or its accompanying target audience. The picture book calls attention to an especially pernicious form of peer harassment, what is known as sexual bullying. Encompassing behaviors ranging from snapping a girl's bra strap or calling her a slut to labeling a boy a faggot or forcing a classmate to engage in unwanted erotic activity, sexual bullying is one of the most hurtful types of schoolyard harassment. Through its presentation of a preadolescent protagonist being teased by his classmates for having a small penis, *Little Zizi* gives voice and visibility to a serious but widely ignored topic: the sexualization of boys. While young girls are commonly seen as the targets of socio-culture pressures to act, dress, and view themselves in highly eroticized ways, the narrative demonstrates that such pressures, along with personal problems and bodily anxieties that they produce, are also present among their male peers. Furthermore, this message disrupts the seemingly singular focus in *Little Zizi* on heterosexual procreation and instead opens up the book to explorations of male homoeroticism and the nonheteronormative child.

Chapter 4 spotlights Paul M. Kramer's *Maggie Goes on a Diet* (2011). As many previous discussions have articulated, the picture book fails miserably at presenting a positive portrait of pediatric health. However, my discussion makes a case that it succeeds in accomplishing another and far more elusive task in the realm of narratives for young readers: the presentation of a wholly autonomous child character. Kramer's protagonist has the authority to make decisions about her life as well as the agency to implement them. The shortfalls in *Maggie* are the result of the adult author's failings—his naivety, lack of previous knowledge about the subject, and failure to do adequate research—rather than those of the youthful protagonist. In so doing, the picture book inverts conventional distinctions between adult and child, especially with regard to their social subject position and power relation. Children are routinely relegated to a subjugated status because they are seen as lacking important knowledge, wisdom, and experience. In *Maggie*, though, these traits are ultimately, if unintentionally, ascribed to adults. Previous criticisms of Kramer's picture book has lamented how his young protagonist was unable to escape the cult of thinness; but, in their singular focus on this issue, they have overlooked how she was able to elude an arguably even more powerful cultural force: adult control. Maggie may not be a role model for pediatric nutrition, but my chapter argues that she is a daring new type of unfettered child protagonist.

Chapter 5 spotlights Janice Barrett Graham's picture book *Me Tarzan, You Jane* (2011). Illustrated by Andrew S. Graham and Lili Ribeira, the text uses the central characters from Edgar Rice Burroughs's well-known narrative about the King of the Jungle to offer a Christian-based critique of nonheteronormative gender and sexuality identities. During this process, *Me Tarzan, You Jane* provides a vivid illustration of how the ex-gay movement in the United States is reinventing itself as what might be called the pre-gay movement—or, perhaps more accurately, the *ex-pre-gay* movement. As it has become increasingly untenable to claim that same-sex desires in adults can be eradicated, individuals who remain committed to combating homosexuality have turned their attention to a new and ostensibly more efficacious cause: preventing its emergence in the first place through early intervention with young children who exhibit gender nonconformity. The confidence with which Graham's narrative claims that behaviors that are predictive of homosexuality can be both easily identified and quickly eliminated re-energizes the longstanding efforts by the ex-gay movement to medicalize homosexuality while they also serve to pathologize nonconformist children and unconventional childhoods. Finally, given the book's use of characters, scenes, and settings from Edgar Rice Burroughs's politically problematic novel about a white man raised in the jungle by apes, coupled with Graham's repeated framing of same-sex attraction as "wild" and "uncivilized" behavior, *Me Tarzan, You Jane* reveals how the anti-gay rhetoric and even rationale are heavily imbricated with other discourses of intolerance, namely racism, white Western imperialism, and xenophobia.

Finally, the Epilogue speculates about not simply the literary place and socio-political impact of niche market picture books as the twenty-first century progresses, but their economic significance. As narratives that exist outside of conventional corporate power structures—and, thus, their means of material, economic, and especially ideological control—these texts embody an important alternative to the highly commercialized, heavily commoditized, and increasingly intellectually vapid books released by mainstream, corporate-owned publishers. In contrast to these narratives that have media and merchandising tie-ins, niche market picture books are not part of a synergistic, multiplatform product campaign that is designed to further a licensed brand. Instead, texts like *It's Just a Plant* and *My Beautiful Mommy* embody important venues for the expression of unconventional and often unpopular ideas. That said, framing niche market picture books as a salvific counterpoint to the increasing influence of big business on children's literature has the potential to be not merely overly hopeful but also somewhat naïve. After all, the first principle of Western capitalism is identifying what consumers want (or, in some cases, telling consumers what they want) and then selling that item to them—a task that niche market products arguably do even more effectively than mass-produced ones. Creating a niche is creating a new base of consumers, either by attending to an underserved existing market or by engendering an entirely new consumer category. Regardless of the specific pathway followed, the niche market model can be seen not so much as circumventing the capitalistic process but returning to its starting point.[9] Accordingly, the Epilogue will explore the way in which niche market picture books embody both change and continuity in their expression of artistic freedom, their articulation of iconoclastic ideology, and their negotiation of consumer capitalism.

In *Purple Cow: Transform Your Business by Being Remarkable*, Seth Godin reiterated longstanding axioms for American business: "Playing it safe. Following the rules. Those seem like the best ways to avoid failure" (55). In the economic climate of the twenty-first century, however, these guidelines no longer apply. In the words of Godin: "In a crowded marketplace, fitting in is failing. In a busy marketplace, not standing out is the same as being invisible" (*Purple* 56).

While the niche market picture books featured in *The Big Smallness* spotlight disparate subject matters, they are united by their shared awareness of this maxim. As Diane Carver Sekeres has written, in 2009 alone, "30,000 new titles and editions a year for juveniles [were] produced" (401). Within this climate of superabundance, books for young readers need to do something notable to distinguish themselves. For better or worse, titles like *My Beautiful Mommy* and *Maggie Goes on a Diet* do just that. As Susan Friedmann has written, the key to finding "riches in niches" is "a belief in taking risks and moving outside the security of the pack" (10). Whatever else these narratives may strive to accomplish, taking a risk is certainly one of them. *The Big Smallness* meets these texts where they are, exploring the ways in which niche market picture books engage with controversial subject matter, the U.S. culture wars, and, ultimately, the children's literary landscape.

Notes

1. A similar observation could be made about discussions concerning the innovations to picture books that have been precipitated by postmodernism. Lawrence R. Sipe and Sylvia Pantaleo in their book *Postmodern Picturebooks: Play, Parody and Self-Referentiality* (2008) have discussed how elements like playfulness, pastiche, and parody, along with intertextuality, nonlinear chronology, and indeterminancy, have dramatically transformed illustrated narratives for young readers (1–8). However, the ethos of niche marketing, which is so closely connected to the postmodern traits of atomization, fragmentation, and rejection of universality, is not among them. Likewise, Eliza Dresang has demonstrated the "radical change" that has arisen within children's literature from the "interactivity, connectivity, and access" of the digital age (41). Once again though, niche marketing—a concept that is thoroughly enmeshed with the rise of new media and expansion of digital technologies—is not included.

2. Joel Taxel's essay "The Economics of Children's Book Publishing in the 21st Century" (2011) offers one corrective to this problem by spotlighting the juvenile book industry. However, his engagement with amateur authored, small press, niche audience books is not sustained: it appears in his consideration at a few points, but it is certainly not the primary or even secondary focus. Instead, the bulk of his essay spotlights events occurring within mainstream, corporate-owned children's publishing houses.

3. That said, as Lindsay Brooke and others have documented, subsequent owners of the Model T did customize and even personalize their vehicles in a variety of ways: from modifying the engines to altering the appearance of the car by changing the lights, seats, and running boards. Moreover, the Ford Motor Company, along with a number of third-party manufacturers, also sold supplemental "styling kits" (Brooke 110). These kits permitted owners to make a variety of both aesthetic and utilitarian changes, such as converting the vehicle into a tractor or making it into a snow-ready half-track (Brooke 119). Nonetheless, these options existed only as after-market modifications; they were not offered as showroom versions of the Model T.

4. These comments ought not to imply that books targeting more specific subjects for a more selected readership did not exist during this period. For example, Julia K. Mickenberg and Phillip Nel's *Tales for Little Rebels: A Collection of Radical Children's Literature* (2010) reprints a wide variety of narratives written and released during the early twentieth-century that contain socialist and/or communist perspectives and are intended for a readership of politically

like-minded parents and their children. That said, none of these texts attained the mainstream success or public popularity that the niche market picture books that I am profiling in this project enjoy. Instead, titles like "ABC for Martin" (1935), which offered juvenile readers a proletariat spin on the alphabet book—"A stands for Armaments—war-mongerers' pride; B is for Bolshie, the thorn in their side" (qtd. in Mickenberg and Nel, *Tales* 20)—remained on the margins of American society, confined largely to the socio-political community that these books were addressing.

5. Along these same therapeutic lines, in 1990, Doris Sanford released *Don't Make Me Go Back, Mommy: A Child's Book about Satanic Ritual Abuse*. The narrative appeared in response to widespread media coverage—and growing national panic—about an alleged epidemic of cult-related satanic abuse of children, especially at preschools and day care centers. As the commentary about the book by the author indicates, *Don't Make Me Go Back, Mommy* was both based on the clinical treatment of victimized children and primarily intended for use by other therapists: "The words of the text and the objects and situations illustrated are based on months of intensive research into the nature and practice of satanic ritual abuse. Any child who has been ritually abused will recognize the validity of this story" (qtd. in "'Don't Make Me'").

6. Of course, narratives written by, about, and for African American children date back much earlier and have a rich and lengthy history. In 1922, for example, W. E. B. Du Bois launched *The Brownies' Book*, which was the nation's "first major African American children's magazine" (Smith, par. 2). For more on the history of black children's literature in the United States, see Rudine Sims Bishop's *Free Within Ourselves: The Development of African American Children's Literature* (Heinemann, 2007), Michelle Martin's *Brown Gold: Milestones of African American Children's Picture Books, 1845–2002* (Routledge, 2004), Katharine Capshaw Smith's *Children's Literature of the Harlem Renaissance* (Indiana University Press, 2004) and, as Katharine Capshaw, her *Civil Rights Childhood: Picturing Liberation in African American Photobooks* (University of Minnesota Press, 2014).

7. That said, more recent sales figures indicate that interest in storytelling apps and ebooks has been declining. See, for example, John Biggs's article "Publisher Revenues Down as EBook Buying Slows," in *TechCrunch* (3 March 2015).

8. I would like to thank an anonymous early reader of this manuscript for calling attention to these implications and pushing my thinking in this direction.

9. Again, I am indebted to an anonymous early reader of this manuscript for calling attention to these implications and pushing my thinking in this direction.

1 The Straight Dope

Ricardo Cortés's *It's Just a Plant*, Marijuana Use, and the Question of Prohibition Politics

From their origins, picture books have been associated with didacticism. From early examples like Heinrich Hoffman's *Struwwelpeter* (1845), which demonstrated the evils that befell children who did not behave, to contemporary classics like Dr. Seuss's *One Fish, Two Fish, Red Fish, Blue Fish* (1960), which offers instruction in both counting and color identification, these narratives routinely seek to educate as much as they strive to entertain.

While picture books have spotlighted an array of informational subjects over the decades, they expanded into a new and far more niche realm in early 2005 with the publication of *It's Just a Plant*. Written and illustrated by Ricardo Cortés, the narrative was, as its subtitle explained, "A Children's Story about Marijuana." The text begins when an elementary-school-aged girl named Jackie discovers her parents smoking cannabis. Reflecting contemporary desires to be more open and honest with children, rather than lying to the young girl about what they are doing, her mother tells her the truth: "This is a 'joint.' It's made of marijuana."[1] Hearing about this substance for the first time, Jackie asks her parents a plethora of questions about it. To help her daughter obtain answers, her mother takes her on a bike ride around town to learn more about the plant: they make stops to talk with a farmer who cultivates cannabis, a doctor who prescribes it for her patients, and a group of young men from the neighborhood who use it recreationally. During this process, Jackie—and, by extension, the book's child readers—learn what marijuana looks like, how it grows, what parts of it are used for different purposes, the effects it has when smoked or eaten, and even the different names by which it is known. "'I call it ganja,' said one of the men … 'And I,' said another,' call it La La.' 'I call it cannabis sativa,' said the third." Of course, another key issue that Cortés's text addresses is marijuana's criminalization. This information comes, appropriately, from a law enforcement officer whom Jackie meets: "'Young lady,' answered the policeman, 'These men were smoking what I call grass. And that is against the law.'"

Akin to all of the other niche market picture books profiled in this project, *It's Just a Plant* was not released by a mainstream press. Instead, the narrative was published by Magic Propaganda Mill, a small, independent imprint that the author-illustrator cofounded with Ramona Cruz and which releases only books that he has written. *It's Just a Plant*, in fact, was the press's first publication. Cortés's decision to focus on cannabis in his picture book was far from an arbitrary choice. Echoing the confluence between niche market modes of production and the American culture wars that I traced in the "Introduction," the narrative was written and released during a time of increased national controversy over marijuana laws. In spite of the more than seventy-year federal ban on growing, possessing, or selling the plant, "Marijuana is the most commonly used illegal drug in the United States" (Gottfried 4). As Christine Van Tuyl has written, "More than 100 million Americans aged twelve or older—or 40.2 percent of the population—have tried marijuana at least once in their lifetimes" ("Foreword" 9). In addition, "More than 3.2 million Americans smoke it on a daily basis" (Van Tuyl, "Foreword" 9; Van Tuyl, "Facts" 111). Furthermore, according to Ed Rosenthal and Steve Kubby, "Over 65 million Americans use it either occasionally or regularly" (ix). Given these statistics, one former judge conceded: "Cannabis has achieved a status similar to that of alcohol in the waning days of Prohibition" (Gerber xvi). In examples ranging from the admissions by prominent public figures such as Newt Gingrich, Al Gore, and Michael Bloomberg that they have used it[2] to the presence of marijuana-themed clothes, stickers, and even water bongs for sale at stores in any local mall, it seems clear that, official legislation aside, "Marijuana is part of American culture" (Rosenthal and Kubby ix).

It's Just a Plant reflects this reality. Rather than pretending that the criminalization of cannabis curtails widespread usage, Cortés's picture book acknowledges the fact that many men and women—including those who have children—smoke it on occasion. In fact, in an interview shortly after the release of his book, the author-illustrator pointed out an eye-opening statistic: "there are over six million parents out there that are smoking marijuana" ("Personal Story"). Cortés wrote his narrative for this niche audience. As he remarks on his website: "Many parents have tried marijuana, millions still use it, and most feel awkward about disclosing such histories (many duck the question) for fear that telling the truth might encourage them to experiment too" ("About the Book," par. 2). As a result, his picture book is geared for this specialty demographic who are facing this exact conundrum. In the words of Cortés again, "*It's Just a Plant* is a book for parents who want to educate their children about the complexities of pot in a thoughtful, fact-oriented manner" ("About the Book," par. 5).

Of course, Cortés was not the first person to broach the subject of marijuana with young people. By 2005, when his text was released, an array of printed and visual materials discussed the subject. These examples included the infamous *Reefer Madness*-style movies of the 1930s, the "Just Say No" campaigns during the 1980s, and the juvenile nonfiction books like *Drug Facts: Marijuana* released in the opening decade of the twenty-first century. That said, *It's Just a Plant* offers a vastly different message about marijuana. As the title of the book suggests, Cortés does not call attention to the widespread use of cannabis in order to condemn it. Protagonist Jackie learns that marijuana is illegal, but this fact is not the final word on the subject. Instead, the book encourages her—and, by extension, its youth audience—to question prohibition politics. Drawing on reasons ranging from the enjoyment that marijuana safely provides to millions of responsible adults to its longtime use as a raw material for making clothes, fuel, medicine, and rope, the picture book challenges the criminalization of cannabis. As the author-illustrator has said about the aim or intent of his text, the "'drug facts' [that] children learn in school can be more frightening than educational blaming pot for everything from teenage pregnancy to terrorism. A child's first awareness of drugs should come from a better source" ("About the Book," par. 4). *It's Just a Plant* serves this precise purpose. The picture book breaks from the longstanding literary treatment of and mainstream messages about marijuana control.

This perspective has caused *It's Just a Plant* to become both famous and infamous. To date, Cortés's text has gone through three editions and been translated into more than a dozen languages ("Marijuana for Kids," par. 5). Although the book is published by a small independent press, it echoes the niche marketing model of distribution by being available for sale at major online booksellers like Amazon and Barnes & Noble; it was also featured, for a period in 2007, "as a kitschy offering at the Urban Outfitters chain" (Garofoli, par. 48). Similarly, recalling the common means by which niche market materials generate buzz and garner publicity, this controversial book about a controversial topic has been a media sensation, with discussions of it appearing in print, radio, television, and especially Internet venues. *It's Just a Plant* has been reviewed in magazines and newspapers across the country, and its author has been profiled in media venues ranging from *The Village Voice* to *The O'Reilly Factor*.[3] Assessments of the book have been as divided as the divisive subject that it addresses. Cortés's narrative has been praised for offering an alternative way to approach an important, but often difficult, subject for parents to discuss with their children. As Martha Rosenbaum, the director of the Drug Policy Alliance, has written: "many parents worry about how much to admit about their own past or present marijuana use. They fear 'opening the door' if they say anything at all that is remotely positive about their experiences, and that their children will believe they condone drug use if they offer neutral information and ongoing, supportive conversations" (par. 3). *It's Just a Plant* offers a much-needed means for doing so. In the words of Rosenbaum, the text "provides parents of young children with a realistic tool that enables them, through reading together, to open early discussions about marijuana" (par. 5).

By contrast, when the narrative is examined by individuals positioned on the other side of the culture wars debate about this subject, *It's Just a Plant* has been heavily criticized and even outright condemned. Viewed from this socio-political perspective, the picture book has been rebuked as a poignant example of permissive parenting and the declining state of morality in the United States. In 2005, for instance, Republican Congressman Mark Souder denounced the book for what he cited as its pro-marijuana message, even reading passages of the text into the Congressional Record (Garofoli, par. 46). Meanwhile, Bill O'Reilly suggested that Cortés was irresponsible for writing a children's book about cannabis. As he told the author-illustrator when interviewing him on his cable show: "I don't know if a sympathetic book to marijuana does [young people] any good" (Cortés, "Personal Story"). Echoing this viewpoint, the nationally circulating magazine *Entertainment Weekly* titled its review of the book "Outrage of the Week" ("Outrage" 91).

In the pages that follow, I argue that *It's Just a Plant* is controversial for reasons that extend far beyond the book's niche focus on questioning the criminalization of marijuana. The tumult surrounding Cortés's narrative emanates from a second equally powerful, but as-yet unspoken, source: its advocacy for child agency. In stark contrast to the steadfast prohibition about marijuana in materials for young people, *It's Just a Plant* makes a case that individuals, including children, have the right to decide about this issue for themselves. Cortés has his protagonist Jackie and, by extension, his child readers, talk with a marijuana grower, doctor, and users so that they can learn about the plant from a variety of different perspectives, ask questions, and generate their own opinions about it. While *It's Just a Plant* does not condone marijuana use among youth, it also does not condemn it among adults. Rather, Cortés's text makes the case that individuals ought to be able to learn about the issue and, ultimately, make their own informed decision about it. Even more radically, *It's Just a Plant* urges young people who disagree with current public policy about cannabis to work toward social change. For all of the lip service paid in the United States during the twenty-first century to empowering children, valuing their opinions, and encouraging their ambitions, it is ultimately this message about child activism and even youth civil disobedience that makes *It's Just a Plant* threatening, at least as much as its ostensible focus on marijuana—and perhaps even more so.

Reefer Madness: The Criminalization—and Demonization—of Marijuana in the United States

As Solomon H. Snyder has aptly noted, "The history of marijuana is one of *déjà vu*" (v). Both positive and negative attitudes about the plant fade and then reappear, establishing a cyclical pattern where cannabis is valued followed quickly by a period in which it is vilified.

This process long predates the appearance of marijuana in the United States. As Randi Mehling reminds us, "For thousands of years, cannabis has enjoyed historical significance as a recreational drug, a useful fiber, an oil, an edible seed, and a medicine" (8). The first documented instance of cannabis cultivation dates back 12,000 years ago (Mehling 8). According to W. Scott Ingram, "The Chinese were the first people to use cannabis for food, clothes, paper, and medicine" (37). Western trade routes brought the plant to Europe: "In the nineteenth century, the British imported these therapeutic strategies from their Indian colonies" (Snyder v).

By this point, cannabis had long been present in the United States. As Ted Gottfried reveals, "Hemp was a major crop for American colonists. They used it to make paper, clothing, and rope" (6). Indeed, in an etymological fact that has been largely forgotten today, "the word *canvas* comes from the word cannabis" (Ingram 19). The plant was such a crucial raw material for the Anglo-European settlers in North America that, as Rudolph J. Gerber has noted, "America's first law on marijuana, dating from 1619 in Virginia, required farmers to grow hemp" (2). An analogous situation applied to the New England area. As Ingram has documented, "Cannabis ... was one of the first crops grown in the Massachusetts Bay Colony" (43).[4]

The outbreak of the American Revolutionary War only heightened the need for cannabis. Cut off from British imports as well as from many former sources of trade, "[r]ope and sails (also made from hemp fiber) were so important that some colonial assemblies declared that any man who raised hemp or worked in a ropewalk for at least six months did not have to serve in the military" (Ingram 45). Furthermore, "Thomas Jefferson once claimed that America's future depended upon hemp agriculture" (McMullin 13). As a result, it was cultivated widely. "Entries from George Washington's diary in 1765 show that he personally planted and harvested cannabis for both fiber and medicinal purposes," Mehling documents (10). Moreover, according to Gerber, "Jefferson probably wrote The Declaration of Independence on hemp paper. Betsy Ross made her first American flag of hemp fabric" (2).

In the tumultuous Federalist period, cannabis acquired a new significance. As Ingram has discussed, "Hemp ... was more than just fiber for clothes, rope, and sails. It was used for money as well. Paper money had almost no value in the colonies. ... One trade item that had value for every colonist was hemp. It became the 'money standard' for the first decade of the new United States" (45). By the end of the eighteenth century, however, the use of cannabis as a raw material for items like rope, clothes, and sails began to decline. In the words of Gottfried: "The invention of the cotton gin in 1793 meant the end of hemp as an American crop. With the cotton gin, farmers could more easily separate cotton fiber from the cotton plant. Cotton became cheaper to produce than hemp. Many hemp plantations switched to growing cotton" (6).

This shift, however, did not mean the end for cannabis. Akin to its usage in China, India, and Great Britain, the plant acquired a new life as a treatment for physical ailments and, of course, as a recreational intoxicant. According to Connolly, by the late nineteenth century, "people had discovered the drug's other properties—it seemed to create feelings of pleasure and make people feel good. A new chapter in marijuana use was about to begin" (9). Growing awareness about the relaxation that many people experienced when they smoked marijuana in a cigarette, consumed it as an oil added to food, or inhaled the vapors from burning it in a hard resin form known as hashish, changed popular perceptions about the plant forever. Charles Baudelaire, the nineteenth-century French poet, famously wrote about how smoking hashish loosened his inhibitions and furthered his creative abilities.

Back in the United States, recreational use of cannabis became associated not with aristocratic writers and artists, but with the growing cohort of new immigrants from Mexico. Within this context, cannabis acquired both a new name—"marijuana" or, as it was then more commonly spelled, "marihuana"—and a whole new reputation. After centuries of cannabis being valued as a crop used for food, oil, fuel, and medicine among Anglo-European Americans, now, in the hands of Mexican immigrants, it was vilified. As Ingram has discussed, "Although most Americans knew the terms *cannabis* and *hemp*, the term *marijuana* and its use by newcomers led to an anti-immigrant backlash" (49). Rudolph Gerber expands on this assessment: "Law enforcement's campaign against this 'marijuana menace' targeted foreigners, inferior races, sexual deviants, and social misfits" (3).

Regardless of the specific user, cannabis was linked with a whole host of pernicious physical and psychological effects. Indeed, one expert characterized cannabis as "a diabolical substance, a drug that could enslave a man in its addiction, destroy his moral fiber, turn him into a degenerate and a parasite, and unleash the mad dog that hitherto had been securely restrained in his erstwhile healthy body" (Abel, par. 12). These sentiments reached a fevered pitch during the 1930s. "In 1936, a movie called *Tell Your Children* was financed by a small church group who wanted to deliver a strong cautionary message to parents about the 'evils' of marijuana in a mock documentary format. Soon after the film was shot, it was re-edited and released as *Reefer Madness*" (Mehling 12–13). The film shows, among other scenarios, a jazz musician smiling cravenly after smoking a joint, a teenaged girl brought to sexual ruin by reefer, and a formerly upstanding young man partaking in a killing spree while under the influence of the drug. *Reefer Madness* was certainly the most famous (or infamous) scare film about marijuana, but it was far from the only one. A number of other marijuana-themed movies were released during this era. Bearing titles like *Devil's Harvest* and *Marijuana: Weed with Roots in Hell*, their viewpoints on cannabis were clear (Gerber 6).

While the national frenzy over marijuana was certainly fueled by the increased racial, cultural, and class conflicts precipitated by the Great Depression, it was also greatly aided by the advocacy of one particular person: Harry J. Anslinger. The founding director of the Federal Bureau of Narcotics from 1930 until 1962, he was one of the most vocal opponents of marijuana. Indeed, as Gerber has written, "Almost single-handedly, Anslinger planted the seeds of our nation's legal pot jungle" (4). Calling marijuana nothing less than "this killer weed" (qtd. in Gerber 4), Anslinger published articles on the subject with dramatic titles like "Marihuana as a

Developer of Criminals." In these essays, Anslinger explained how cannabis was the cause of a whole host of craven behaviors. As he mused in the opening paragraphs to an article called "Marihuana: Assassin of Youth": "How many murders, suicides, robberies, criminal assaults, holdups, burglaries, and deeds of maniacal insanity it causes each year, especially among the young, can be only conjectured" (Anslinger 63).

The nation's young people were not the only demographic group susceptible to the corrupting influence of weed. Echoing the racism and xenophobia of the day, Anslinger argued that racial and ethnic minority groups were also vulnerable. As Gerber has discussed, "Anslinger's arguments linked marijuana to unwelcome minorities." He wrote of "'ginger-colored niggers' using pot" (8). Later, during Congressional testimony, Anslinger elaborated: "Most marijuana smokers are Negroes, Hispanics, Filipinos, and entertainers. Their satanic music, jazz and swing result from marijuana usage. This marijuana causes white women to seek sexual relations with Negroes" (qtd. in Gerber 9).

Largely through Anslinger's efforts, the United States passed the Marihuana Tax Act in 1937.[5] The bill technically only required those who wished to grow, use, or otherwise possess cannabis to pay a fee to the Department of the Treasury and receive a tax stamp. But, since such stamps were never granted, the act effectively outlawed cannabis. Moreover, as David Solomon points out, the fact that the Marihuana Tax Act contained more than sixty pages "of administrative and enforcement procedures" that included broad powers to enact "affidavits, depositions, sworn statements, and constant Treasury Department police inspection in every instance that marijuana is bought, sold, used, raised, distributed, given away, and so on," made clear that criminalization, not taxation or even regulation, was the intent of the act all along (par. 2).

The Depression-era hysteria over "reefer madness" and the Marihuana Tax Act that arose from it set the tone for national attitudes regarding cannabis until the 1960s. As Ingram has written, "baby boomers rejected the conservative attitudes of their parents and other adults. One way in which they rebelled was by using marijuana" (21). Many young people felt that since the older generation had misled them about socio-political issues like the Vietnam War, it was possible that they had lied to them about other subjects, such as the hazards of drugs like marijuana. In the wake of such attitudes, "Cheech and Chong became the embodiment of a new culture honoring the 'stoned' anti-war, anti-government protester" (Gerber 22).[6] Within this environment, "Young people used marijuana more openly, smoking it at concerts and war protests" (Gottfried 16).

They were not alone. A growing number of Americans outside of the student protest movement and hippie counterculture were also questioning the criminalization of marijuana. In a powerful index of these changing attitudes, then-President John Kennedy forced Anslinger to resign in the face of evidence that many of his arguments regarding the ills of marijuana were inaccurate. As Gerber reveals, "Research commissions, most notably the 1962 White House Conference on Drug Abuse, again found no direct link between pot and violent crime or hard drugs" (18). In the wake of such discoveries, by the end of the decade, the American public was largely questioning the criminalization of marijuana. In a telling index of this phenomenon, "[o]n September 7, 1970, *Newsweek* ran a cover story entitled 'Marihuana: Time to Change the Law?'" (Gerber 19).

This change would never occur. Averring Solomon Snyder's opening assertion that the "history of marijuana is one of *déjà vu*," the growing acceptance of cannabis during the era of the Vietnam War precipitated a backlash. "Many people were outraged," Gottfried has documented, "[t]hey blamed marijuana for firing up rebels on college campuses and causing race riots in inner cities" (16). In response, Republican presidential candidate Richard M. Nixon made the issue of drug control one of his central platforms: "In a 1968 campaign speech in California, he called drugs 'the modern curse of youth' capable of 'decimating a generation of Americans,' adding later that pot users were like 'foreign troops on our shores'" (Gerber 21). When Nixon took office the following year, he turned this campaign promise into legislative reality. Announcing a nationwide "War on Drugs," Nixon declared the growing popularity of illegal substances like LSD, marijuana, and mushrooms "public enemy number one" (Van Tuyl, "Foreword" 9). As one of its first steps, "[t]he Nixon Administration then passed the Controlled Substance Act of 1970 and established the Drug Enforcement Administration (DEA), a 'super agency' that would handle all aspects of the drug problem" (Van Tuyl, "Foreword" 10). And it did. The Controlled Substances Act made the criminalization of marijuana, which had long been a *de facto* result of the Marihuana Tax Act, now *de jure*. Moreover, it categorized cannabis as a Schedule I drug, which meant "that is a dangerous, addictive substance with no known medical application," despite an abundance of scientific evidence demonstrating otherwise (Van Tuyl, "Foreword" 9).

The aggressive prosecution mandated by the Nixon Administration and the harsh penalties imposed by the DEA eventually led to another period of softening public and political attitudes about cannabis. Akin to the postwar period, "A popular sense developed that pot use had been overcriminalized" (Gerber 18). Such sentiments grew so strong, in fact, that, "[i]n 1976, Jimmy Carter actually campaigned on the decriminalization of marijuana. Carter's head drug policy maker, Peter Bourne, publicly stated that he did not view marijuana—or even cocaine—as a serious public health threat" (Van Tuyl, "Foreword" 10). Indeed, as Van Tuyl reports, "Policy reform advocates attempted to get marijuana rescheduled several times and introduced bills in Congress, but none of their efforts were successful" ("Foreword" 10).

The inauguration of President Ronald Reagan in January 1981 marked another new chapter in the nation's demonization of cannabis. This time, however, anti-drug measures would be spearheaded by another figure in the White House: "Dismayed by increased used of cocaine and crack in the early 1980s, then-First Lady Nancy Reagan launched her 'Just Say No' antidrug campaign in 1984" (Van Tuyl, "Foreword" 10). This new war on drugs quickly put marijuana in the crosshairs. In remarks that recalled earlier attitudes about cannabis use, "Carlton Turner, Reagan's first director of the ONDCP [Office of National Drug Control Policy], believed that marijuana use was inextricably linked to 'the present young-adult generation's involvement in anti-military, anti-nuclear power, anti-big business, anti-authority demonstrations'" (Van Tuyl, "Foreword" 11). Through these tactics, Reagan was able to demonize marijuana even more than during the Depression era and expand its criminalization accordingly. As Van Tuyl discusses, "a public-health approach to drug control was replaced by an emphasis on law enforcement. Drug abuse was no longer considered a form of illness, as all drug use was deemed immoral and deserving of staunch punishment" ("Foreword" 11). In 1986, for instance, "President Ronald Reagan signed a $1.7 billion drug bill along with requirements for mandatory sentencing of drug offenders" (Van Tuyl, "Foreword" 10).

To greater or lesser extents, all subsequent presidential administrations have followed the policies first established by Nixon and then expanded upon by Reagan with regard to marijuana. During the 1990s, in fact, "[t]he drug war soon became a bipartisan effort, supported by liberals and conservatives alike" ("Foreword" 11). Indeed, while presidents Bill Clinton, George W. Bush, and Barack Obama all admitted to youthful experiments with marijuana,[7] they upheld longstanding federal drug laws. In some ways, their administrations even heightened the criminalization of cannabis. While Reagan is more commonly associated with waging the "War on Drugs," "The number of Americans arrested each year for marijuana offenses increased by 43 percent after Clinton took office, with more arrests during his first three years than during any other three-year period in history" (Gerber 69). Meanwhile, Barack Obama's administration "asked Congress for $26.2 billion" to combat substance abuse in 2012 (Purcell 30). Although only $25.2 billion was ultimately approved (Office of National Drug Control Policy, "The National Drug Control Budget," par. 4), this figure still marked the moment when the "annual budget for the War on Drugs ... multiplied 50 times" since Richard Nixon first inaugurated it in 1971 (Purcell 30). As such details demonstrate, the national campaign against substances like marijuana shows no signs of letting up or slowing down.

To Be Blunt: Confronting Marijuana Policy, Practice, and Paranoia in *It's Just a Plant*

From the opening page of *It's Just a Plant* to its final utterance, Ricardo Cortés engages with this long and often contradictory history of marijuana policy, practice, and, of course, paranoia. The author commences his book with a detail that is simultaneously the most mundane and the most controversial: the fact that many adults, including those who have children, smoke marijuana occasionally for pleasure. As Joe Garofoli has written, "Pot-smoking parents are everywhere. … They take their regular turn in the carpool, and maintain their lawns and serve as lectors at their church. They're not tough to find" (par. 7). In short, they are our neighbors, family members, and friends. Moreover, they are not habitual stoners who live each day in a fog of pot smoke. On the contrary, as Garofoli asserts: "They smoke marijuana occasionally— socially, 'like a glass of wine' is a common comparison" (par. 4).

Cortés locates the parents in his book within this cohort of men and women. The author makes clear that Jackie's mother and father are not dazed potheads, as marijuana users are so often portrayed in the media. Rather, they are loving parents and responsible adults who have created a happy, healthy home for their daughter. In *How Picturebooks Work*, Maria Nikolajeva and Carole Scott discuss the complex interaction that occurs between text and image in these narratives. As they assert, the illustrations in picture books are far from "merely decorative" (2); on the contrary, they are rich sites of narrative meaning. Nikolajeva and Scott explain that while the images in picture books may possess a variety of relationships to the printed text—including symmetrical, complementary, counterpoint, and contradictory—a prevalent one is "enhancing" (6–21). The images in picture books frequently augment the information conveyed by the words on the page, depicting details and even introducing elements that are not explicitly mentioned. Indeed, as Perry Nodelman has commented, "the pictures in picturebooks are almost always more complex, more detailed, more sophisticated than the texts are" ("Words" 17).

This observation certainly applies to the illustrations throughout *It's Just a Plant*. The images consistently enhance and even amplify the message of the printed text. On its opening page, for example, *It's Just a Plant* informs its readers: "Jackie loved to go to sleep at night. Before she got tucked in, her mother would help her walk on her hands … all the way to bed." The illustration that accompanies these remarks shows Jackie's mother putting the protagonist to bed (Figure 1.1). The elementary-aged girl is doing a handstand and laughing joyously while her mother holds her feet, a warm smile on her face. The room where this scenario is taking place is clean, bright, and well furnished: it has comfortable chairs, interesting pictures on the wall, and a stylish throw rug. In short, it could be the living room of almost any home in the United States. Many of the subsequent illustrations likewise reinforce that the protagonist has a happy home environment; loving parents; and a secure, content, and even child-centered family life. One drawing, for example, shows the father cradling Jackie and flying her "airplane-style" off to bed, a huge smile beaming across her face. Likewise, another illustration shows the family sitting at the table together eating a meal; both the mother and father are focused on their daughter and are looking at her warmly. Finally, the artistic medium and aesthetic appearance of Cortés's artwork on this page and throughout the book also serve this ideological purpose. As Lynd Ward once remarked about picture books, the illustrations are "a part of the flesh of the book in their technical creation, a part of the spirit of the book in the way they have come into being" (qtd. in op de Beeck xiii). Not only do the drawings throughout *It's Just a Plant* have fun, vivid colors, but many of them have also been made with common children's art supplies: markers, colored pencils, and crayons. Consequently, one can imagine Jackie having drawn or, at least, colored these images. This viewpoint offers an alternative perspective about the oft-mentioned "amateurish" nature of Cortés's artwork. For example, Susan Lissim, in her review for the *School Library Journal*, criticized the book for having illustrations that were "awkwardly drawn" (164). Rather than being poorly rendered, Cortés's images can be seen as child-focused.

Figure 1.1 From *It's Just a Plant* by Ricardo Cortés. Reprinted with permission.

After establishing Jackie's parents as regular, responsible, and loving people instead of drug-addicted fiends, the narrative presents the young girl's discovery of their pot usage in an equally realistic manner. Cortés writes: "One night Jackie woke up past her bedtime. She smelled something funny in the air, so she walked down the hall to her parents' bedroom." The image on the facing page shows her standing in the entryway to her parents' room, holding open the door to investigate (Figure 1.2). Nikolajeva and Scott discuss how picture book illustrations, especially when they are "extradiegetic-heterodiegetic" or "'omniscient' and not participating in the story" function as a type of "visual narrator" (119): directing the reader's gaze, guiding their engagement with the story, and shaping their intellectual as well as emotional reaction. Cortés makes full use of this potential in the drawing that shows Jackie peering into her parents' bedroom. The illustration places the viewer in the same subject position as the protagonist. The young girl is standing with her back to the viewers, so that we are looking over her shoulder to see what she sees: namely, her mother and father sitting in bed smoking.

Figure 1.2 From *It's Just a Plant* by Ricardo Cortés. Reprinted with permission.

On the following page, Jackie asks her parents if they are sharing a cigarette. In a brave act of honesty—and one that is not present in any previous books on the subject for young people—her mother calmly and matter-of-factly answers: "'No, baby,' said her mother. 'This is a *joint*. It's made of marijuana.'"[8] The drawing on the facing page builds on some of the book's previous themes. As Jackie's mother offers this explanation, the young girl is lying between her mother and father on their bed. In keeping with previous portrayals of Jackie's parents as thoughtful and caring individuals, the mother lovingly holds her daughter's head in her lap as they talk. Moreover, she is looking down at Jackie and has a big warm smile on her face. The physical closeness and emotional intimacy that the family displays in this scene mirrors the conversational candidness and socio-cultural honesty that they share about subjects like marijuana use.

While the candor expressed by the parents in Cortés's book may seem radical, it actually reflects the mundane reality that marijuana exists in American culture and that a significant percentage of the population uses it. As Marsha Rosenbaum has written, print, visual, or online materials that pretend otherwise are not only inaccurate and ineffective but often do more harm than good: "To deny the reality of the role of drug use in our culture, to cling to worn out doomsday messages, and deny our kids help and support when they need it, is to expose them to risk and danger far beyond marijuana use" ("An Epilogue," par. 5). Journalist Joe Garofoli echoes this claim. As he has reported, "many kids are tuning out the government's zero-tolerance message" (par. 6). In spite of growing up amidst the "Just Say No" campaign, "[s]chool kids of the late 1990s were more likely to smoke pot than teens a decade earlier" (Gerber 69). As the U.S. Department of Health and Human Services reported after surveying roughly 18,000 young people, "marijuana use among youth ages twelve to seventeen rose 105 percent from 1992 to 1994 and 37 percent between 1995 and 1998" (qtd. in Gerber 70). This trend has largely continued in the new millennium. Writing in 2007—just two years after the initial release of *It's Just a Plant*— Joe Garofoli revealed: "Last year, the Government Accountability Office, the investigative arm of Congress, found that the federal government's $1.4 billion anti-drug campaign wasn't working" (par. 6).

Such statistics indicate that, while the taglines for federally funded anti-drug commercials such as the now-famous "This is Your Brain … This is Your Brain on Drugs" may have been absorbed into the nation's popular culture, their messages were not. According to Maia Szalavitz, in fact, "If anything, experts say, the latest ad campaign's overblown claims could damage credibility with teens, undermining warnings about other, more dangerous illicit substances" (24). Indeed, in details that are arguably far more shocking than the fact that some parents occasionally smoke marijuana, research conducted by the National Institute on Drug Use "showed that, not only were the ads unsuccessful, but they also actually seemed to increase the likelihood that some groups of young people would try marijuana. In fact, the more times young people saw the ads, the more likely they were to become curious about marijuana and to try it" (Ingram 29). In comments that once again recall the history of marijuana policy and practice as one marked by "*déjà vu*," Ingram went on to say about these findings: "In some ways, this is similar to what happened in the 1960s when young people were warned that marijuana was a 'deadly poison' and became curious about the drug as a result" (29). As Paul Armentano has commented: "by overstating marijuana's potential risk, America's policy-makers and law enforcement community undermine their credibility and ability to effectively educate the public of the legitimate harms associated with more dangerous drugs" (22).

Ricardo Cortés seeks to avoid making the same mistake in *It's Just a Plant*. Thus, not only do the parents in his book openly discuss their marijuana use with their daughter, they arrange for her to meet various individuals who can tell her even more about the plant. The first place that Jackie's mother takes her to learn more about marijuana is a local farm owned by a friendly man named Bob. Once again, Cortés uses the book's illustration to help humanize his characters and dispel Anslinger-style fears. The facing page provides a bust-style depiction of Farmer Bob. This close-up profile allows reader to plainly see that the farmer is not a scary or maniacal "drug-pusher." Rather, he is a middle-aged bald man with bright blue eyes and a rosy complexion who is wearing a simple gray sweater. Moreover, in the background behind him are tall stalks of corn, a crop that is not only seen as wholly innocuous today but whose versatility can be compared to the historical uses of hemp. After giving Jackie a tour of his more conventional crops like apples, strawberries, and corn, the farmer shows her his cannabis plants: "Finally he reached a pot with a sweet, skunky smell. 'This,' said Bob, 'is a marijuana plant.'" The illustration on the facing page shows Farmer Bob and Jackie standing in the middle of his large garden. Numerous containers of cannabis in various stages of development can be seen on the ground.

Although this scenario is fictional, the premise behind it is not. A study conducted by DrugScience.org in 2006—the year after *It's Just a Plant* was published—revealed that marijuana "was the top cash crop in 12 states and among the top three cash crops in 30 states" (Ingram 23). In some locales, such as California, cannabis plays a significant, albeit unofficial, role in the agricultural economy. According to Sean Connolly, "Marijuana is California's largest cash crop. Officials estimate that it is worth $3–$5 billion each year. Compare this amount with the leading legally produced crops: grapes ($2.6 billion), lettuce ($1.4 billion), and flowers ($1 billion)" (13). When the value of marijuana cultivation is viewed nationally, these figures are even more astounding. Ingram reports: "A 2006 article in the *Los Angeles Times* noted that 'the market value of pot produced in the U.S. exceeds $35 billion—far more than the crop value of such important farm products such as corn, soybeans, and hay'" (29–30).

While it is commonplace to refer to marijuana in the singular, as if it were a solitary species of plant, cannabis actually comes in a number of forms. As Randi Mehling has written: "The three most prevalent varieties of the Indian hemp plant are *Cannabis sativa* (*C. sativa*), the most common of the three varieties, which is tall, loosely branched, and grows as high as 20 feet; *Cannabis indica*, which is three or four feet in height, pyramidal in shape, and densely branched; and *Cannabis ruderalis*, which grows to a height of about two feet with few or no branches" (14). It is the first kind, *Cannabis sativa*, however, that is the most commonly grown, and thus is the one to which we tacitly reference when we discuss marijuana.

Jackie learns about the different kinds of cannabis from Farmer Bob. Although he does not mention the names of these varieties, he does describe them in some detail. "It can be very, very tall with long jagged leaves," Farmer Bob explains, "Or it can be short, blue and purple!" Moreover, echoing the plant's long history both in the United States and in countries around the globe, he goes on to inform her: "Like fruits, vegetables, cotton and grains, marijuana has been cultivated by people for hundreds of years." The image on the facing page serves to further demystify marijuana. The drawing shows a close-up of a marijuana plant as Farmer Bob tends to it (Figure 1.3). The illustration appears against a plain white backdrop, with no other details, border, or background images to distract readers from being able to look at the plant closely, see its various qualities and inspect its identifying traits, akin to a botany textbook. Once again, this illustration works to dispel common fears and longstanding anxieties surrounding cannabis. The calm, clear, and matter-of-fact portrait reveals that marijuana is not some fiendish terror; rather, as the title of Cortés's text announces, it is just a plant.

Figure 1.3 From *It's Just a Plant* by Ricardo Cortés. Reprinted with permission.

Of course, what really interests Jackie—as well as, undoubtedly, Cortés's readership—is not so much how people grow marijuana, but why they consume it. Farmer Bob tells the young girl about the dried leaves and flowers of cannabis plants on the following page: "People eat and smoke them. ... Some people say marijuana makes them feel happy. Others say it's 'dreamy.' Actually, the flower has different effects on different people who try it." Significantly, and in a detail that challenges Anslinger-era stereotypes that individuals who participate in marijuana production are avid consumers of the substance themselves, Farmer Bob does not partake of cannabis himself. Cortés's text relays the following exchange: "'Why do you use it, Farmer Bob?' asked Jackie. 'I don't.' he said. 'It just puts me to sleep!'" Then, in an indication of how marijuana use can be found in a wide cross-section of the population, Farmer Bob goes on to list various types of men and women who partake of it: "artists, doctors, writers, scientists, even presidents." The illustration that accompanies this passage reinforces this message about the diversity of cannabis users (Figure 1.4). The drawing shows a large group of people sitting around a hookah, talking and laughing. The men and women represent a wide range of ages, races, and ethnicities. These include a young woman who is dressed in a shirt emblazoned with a university logo, an Asian man with tattoos, a Jewish gentleman with curly sideburns wearing a yamekah, and a young black man sporting a hat with the red, green, and yellow colors of Rastafarians. Moreover, an array of famous figures, including Willie Nelson and Bill Clinton, appear in various locations throughout the illustration. Finally, the perspective that Cortés employs in the drawing is significant. Perry Nodelman has commented: "Whereas the texts of picturebooks tend conventionally to focalize events through their child protagonist, the pictures usually show that same child as seen from a distance and, therefore, presumably, by someone else—someone whom, it seems, has the ability to record all the visual surrounding details the child is not necessarily conscious of" ("Words" 17). Cortés's drawing of the men and women around the hookah does not adhere to this tendency. The image is rendered from the perspective of a person who is sitting on the floor with the group around the hookah or—in an alternative and even more likely possibility— who is looking at the scene from the height and accompanying viewpoint of a child like Jackie. Indeed, giving further credence to this possibility, the protagonist is not present in the drawing. This low-level perspective does not make the adult figures seem imposing. Instead, it invites readers to meet them, quite literally, where they are.

Of course, recreational enjoyment is not the only reason why individuals use marijuana; they also do so for medicinal purposes. As Jordan McMullin has written, as early as the first century A.D in China, cannabis was a treatment "for more than one hundred ailments, including beriberi, constipation, malaria, and even absentmindedness" (14). Cannabis likewise held an important medicinal role in many areas of Southeast Asia. "In India cannabis was used to restore appetite, cure fevers, induce sleep, and relieve various kinds of pain," McMullin reports (14).

Figure 1.4 From *It's Just a Plant* by Ricardo Cortés. Reprinted with permission.

Western trade and colonialism brought cannabis to Europe where its medicinal uses quickly spread. As Sean Connolly explains, "In England, Queen Victoria's doctor even recommended it to her to reduce the pain of menstrual cramps" (9). In fact, in an article published in the first issue of the British medical journal *The Lancet* (1890), Sir Russell Reynolds, the monarch's personal physician, said about marijuana: "When pure and administered carefully, it is one of the most valuable medicines we possess" (qtd. in Connolly 9).

Cannabis was also a common curative for generations of Americans. In a detail that has largely been forgotten to history, "[p]hysicians in the United States had liberally prescribed marijuana throughout the nineteenth century" (McMullin 14). As W. Scott Ingram documents, "The Ohio Medical Society reported in 1857 that people using cannabis products claimed that it cured 'hysteria ... whooping cough, asthma ... chronic bronchitis ... muscular spasms, epilepsy ... and appetite loss'" (48). By the 1880s, "dentists found hemp to be an excellent topical anesthetic for performing dental procedures on their patients" (Mehling 11). Far from a fringe phenomenon, the medicinal use of marijuana was mainstream. As McMullin has documented, as early as 1850, cannabis "was included in the U.S. Pharmacopeia as a medicine, and solutions and tinctures containing cannabis were frequently prescribed for relieving pain and inducing sleep" (9). Moreover, many of these products "were made by well-known pharmaceutical firms that still exist today, such as Squibb (now Bristol-Myers Squibb) and Eli Lilly" (Medical Marijuana Policy Project 44).

While the introduction of new painkillers, such as aspirin, caused marijuana to fall from favor by the late 1800s (Connolly 9), its medicinal qualities were not forgotten. Even during the height of the anti-marijuana campaign of the 1930s, the clinical value of cannabis remained in the minds of citizens and scientists alike. Much to the annoyance of Harry J. Anslinger, for instance, during Congressional hearings prior to passage of the Marihuana Tax Act, "[a] physician from the American Medical Association pled for continued permission for medical use of marijuana, then in use only in some medical circles" (Gerber 8). In a direct challenge to Anslinger's authority, "Dr. William Woodward observed that, in these medical circles, marijuana was considered harmless medicine. In fact, some leading drug companies were distributing small packets of marijuana commercially, and some pharmacies were selling it legally" (Gerber 9–10). Of course, Dr. Woodward's testimony was ignored and cannabis was criminalized in 1937, an event which, as Solomon H. Snyder notes, "essentially eliminated all medical research in the field for almost 30 years" (v).

Ironically, it was during attempts to provide scientific evidence about the ills of cannabis in the 1960s and 1970s that scientists unwittingly rediscovered its clinical potential. As skeptic Jane Bingham grudgingly conceded:

> Marijuana is said to help with symptoms associated with multiple sclerosis and Parkinson's disease. It also seems to reduce painful eye pressure in the eyes of glaucoma sufferers. The drug may also reduce the headaches and nausea that many people experience during chemotherapy. Some people claim that marijuana is more effective than other medical drugs in combating pain and nausea because it helps patients to relax. (36)

As a result, marijuana has been used in recent years to ease the symptoms associated with a variety of conditions, including AIDS, cancer, glaucoma, multiple sclerosis, epilepsy, and chronic pain (Medical Marijuana Policy Project 42–43). Akin to its usage during the nineteenth century, the clinical use of cannabis has attained professional legitimacy: "Organizations supporting some form of physician supervised access to medical marijuana include the American Academy of Family Physicians, American Nurses Association, American Public Health Association, the *New England Journal of Medicine* and many others" (Medical Marijuana Policy Project 47).

In the wake of mounting scientific evidence of marijuana's ability to ease the pain and suffering of seriously ill patients, the Food and Drug Administration permitted the inclusion of marijuana in its Investigational New Drug (IND) program in 1975. For the first time since the passage of the Marihuana Tax Act in 1937, the IND approved a small cadre of individuals to legally purchase, receive, and use cannabis from a federally

grown crop. This seemingly groundbreaking initiative was ultimately ineffective. From its inception, the IND was so tightly restricted that only a
small number of patients were ever helped by it. Then, in what would
constitute a fatal blow to the initiative, "[i]n 1992, in response to a flood
of new applications from AIDS patients, the George H. W. Bush Administration closed the program to new applicants, and pleas to reopen it
were ignored by subsequent administrations. The IND program remains
in operation only for the seven surviving, previously-approved patients"
(Medical Marijuana Policy Project 46).

Real change in medical marijuana policy would not come until four
years later when, in 1996, "California voters approved Proposition 215,
the Compassionate Use Act." The purpose of the law was "'[t]o ensure that
seriously ill Californians have the right to obtain and use marijuana for
medical purposes where that medical use is deemed appropriate and has
been recommended by a physician who has determined that the person's
health would benefit from the use of marijuana'" (Ruschmann 25). In the
years following the passage of Proposition 215, support for similar legislation steadily increased. The results of a Gallup poll in November 2005
"found that 78% of Americans support 'making marijuana legally available
for doctors to prescribe in order to reduce pain and suffering'" (Medical
Marijuana Policy Project 47). These statistics were far from an anomaly:
"For over a decade, polls have consistently shown between 60% and 80%
support for legal access to medical marijuana" (Medical Marijuana Policy
Project 47). At the time of this writing, in fact, twenty U.S. states, plus
the District of Columbia, have legalized the medical use of marijuana in
some form (Office of National Drug Policy Control, "Marijuana Resource
Center," par. 1).

It's Just a Plant engages with this issue. It is no coincidence that, after
Jackie and her mother finish talking with Farmer Bob, their next stop is
a medical office. The female physician, who has the suggestive name of
"Dr. Eden," explains to Jackie why she prescribes cannabis to her patients:
"'Marijuana,' said Dr. Eden, 'is used for different reasons. Like many plants,
it can be a medicine, and it is sometimes called a drug.'" While the doctor
does not mention any particular diseases or specific ailments for which
cannabis is used as a treatment, she does mention some of the ways that it
helps people to feel better. "'It can heal the eyes of some people,' Dr. Eden
asserts, 'help other people relax, and it calms the stomach and helps many
people eat when they need to.'" In spite of these many positive effects,
Dr. Eden is careful to point out that cannabis is not suitable for all of her
patients. As she makes a point of telling Jackie: "'Marijuana is for people
who can use it responsibly. It gives many people joy, but like many things,
it can also make someone sick if it is used too much. I do not recommend it
for everyone.'" In keeping Cortés's use of illustrations throughout the book,
the drawing that accompanies these lines reinforces the candid and even
serious nature of their conversation. The image on the facing page shows
Dr. Eden and Jackie sitting in her exam room in simple wooden chairs that

face each other while having their conversation (Figure 1.5). Once again, Cortés's use of perspective is important: the scene is presented in profile, as if the fourth wall to the room has been removed. The result is that readers feel like they could be occupying the chair that would triangulate with that of Dr. Eden and Jackie. To be sure, they are eye-level with the child protagonist. Not only does this point of view make the scene less frightening, but it also pulls them into the story, inviting them to imagine that they are part of the discussion.

Figure 1.5 From *It's Just a Plant* by Ricardo Cortés. Reprinted with permission.

Given both the medicinal and the recreational uses of marijuana, Cortés's young protagonist is baffled to learn that it is illegal. "Jackie couldn't believe it! 'Mommy ...' she said breathlessly, 'is that all true,'" the youngster inquires upon learning that growing, selling, or possessing marijuana is a crime that could result in a fine, a jail sentence, or both. In a turn of events that seems somewhat unlikely but serves the didactic aim of the book, the policeman who informs Jackie of these facts shares her sense of disbelief. Calling attention to the longstanding history of cannabis in the United States, he explains: "'People were once allowed to smoke, marijuana,' began the police officer. 'There was a time when the government even told farmers to grow it. Back then it was called Hemp.'" The officer makes it clear, however, that he does not know such facts not merely from abstract history lessons but from personal experience. As he tells Jackie with some pride, "My grandfather grew hemp and made rope from the fiber of the plant's stalk. Other people made cloth and paper with it. My grandmother once ran a café where she would read all day, drink tea with toast, and sell cakes made of homegrown grass.'"

Of course, these seemingly halcyon conditions for cannabis consumption soon came to an end. As the officer goes on to explain: "'Then one day, a small but powerful group decided to make a law against marijuana,' continued the officer." Although the policeman never explicitly mentions Harry J. Anslinger or his crusade against cannabis in the 1930s, his account of the criminalization is highly suggestive of this figure's career and its legacy: "'Doctors who used it as medicine tried to protest, but the politicians and lawmakers did not listen. Marijuana became an illegal plant.'" Finally, in remarks that reflect federal anti-drug policy during the latter half of the twentieth-century, and especially under Presidents Nixon and Reagan, the officer informs Jackie how "'our government started War [sic] around the world to stop people from growing it.'"

* * *

In spite of Cortés's effort to resist the longstanding demonization of marijuana and instead present a more factual and even realistic portrayal of its presence in American culture, not every section of the book adheres to this ethos. First, contrary to the police officer's account about the history of cannabis in the United States, hemp and marijuana are not synonymous terms—or substances. As W. Scott Ingram explains, "One name that is sometimes substituted for marijuana is *hemp*. Although the two names are used as synonyms, hemp is actually a very different kind of cannabis that has far lower levels of cannabinoids than marijuana smoked by users today" (19; emphasis in original). As a result, he continues, "A person would have to smoke extremely large amounts of hemp in order to feel anything" (Ingram 19). The type of cannabis grown in colonial and Federalist America—whether by choice or by law—was hemp not marijuana. Moreover, it was cultivated exclusively for industrial purposes: as raw material to make items like rope, clothing, and sails. As Ingram, Gerber, and McMullin all mention, both regular citizens and prominent public figures like George Washington and Thomas Jefferson did not smoke the hemp they grew, nor would it have ever occurred to them to do so. So, Cortés's equation of hemp and marijuana is misleading or, at least, not entirely accurate.

In addition to errors regarding the botany of cannabis, Cortés's book contains some oversights in the presentation of its place in the criminal justice system. After Jackie and her mother leave Dr. Eden's office, they begin their journey back home. Before they have traveled far, however, "Jackie stopped to sniff the air. 'I know that smell!' she said." When readers turn the page, they see an illustration of a group of young black men standing on the street in front of a Chinese restaurant; one of them is clearly holding a joint. "'YOU'RE SMOKING MARIJUANA'" the protagonist exclaims. Before long, two police officers also smell the smoke and approach. In a dramatic description that seems patterned after contemporary reality crime shows like *COPS*, Cortés writes: "two police officers drove up and told all the men to turn around and put their hands up against the wall!" The drawing on the facing page shows the men complying with this command: It depicts one of the figures with his back to the readers, his legs spread apart on the sidewalk, and his hands up against a graffiti-covered wall (Figure 1.6). Framed between the right border of the drawing and the figure of Jackie, readers can see that the man standing to his right has already been handcuffed; he is still facing the wall but his hands are in metal cuffs behind his back. In a surprising reversal, however, the officers ultimately decide not to take the men into custody. Instead, they elect to exercise their enforcement discretion. As the second officer informs Jackie a few pages later: "'we're going to let these men go, with a warning.'"

Figure 1.6 From *It's Just a Plant* by Ricardo Cortés. Reprinted with permission.

While this encounter may have ended happily for the black men in Cortés's picture book, it is not an accurate reflection of many similar scenarios in real life. As Paul Ruschmann has written, "According to the 2002 National Survey on Drug Use and Health, 14 percent of regular users are African Americans. The Sentencing Project, however, found that African Americans account for 30 percent of those arrested for marijuana violations. To put it another way, whites are more likely to be 'let off'" (78). Rudolph J. Gerber, a former judge, echoes these sentiments: "Law enforcement directed at pot resembles pot growing and use: It is haphazard, discretionary, and geographically uneven" (61). While socio-economic class plays an important role in determining a person's probability of prosecution, their race, ethnicity, and even geographic locale are far more influential factors. In regions throughout the United States, "Black and Hispanic Americans continue to be overrepresented among outdoor pot sellers because of their concentration in inner cities and their relative scarcity on college campuses" (Gerber 63). As Gerber goes on to discuss: "These factors help explain why white high school and college-age students compose the highest number of pot users, but inner-city blacks and Hispanics compose the most numerous arrestees" (63). Unfortunately, Cortés's text does not represent this reality and, for an author-illustrator who is acutely interested in issues of social justice, this missed opportunity seems especially noticeable—and regrettable.

Just Say Maybe: *It's Just a Plant* Turns Youth Education into Agency—as Well as Activism

For generations, print, visual, and media discussions about marijuana for young people have contained a clear abstinence-only message. Echoing the campaign of Harry J. Anslinger in the 1930s, these materials employ scare tactics to convince juveniles about the hazards of cannabis. Ted Gottfried employs such techniques in his juvenile-audience book *Drug Facts: Marijuana*. Even though only a tiny fraction of individuals who use marijuana are ever arrested—Paul Ruschmann, writing in 2011, places this figure at three percent (78)—Gottfried begins his treatment with the theoretically true but statistically unlikely statement: "You can go to jail for using it. You can go to jail for having it in your possession. You can go to jail for selling it" (4). Meanwhile, Randi Mehling takes a slightly different tact in his youth-audience text *Marijuana*, but the end result is the same. Ignoring the reality that millions of young people have tried marijuana and suffered no ill effects, the author informs his juvenile readers: "Consequences of the short-term effects of marijuana can greatly influence a teen's future life" (Mehling 23).

Such approaches permeate even more recent texts about cannabis for young people that have been written and released amid the growing wave of legalization for medicinal use. Jane Bingham's *Marijuana: What's the Deal?* (2006), for example, contains numerous supposedly true "personal stories" that could have come directly out of Depression-era scare films like *Reefer Madness*. In one such testimonial, a young man named "Joe" dreamt of becoming a doctor. However, after he started smoking marijuana, he stopped caring about classwork did poorly on his exams, and was unable to get into medical school. As Bingham reveals, "Now he's 26 and working as a security guard in the hospital where he had planned to complete his training. Joe now realizes he's thrown away his chance to do the one thing he really wanted to do" (30). If such personal anecdotes fail to convince juvenile readers, the text includes more general and, arguably, more frightening proclamations, such as "Some dealers even add crack or heroin to marijuana joints so that the smoker becomes dependent on these drugs" (Bingham 35). These details demonstrate that although Bingham's narrative opens with the assertion that "[t]his book has the information you need to help you make your own decisions about marijuana" (4), it is clear what those decisions ought to be.

It's *Just a Plant* rejects this approach. Rather than denying the widespread nature of marijuana use, Cortés acknowledges it. Likewise, instead of pretending that one puff of a marijuana cigarette will lead young people to ruin, the author-illustrator takes a more realistic approach. As Cortés has said about cannabis: "it's about a plant that most children will encounter in their lives. Before they investigate on their own, shouldn't they be prepared?" ("FAQs"). His picture book aims to do just that. In remarks that may be unsettling but are nonetheless true, Cortés observes: "Marijuana is around kids! Some children are trying their first 'hit' of marijuana at ten years old, and awareness of the plant begins even earlier (through pop culture or by simply opening a parent's door late at night)" ("FAQs").

That said, although It's *Just a Plant* rejects prohibition politics, Cortés has repeatedly emphasized that it does not advocate for cannabis use among young people. In remarks that the author-illustrator has reiterated in numerous articles and interviews, he asserts:

> It's *Just a Plant* explicitly addresses the potential harm of drug abuse and insists that marijuana is not to be experimented with by children. As with books that teach kids about sex, It's *Just a Plant* encourages parents to explore the topic and children's questions about it, all the while reminding them that trying "pot" is an experience for responsible *adults*. ("FAQs"; emphasis in original)

Indeed, when young Jackie excitedly announces "I'm going to plant some marijuana at home!" after meeting with Farmer Bob, her mother quickly puts a stop to such ambitions. She tells her daughter, "'We'll talk about it later,'" a phrase that every child recognizes as a synonym for no.

A few pages later, when Jackie meets with Dr. Eden, this admonition appears even more directly. After the physician has finished describing the many ways that marijuana helps her patients, Cortés's protagonist asks: "'Will it help me if I use it?'" Dr. Eden's answer is as clear as it is unequivocal: "'No,' said the doctor." As she then goes on to explain: "'I think you can understand that there are some experiences that are okay for an adult, but definitely not for children. Using marijuana is a decision for an adult to make, like driving a car or drinking a glass of wine." As a result, Dr. Eden tells Jackie: "You should make the choice whether or not to try it when you are older and more mature."

Consequently, *It's Just a Plant* offers what can be seen as a modification on a well-known mantra. Instead of telling young people to "Just Say No," the picture book encourages them to "Just Say Maybe" and to do so later, when they are older. Given the widespread nature of marijuana use, it is likely that young people will try cannabis. Thus, rather than advocating for the unrealistic position of abstinence, Cortés makes a case for the more realistic one of informed consent.

In so doing, *It's Just a Plant* advocates for a position that is just as radical as its stance about marijuana: that of youth agency with regard to this issue. In contrast to previous books for young people about marijuana, Cortés does not tell his juvenile readers what position to take with regard to cannabis. Instead, he offers them information about cannabis from a variety of different perspectives and allows them to decide for themselves how they feel about it. They may chose, like Jackie's mother and father, to smoke cannabis occasionally for pleasure. Alternatively, they may find themselves in a position akin to Dr. Eden and use or prescribe marijuana for medical purposes. Or, finally, they may follow in the footsteps of Farmer Bob and refrain from partaking in cannabis altogether. Cortés stresses that this decision ultimately belongs to them—not to parents, physicians, police officers, or (in a telling *mea culpa*) even authors of books about marijuana.

In so doing, Cortés's text makes a strong and all-too rare case for the rights, maturity, and even intellectual capacity of children. Perry Nodelman has written about how adults resist giving true agency to young people: "By and large, we encourage in children those values and behaviors that make children easier for us to handle: more passive, more docile, more obedient—and thus, more in need of our guidance and more willing to accept the need for it" ("The Other" 30). As he goes on to discuss, most narratives for young readers reflect this ethos, urging boys and girls to accept adult authority, not challenge it. In the words of Nodelman, "It's no accident that the vast majority of stories for children share the message" ("The Other" 30).

It's Just a Plant breaks from this trend. Whereas previous books about drug control also placed young people in the position of a learner and accordingly offered them information about marijuana, it did not allow them to employ this knowledge in an agentic way. Instead, it expected young people to use the material that they were being given to make the decision that the book wanted them to make. In this way, education did not give young people more agency or autonomy. Instead, being cast in the role of "student" about national drug policy was synonymous with being placed in a position of subservience to adult control and official authority. They might be educated about marijuana, but they could only learn what the powers-that-be had decided that they should know, with no alternative viewpoints or competing perspectives. Moreover, this information did not empower young people to make their own decisions about this issue; instead, it was used as a means to justify and even compel them to accept the choices that had already been made for them.

It's Just a Plant does not follow this pattern. Unlike previous narratives for young people about marijuana, the niche market picture book repositions the child learner as someone who is not simply obtaining knowledge, but power. Rather than telling children what they should think and how they should act, Cortés encourages them to gather information, ask questions, and make decisions for themselves. Moreover, given the subject matter of his picture book, the author-illustrator is not simply permitting children to question adult authority, but to challenge nothing less than current civic law. In *The Pleasures of Children's Literature*, Perry Nodelman and Mavis Reimer articulate some of the broad issues with which all books for young readers engage, including "What part does literature play, or can it play, in the process of people understanding themselves and their world?" and "How much can or should children understand about themselves and their world?" (x). With its frank discussion about cannabis, *It's Just a Plant* provides a more candid and more daring response to these questions than any of its predecessors. Whereas many children's books strive to protect or shelter young people from controversial subjects like marijuana policy and practice, Cortés's text believes that these narratives have a responsibility to help young people learn about and even debate them.

In keeping with the overall iconoclastic qualities of *It's Just a Plant*, the finale to the picture book goes one step further. If young people decide that they disagree with existing public policy regarding marijuana, the author-illustrator informs them that they can advocate for social change. As Jackie's mother explains: "'The government can make a mistake when they make a law. ... Thankfully, we live in a country where we have the right to change the law if it doesn't work. We might change a law by writing petitions and voting.'" The illustration that accompanies these lines shows a group of people protesting outside of the Capitol Building in Washington D.C. (Figure 1.7). A woman in the foreground is signing a petition titled "Time for a Change," while the individuals in the background are holding up signs emblazoned with a variety of messages. There are anti-war slogans like "Schools Not War" and "Bikes not Bombs." In addition, there are some civil rights banners such as "Freedom of Religion" and "Civil Rights are Human Rights." Finally, there is one placard emblazoned with the pro-medicinal marijuana message "Don't Tread on My Garden!" Not coincidentally, the man standing near this sign is wearing a lapel pin that bears the symbol for the American Medical Association.

Figure 1.7 From *It's Just a Plant* by Ricardo Cortés. Reprinted with permission.

Jackie's mother is not the only figure who encourages her to question the cultural-judicial status quo and work for social change. So, too, does the police officer that she meets. As he tells the young girl, "'Many police officers don't agree with the law against marijuana. But our job is to enforce rules, not to change them. If you think the law is a mistake, then maybe you should work to change it.'" She takes this advice to heart. As Cortés writes on a following page: "'When I grow up,' announced Jackie, 'I am going to vote so I can make all laws fair.'" Her father pushes her even further along in this line of thinking: "'There are other ways to help make change,' said her dad. 'Maybe you will be a lawyer, or the Mayor [*sic*].'" It is with this sentiment, as Jackie falls asleep listing the myriad different professions that she might be when she becomes an adult, that Cortés's book ends.

Jackie E. Stallcup, in an essay addressing the issue of agency in recent picture books, argues that even in narratives that ostensibly seek to empower children there "are unspoken issues of authority and control that add layers of complexity and suggest parallels with older texts that sought to control children" (126). Contrary to the seemingly iconoclastic aims of these texts, "the goal of securing adult authority has not changed—only the means of attaining it have been inverted" (Stallcup 126). Echoing the longstanding tradition of adults controlling nearly every facet of children's lives—from what they wear and when they go to sleep to what they eat and how they are to behave—"many of these books consolidate and disseminate adult authority while diminishing the possibilities for children's empowerment and emotional growth" (Stallcup 127).

This phenomenon is even more pronounced when it comes to children's activism. As Patricia N. Desjardins has written, "nearly all nations at least symbolically acknowledge the capabilities and rights of children to actively engage their citizenship" yet an array of "obstacles confront children who attempt to exercise these rights" (3). She elaborates: "Despite growing recognition of children's capabilities and competencies, prevailing notions of children as vulnerable and incompetent beings remain a powerful force in sustaining the relationship that exists between children and adults that precludes children from having a voice. Thus children are excluded from important decision-making processes as their need for protection is emphasized over other rights" (Desjardins 4).

For this reason, the focus of many print, visual, and media discussions about youth activism spotlight not the methods by which young people can engage in civic culture, but the ways that they can combat adult resistance to such activities. As Aarti Subramaniam and Fe Moncloa have written, community leaders need to create a "'participation-friendly' culture" that permits young people's civic action. To do so, however, adults must relinquish a certain amount of control—a condition that makes many men and women uncomfortable. For this reason, Jennifer L. O'Donoghue and Karen R. Strobel have proposed that adults need to negotiate the realms of "directivity and freedom," striking a balance between providing young people with suitable guidance, appropriate supervision, and helpful structure and allowing them the autonomy to think, speak, and act on their own.

Ricardo Cortés's *It's Just a Plant* offers a commentary about marijuana. But, in so doing, it takes a larger and more radical stance on children's personal agency, intellectual autonomy, and civic action. In the United States, it is commonplace for parents, politicians and—as the lyrics to a hit song from the 1980s attests—even popular musicians to assert how "children are our future." Cortés's picture book does more than simply give lip service to this statement. It offers an example of what it looks like to put these words into practice. While the message about questioning the criminalization of marijuana certainly makes *It's Just a Plant* controversial, it is this additional one about encouraging children to question adult authority and even current civic law that causes the book to be truly radical and, for many, truly alarming. In this way, while Cortés's picture book spotlights the niche market subject of marijuana, the implications of his discussion reach far beyond this realm.

Notes

1. *It's Just a Plant* is not paginated. Accordingly, none of the quotations that I include from the text are assigned page numbers. That said, Cortés's picture book is relatively short and, thus, it should not be difficult for readers to locate these passages.

2. An article that appeared in *The Washington Post* on November 8, 1987, discussed the past cannabis use by both Al Gore and Newt Gingrich. As the reporters document: "Gore, 39, said in an impromptu news conference ... that he had smoked marijuana in college and the Army but that he hasn't touched it in 15 years" (Specter and Dickenson A1). Likewise, a few paragraphs later, they reveal: "Gingrich said he had used marijuana once and that it did not affect him. 'The historical record is that 19 years ago, I used marijuana once at a party ... in New Orleans'" (Specter and Dickenson A1). Finally, Rudolph J. Gerber has documented Bloomberg's now-notorious admission about marijuana: "In 2002, New York City Mayor Michael Bloomberg, asked by a reporter if he had ever smoked pot, responded enthusiastically, 'You bet I did. And I enjoyed it.' Quickly thereafter, the city's billboards featured his larger-than-life picture with this cheerful admission as part of a drug liberalization campaign" (Gerber xvii).

3. See Jamie Pietras's "It's Just a Book," *The Village Voice*, 22 February 2005. Full text is available at http://www.villagevoice.com/2005-02-22/news/it-s-just-a-book/. Meanwhile, Cortés was interviewed on *The O'Reilly Factor* on March 7, 2005. A transcript of their conversation can be found at http://0-www.lexisnexis.com.fintel.roanoke.edu/lnacui2api/api/version1/getDocCui?-lni=4FN7-4R70-TWD3-138H&csi=174179&hl=t&hv=t&hnsd=f&hns=t&hgn=t&oc=00240&perma=true.

4. Later in this chapter, I discuss the botanical, commercial, medicinal, and legal differences between hemp and cannabis. For now, to demonstrate the widespread presence of this plant type in the United States prior to the early twentieth century, I am including hemp and cannabis in the same broad botanical category. Indeed, in contemporaneous discussions about controlled substances, cannabis and hemp are routinely (if erroneously, as I will discuss later) seen as indistinguishable.

5. Once again, the motives for this piece of legislation were not merely concerns about public health and welfare. As Randi Mehling has discussed, "Some experts theorize that pressure from the influential liquor lobby hastened legislation against marijuana in the 1930s. ... The 1937 Marihuana Tax Act and subsequent state laws making marijuana illegal were passed to the delight of liquor manufacturers, who saw the growing popularity of marijuana as a threat to their newly legalized profits" (Mehling 83). Meanwhile, Christine Van Tuyl cites the influence of another powerful business lobby. Both while the Marihuana Tax Act was being debated and especially after its passage "many commentators conclude[d] that the law has passed just to prohibit industrial hemp from competing with paper, cotton, and newly discovered plastics like nylon" (9–10).

6. Of course, Richard "Cheech" Marin and Tommy Chong reintroduced while they simultaneously complicated the longstanding racialization of marijuana use. The comedy duo was exceedingly popular with young, white, middle-class American audiences, but they were not Anglo-European. Marin's family hailed from Mexico. Moreover, one the trademarks of his comedy routine was his implementation of a heavy (and wholly artificial) Spanish accent. Meanwhile, as

Darby Li Po Price has written, "Most people think of Chong as a Chicano-even though he has a Chinese last name" (100). For more on the perception as well as the performance of racial identity in the Cheech and Chong comedy duo, see Norman K. Denzin's *Reading Race: Hollywood and the Cinema of Racial Violence* (London: Sage, 2002) and Darby Li Po Price's "Humorous Hapas, Performing Identity," *Ameriasia Journal* 23.1 (1997): 99–111.

7. As journalist Steve Chapman has reported: "Both George W. Bush and Bill Clinton admitted to smoking marijuana, as did Al Gore and John Kerry. Obama has admitted doing the same" (par. 7). He goes on to discuss the specific circumstances of their youthful indiscretions with cannabis along with the irony that such admissions have been both forgiven by the public and not influenced their stance on drug control policy.

8. There is a preview version of *It's Just a Plant* that can be examined for free online through the website for Magic Propaganda Mill. This edition contains some alterations and even omissions from the printed version of Cortés's book. However, this online edition is not a complete version of *It's Just a Plant*; it is just a preview.

2 Nip/Tuck Truth

My Beautiful Mommy, the Medicalization of Motherhood, and the Harmful Condition of Childhood Innocence

Beginning in the 1990s and accelerating rapidly throughout the opening decade of the new millennium, both the number and the variety of cosmetic surgery procedures performed on individuals in the United States increased exponentially. As Victoria Pitts-Taylor has written, "in the United States in 2005, there were nearly two million aesthetic operations—more than quadruple the number in 1984—along with over eight million nonsurgical procedures like Botox and skin resurfacing" (3). While these figures are already astoundingly high, they do not represent the true number of actual aesthetic procedures performed. In the words of Pitts-Taylor once again: "Patients getting cosmetic surgery increasingly have multiple procedures during the same operation—in 2004, for example, one-third of cosmetic surgeries involved multiple procedures. It is now ordinary for a cosmetic surgeon to package procedures, like a chin implant to go with rhinoplasty, or a breast lift to go with a tummy tuck" (3).

Although men constitute a growing number of cosmetic surgery patients,[1] women still form the overwhelming majority. As Kathy Davis has observed, "the media makes its message clear: no one is so beautiful that she cannot become even more so with the help of surgery" (18). Such beliefs have made an impact. Throughout the opening decade of the new millennium, the American Society for Aesthetic Plastic Surgery reported that roughly 90% of all procedures were performed on women ("Statistics").

Of course, some of the women who undergo cosmetic procedures have children. This situation raises a dilemma about how to handle the issue. Unless the mother plans to spend weeks away from her family while healing, the child is surely going to notice that she has undergone some type of medical treatment. After all, there will be bandages, bruising, and a period of convalescence. Moreover, even if the mother is able to conceal her recuperation from her child, her physical appearance will be altered by the procedure in some way. As a result, many mothers undergoing cosmetic surgery struggle with how to discuss the issue with their son or daughter. What do they say about plastic surgery? When should they bring it up? How do they even broach the subject?

In the same way that Ricardo Cortés penned *It's Just a Plant* for parents who used marijuana recreationally and wished to talk about this decision with their son or daughter, first-time author Michael Salzhauer composed a children's book for this specialized demographic of mothers undergoing cosmetic surgery and struggling with how to discuss the issue with their children. As New York-based plastic surgeon Dr. Darrick Antell said about the text's target audience: "It's a narrow niche, but there is a need for it" (qtd. in Friedman, par. 6). Salzhauer titled his narrative *My Beautiful Mommy*, and it was billed as the first picture book to address plastic surgery for elementary-aged children. Illustrated by Victor Guiza, the text was released in 2008 by Big Tent Books—a small specialty imprint based in Georgia that identifies itself as a venue for the "self-publisher" ("Fulfillment," par. 1). *My Beautiful Mommy* is told from a first-person perspective and relays the experiences of a young girl whose mother is about to undergo multiple elective aesthetic procedures. Given the didactic purpose of the text, the narrative provides its child readers with a type of "guided tour" or instructive overview of the process. Salzhauer's picture book begins with the mother's initial consultation at the doctor's office, progresses to the day of her surgery, discusses the period of her recuperation, and ends with the removal of her bandages and the unveiling of her new, cosmetically altered self. To help explain the entire cosmetic surgery experience to young readers, the book appropriates a common metaphor from nature: it compares the mother's transformation as that of a caterpillar into a butterfly, complete with likening her postsurgery bandages to a cocoon.

No matter how cutely plastic surgery is framed in *My Beautiful Mommy*, it is a highly controversial subject, especially when it is being discussed with elementary-aged youngsters. Thus, both Salzhauer and his picture book received tremendous media attention. Before *My Beautiful Mommy* had been officially released and then accelerating rapidly after it appeared, the narrative was featured in an array of national magazines and newspapers, including *Newsweek*, *The Atlantic*, *The Huffington Post*, *USA Today*, *The Washington Post*, and *The New York Times*. Similarly, the book was the subject of segments on a variety of news commentary and television talk shows, ranging from *The View* and CNN's *Headline News* to *Entertainment Tonight* and *The O'Reilly Factor*. Meanwhile, the narrative received dozens of customer review posts at online booksellers like Amazon as well as many lively discussion threads on parenting blogs and motherhood boards. Finally, Michael Salzhauer appeared as a guest on various morning shows—including NBC's *Today* show and CBS's *Early Show*—to explain the aim of his book along with his intent in writing it. Echoing the common advertising strategy used by niche market products, these segments collectively helped *My Beautiful Mommy* acquire buzz, generate word-of-mouth, and go viral: throughout the early spring and summer of 2008, the text was the subject of lively discussion at old-fashioned socializing sites like office watercoolers and newfangled social media sites like Facebook and Twitter. In late April 2008, in fact, Amy Hollyfield, in a story for *ABC Morning News* in San Francisco, rightly noted that Salzhauer's book had "lit up" the Internet ("Plastic Surgery").

The mother in *My Beautiful Mommy* is undergoing not simply a random cluster of cosmetic surgery procedures but a specific grouping known as the "mommy makeover." Comprised of a tummy tuck, liposuction, and a breast lift (with or without implants), it is designed to help mothers regain their pre-pregnancy physique. The procedure, which first received this name in the new millennium, has been increasing in popularity during the past decade. As an article in *Newsweek* explained:

> No one specifically tracks the number of tummy-tuck-and-breast-implant combos (or "mommy makeovers," as they're called), but according to the latest numbers from the American Society of Plastic Surgeons, breast augmentation was the most popular cosmetic surgery procedure last year, with 348,000 performed (up 6 percent over 2006). Of those, about one-third were for women over 40 who often opt for implants to restore lost volume in their breasts due to aging or pregnancy weight gain. There were 148,000 tummy tucks—up 1 percent from the previous year.
>
> (Springen, par. 5)

The increasing number of women undergoing cosmetic surgery, coupled with the growing societal belief that parents ought to be more honest and open with their children, demonstrated the need to discuss the subject with young people. As Abigail Jones aptly observed, while much attention has been paid to "the emotional effects plastic surgery can have on patients," few have addressed the question "how does a mother's plastic surgery affect her kids?" ("Mother," par. 6).

My Beautiful Mommy engages with this precise issue. Released on the symbolic date of Mother's Day, the picture book is aimed at children ages four through seven and is intended to ease the fear and anxiety that boys and girls experience when a parent undergoes cosmetic surgery. The jacket flap to the text cites the following eye-opening statistic: "In 2007 more than 400,000 women with young children underwent cosmetic surgery in the U.S. alone." Commenting on this phenomenon, author Michael Salzhauer remarks: "'Parents [facing elective cosmetic surgery] generally tend to go into this denial thing. They just try to ignore the kids' questions completely'" (qtd. in Springen, par. 6). Faced with this lack of information, children "'fill in the blanks in their imagination' and then feel worse when they see 'mommy with bandages'" (qtd. in Springen, par. 6). In this way, *My Beautiful Mommy* was framed—by its author, publisher, and accompanying press materials—as filling a need not yet met by extant books for young readers. As the blurb on the back cover asserts: "If you are a mother with young children and thinking about having plastic surgery—this book is a must-have" (emphasis in original).

These altruistic comments notwithstanding, Michael Salzhauer is not a child psychologist, expert in early childhood education, or even professional writer. On the contrary, echoing the ascendency of the amateur that is a cornerstone to the niche market model of production, he is a first-time children's author. Salzhauer does have a professional life outside of his newfound foray into literature for young people: he is a board-certified cosmetic surgeon with a successful practice in Bal Harbour, Florida. The "About the Author" section at the end of the book explains that Salzhauer "has performed hundreds of beautiful mommy makeovers during his career." In addition, he "hosts a Sunday morning radio call-in show called 'Nip Talk Radio'" (Boodman HE05).

Given Salzhauer's professional stake in the cosmetic surgery industry and his desire to provide the patients in his own practice with a resource to help explain and even justify their decision to have an elective aesthetic procedure, it is perhaps not surprising that *My Beautiful Mommy* is at least as much a public-relations campaign as it is a children's book. Indeed, this aspect of the text was highlighted in many of the print, television, and Internet discussions about it. Fox News, for example, called *My Beautiful Mommy* "marketing for doctors." Likewise, customer reviews on sites like Amazon deemed the narrative "just a glorified advertisement" ("If the Dr.'s Plastic," par. 1). As a consequence, although *My Beautiful Mommy* purports to discuss cosmetic surgery with young people, what it actually—and somewhat unsurprisingly—does is serve as a mouthpiece for the Western beauty industry. The picture book perpetuates the widespread American obsession with the ideal feminine body. Furthermore, it presents cosmetic surgery as a means to obtain it. In this way, while the target audience for Salzhauer's text might have been niche, its message was not.

That said, *My Beautiful Mommy* does more than simply add to ongoing millennial conversations about technoconstructions of the body. In another more serious implication—and one that went largely undetected even amid the intense media attention—the narrative pushes its discussion about Western standards of women's beauty into a new and more alarming realm. Although *My Beautiful Mommy* can be read from a feminist perspective about questions of female agency with regard to elective cosmetic surgery, its more dominant and disturbing message concerns the medicalization of the female reproductive body. Throughout the picture book, a woman's postpregnancy physique is cast as a problem that medical science in general and plastic surgery in particular can solve. Pregnancy and childbirth have long been framed by the largely male medical establishment as debilitating conditions requiring professional treatment. *My Beautiful Mommy* extends such viewpoints to motherhood is as well.

That said, the impetus fueling the problematic messages in *My Beautiful Mommy* stem from much more than merely Salzhauer's status as a plastic surgeon. The perspective that the narrative offers is also heavily influenced by an alternative though equally powerful force: the author's conceptions of children and childhood. Rather than providing a truthful, accurate, and realistic portrait of what children can expect when their parent undergoes an elective cosmetic procedure—as the author purports—*My Beautiful Mommy* provides a highly selective, sanitized, and, at times, distorted one. Salzhauer's desire to inform young people about the experience of cosmetic surgery is overshadowed by his competing and even stronger belief that children ought to be shielded from upsetting information, unpleasant events, and unsavory details. As a result, while *My Beautiful Mommy* offers a telling commentary on the medicalization of women's bodies, it also embeds another tacit but arguably even more revealing message: the impossibility or, at least, incompatibility of writing about a daring new subject for children while still maintaining conventional and highly romanticized views about them.

On the Cutting Edge of Motherhood

Although cosmetic surgery has been part of American life for generations, only in recent decades has it been the subject of increased media attention as well as public notoriety. As Victoria Pitts-Taylor has written, whereas tummy tucks, breast augmentations, and nose jobs were formerly cloaked in secrecy—performed behind closed doors and not publicly disclosed let alone casually discussed—"cosmetic surgery is now culturally ubiquitous. On television, in magazines, and on the Web, there are endless discussions of cosmetic surgery, from makeover shows where participants get multiple surgeries to documentaries and celebrity gossip" (4). Fueled in part by the American interest in self-improvement and in part by the nation's confessional tell-all culture, cosmetic surgery has moved out of the shadows and into the spotlight. In a telling index of this shift, whereas celebrities used to conceal their cosmetic procedures, figures like Cher, Kathy Griffin, and Joan Rivers have openly discussed the numerous nips, tucks, lifts, and injections they have had on their bodies.

Cosmetic surgery is also no longer merely for the rich and famous. As advances in medical technology have made procedures more affordable, cosmetic surgery has been democratized, reaching into the middle class. In a telling index of this shift, "Dr. Alan Matarasso, a plastic surgeon in New York City and a spokesman for the American Society for Aesthetic Plastic Surgery, told *The Economist* in 2003, 'Ten years ago, you could reconstruct a woman's breast for $12,000. Now it can be done for $600'" (qtd. in Kuczynski 16). Reflecting this expansion in the socio-economic pool of potential patients, advertisements about procedures—ranging from Botox and liposuction to facelifts and hair transplants—can be found almost everywhere. As Pitts-Taylor relays, "Beauty and health magazines, local television news programs, and the Internet are replete with consumer information about cosmetic surgery—how to shop for a surgeon, what procedures are better than others, what the latest technology can accomplish" (4). For those who cannot afford cosmetic surgery but want to live vicariously, or for those who would like more information about the experience before deciding whether to go under the knife themselves, they can watch the experience on various television programs. Shows of this nature were especially numerous and exceedingly popular in the years directly preceding the release of *My Beautiful Mommy*. Programs like ABC's *Extreme Makeover* (2002–2007), Fox's *The Swan* (2004–2005), MTV's *I Want a Famous Face* (2004–2005), and the Discovery Channel's *Plastic Surgery: Before and After* (2002–2006) documented an individual's transformation—to strong audience ratings. During its second season, for example, "*Extreme Makeover* produced ABC's highest Adult 18–49 rating (3.2/8) in the hour in more than 7 months" (Rogers, par. 2). By early October, the program's audience size had spiked even more, "up over the prior week by 1.4 million viewers (8.4 million vs. 7.0 million) and by 19% among Adults 18–49" (Rogers, par. 2). When viewed collectively, the proliferation of cosmetic surgery in American popular, print, and material culture "point toward its normalization" (Pitts-Taylor 4). As Elizabeth Haiken has aptly observed, "Today the stigma of narcissism that once attached to cosmetic surgery has largely vanished, leaving in its place the comfortable aura of American pragmatism, with a whiff of optimistic commitment to self-improvement thrown-in" (7).

As cosmetic surgery has become more common in the United States, so too has it become more gendered. Kathy Davis has written that "where previous patients were men disabled by war and in industrial accidents, now the recipients are overwhelmingly women who are dissatisfied with the way their bodies look" (16). She goes on to provide some illuminating statistics: "Nearly ninety percent of the operations are performed on women: all breast corrections, ninety-one percent of facelifts, eighty-six percent of eyelid reconstructions, and sixty-one percent of all nose surgery" (Davis 21). In this way, cosmetic surgery has emerged as one of the largest and most lucrative branches of both American medical practice and the beauty industry. Anthony Elliott has noted that "[i]n the United States alone, it is estimated that cosmetic surgery is an industry generating $15 to $20 billion a year" (21). Public opinion polls indicate that the level of participation in cosmetic surgery is likely to expand further. According to a survey of women conducted on the eve of the millennium, "[m]ore than one-third would like to alter their thighs. One-fourth would like to change their buttocks, and about the same proportion would like to erase their facial wrinkles. Nearly one in five want different breasts and one in seven want different noses" (Sullivan ix). Existing on the nexus of consumer culture and medical technology, cosmetic surgery has become an emblem of the nation's postmodern makeover culture and its attendant belief in the malleability of the self.

My Beautiful Mommy is both a product of this climate and a catalyst for it. The book portrays the appeal of cosmetic surgery, but it also perpetuates its many ethical problems, psychological hazards, and physical dangers. Salzhauer's narrative greatly minimizes or even ignores the numerous potential risks and complications associated with cosmetic surgery. In so doing, *My Beautiful Mommy* is less interested in realistically explaining and accurately portraying cosmetic procedures to young people as it purports and is instead more invested in recruiting the next generation of potential female patients.

* * *

The troubling information about personal appearance and female beauty in *My Beautiful Mommy* begins even before readers open the picture book and examine its first page. The cover image to the narrative presents a full-length portrait of a young, slender woman—the mommy of the title. Echoing longstanding associations of cosmetic surgery with narcissistic vanity, her proportions are not simply perfect, but almost Barbie doll-like in nature: she has a full bosom, a slim waist, and pleasingly curvy hips. Her legs are long and lean, with a slender knee and modest definition around the calf. Her long auburn hair, dainty feet, and creamy white skin—which is without a blemish, freckle, or even hint of body hair—complete the picture.

The clothing that the mother is wearing calls further attention to her body: she is depicted in hip-hugging, form-fitting dark pink pants and a light pink half-shirt, her belly button exposed. Throughout the book, in fact, the mother will retain this attire, wearing snug pants and shirts that expose her midriff. Accentuating both the highly feminized and the fairy-tale nature of this image, the mother is surrounded by whimsical ribbons of sparkly dust. Bright stars or twinkling bits of diamond glimmer in the spotlight. The entire cover of the book is fuchsia-colored, a feature that further genders the text and also furthers its appeal to young girls. At the very least, with its bright pink cover, the picture book does not appear to present itself—contrary to the assertion of its surgeon-author—as being geared for boys and girls equally. Far from being "gender neutral," the narrative clearly seems to be targeting young girls. Finally, when this color palette is combined with the exaggerated eyes and heavy black border that outlines each character, it gives the illustrations a cartoonish appearance. On the cover to *My Beautiful Mommy*, these elements cause the mother to resemble one of the princess characters from Walt Disney's popular animated movies. Author Michael Salzhauer has himself acknowledged the similarities. During an appearance on the *TODAY* show to promote *My Beautiful Mommy* in April 2008, he discussed how illustrator Victor Guiza "Disney-fied" the illustrations. The drawings have a cartoony look, using vivid colors, heavy black outlines, and oversized eyes ("Mommy's Makeover"). Salzhauer explained that the decision to have the illustrations resemble Disney-style animation arose from a desire to give the book a "familiar" look ("Mommy's Makeover"). However, this choice also evokes the problematic messages about women's appearance and the female body that permeate Disney films. Indeed, Loryn Brantz, in an article that appeared on the popular website BuzzFeed, digitally edited the appearance of six of Disney's most popular princesses—including Elsa from *Frozen*, Ariel from *The Little Mermaid*, and Belle from *Beauty and the Beast*—to give them more realistic proportions. The subtitle that

Brantz chose for her post made her intent with these revised versions clear: "Healthier waistlines for them and healthier self-esteem for us growing up."

The mother is not the only character depicted on the cover of Salzhauer's picture book. Her daughter—who serves as the narrator of the story—is standing to her right. In a gesture that simultaneously infantilizes the young girl while it traffics in the historical association of children with cuteness, she is holding a plump teddy bear. Moreover, as she gazes at her new, surgically altered mommy, the youngster has a look of wonder, joy, and even amazement on her face. This depiction of a young girl marveling at the proportionally perfect—because it has been surgically altered—female body foreshadows the message of *My Beautiful Mommy*. Giving further credence to viewing this image as a framing device for the text as a whole, this exact illustration is repeated on the book's title page. In *Children's Picturebooks: The Art of Visual Storytelling*, Martin Salisbury and Morag Styles have commented about how "in the picturebook the visual [imagery] will often carry much of the narrative responsibility" (7). While Salzhauer's written text advances the plot, the illustrations—as this cover image suggests—play a major role in guiding and even modeling how the reader ought to regard these events.

In keeping with Salzhauer's stated goal of easing children's fears when a parent undergoes cosmetic surgery, *My Beautiful Mommy* begins at the beginning: with the visit to the doctor's office. The opening page reads: "Mommy picked me up early from school today. She said we were going to the doctor ... but it wasn't my doctor, Dr. Jill. ... Today we went to a new doctor for Mommy: Dr. Michael."[2] Several pages into the story, we learn that the young narrator has a sibling, a brother named Billy. Although he is older, it is only by a few years. Judging by the illustrations, Billy is still in elementary school. Although the mother's cosmetic surgery will undoubtedly affect her son as much as her daughter, Salzhauer's book focuses on the young girl. In fact, throughout the twenty-two pages that comprise *My Beautiful Mommy*, Billy is mentioned only four times, and it is always briefly and usually as part of the background to the story.[3]

While Salzhauer's decision to focus his book on the daughter may have arisen because she is younger and thus presumably more frightened by the procedure as well as less able to understand what is happening, another and more culturally constructed reason is also possible. By telling the story from the daughter's point of view, the book highlights the highly gendered nature of beauty and the added pressures that women face about their appearance. Indeed, far from simply tacitly acknowledging this fact via the choice of narrator, *My Beautiful Mommy* almost seems to indoctrinate the daughter to this reality. The picture book's initial sentence "Mommy picked me up early from school today" is significant, for it indicates the mother's deliberate decision to include not simply her child but her female child in the process of visiting the plastic surgeon's office.[4] This plot detail raises questions about the book's supposed interest in merely explaining the phenomenon of cosmetic surgery to children versus advertising and promoting it to a specific gendered demographic of them. As reconstructive surgeon Dr. Pete Costantino has written, "Children are still in the process of developing concepts of self-image and beauty and ugliness and so forth. ... They're in a formative phase, and I don't think it's valuable to children to push aesthetic surgery in their face" (qtd. in Friedman, par. 21). Debbie Then, a child psychologist, agrees, commenting that this phenomenon can be especially damaging for young girls given the added pressures that they experience about appearance: "There is a concern that if we focus the attention of young children on this topic, we will encourage very young girls to start obsessing about their looks at an even earlier age than they already do" (qtd. in Friedman, par. 24).

Salzhauer's decision to write his narrative from a first-person perspective with the young girl serving as the story's narrator but have Victor Guiza illustrate the book from a third-person viewpoint—with this character appearing in the images rather than having them drawn from her point of view—adds to this phenomenon. Perry Nodelman has written about the inherent "doubleness" that arises in picture books in which the "I" of the narrative voice does not match how the reader's eye is being focalized by the images ("The Eye" 1). Whereas the first-person perspective presented by the words encourages the child who is reading or listening to the story to identify with the narrator, third-person illustrations serve the opposite purpose: they promote disidentification or, at least, distance from the narrative voice. As Nodelman notes, given that these images are drawn "from the point of view of another person," they offer the perspective "of someone looking *at* the speaker" ("The Eye" 5; emphasis in original). Maria Nikolajeva and Carole Scott discuss the complex interpretive strain that these dual (and even duel) perspectives place on readers: "Picturebooks are supposed to be addressed to a young, inexperienced audience, yet they use within the same story two different forms of focalization, which puts very high demands on the reader" (125). Nodelman argues that the combination of first-person "I" narration and third-person "eye" illustration in a picture book asks children to connect with the young narrator within the text, but then to disconnect themselves from this same figure in the pictures. As he explains, "The child reader is being invited to adopt an adult perspective on the child protagonist he or she reads or hears about and, presumably (since this is how most adults assume child-readers do and should interact with texts), is being invited to identify with. The child viewer is being invited to understand him or herself as adults see and understand him or her" (Nodelman, "Words" 17).

While this combination of child-focalized written text but adult-focalized visual imagery is certainly at play in *My Beautiful Mommy*, the subject matter of the picture book causes it to acquire an additional implication. By having the story told in the young girl's voice but the illustrations requiring readers to look at her physical form, *My Beautiful Mommy* creates a powerful parallel between the way in which the mother's body is being inspected, observed, and scrutinized by the cosmetic surgeon and the way in which the young female narrator is being similarly displayed to the book's audience in the illustrations. In what cannot be seen as a mere coincidence given the topic of Salzhauer's text, both the mother and daughter are being subjected to what Jacques Lacan and Laura Mulvey have famously termed "the gaze."

The second page of *My Beautiful Mommy* continues with this theme but pushes it in a slightly different direction. The illustration depicts the mother sitting across from the cosmetic surgeon's desk; her daughter stands beside her, leaning on the chair (Figure 2.1). The drawing conveys the authority of scientific knowledge along with the power that is conferred on male medical figures: no fewer than eight diplomas tile the wall behind the plastic surgeon. Meanwhile, his certificate from the American Board of Plastic Surgery is prominently displayed on a decorative wood easel atop his desk. Finally, continuing the book's highly gendered color scheme, Dr. Michael's office is painted navy blue, suggesting that boys become medical professionals—like plastic surgeons—and girls seek out their services.[5]

Figure 2.1 From *My Beautiful Mommy*, written by Michael Salzhauer and illustrated by Victor Guiza. Reprinted with permission.

The visual representation of Dr. Michael furthers the association of cosmetic surgery not with the correction of physical problems but with the creation of perfect bodies: with his small head, almost comically broad chest, and huge pectoral muscles, Dr. Michael looks like a comic book superhero. Adding to this vision of vanity, not one but two portraits of a young girl winning a beauty pageant appear in frames on the wall. Finally, the conversation that Dr. Michael has with the mother forms a final element of unease. The speech bubble above the plastic surgeon's head offers the following cartoon-ish rendering of this serious conversation: "Blah, Blah, Blah, Tummy, Blah, Blah, Blah, Nose." While this dialogue is perhaps meant to reflect a child's experience of many adult conversations—glossing over words that do not interest her or that she fails to understand—its vacuous content and flippant tone minimizes the seriousness of cosmetic surgery. Moreover, it also stands in direct contradiction to the book's alleged didactic purpose. If *My Beauti-ful Mommy* is, as its author claims, intended to educate young people about plastic surgery, then the visit to the doctor's office and the chance to meet with the surgeon offers the ideal opportunity to convey this information. As discussed in the previous chapter, this is precisely how Ricardo Cortés utilizes his young protagonist's visit to see Dr. Eden in *It's Just a Plant*. How-ever, in a decision that is confusing and even contradictory, Salzhauer does not capitalize on this seemingly perfect scenario. Instead, he elects to silence the doctor first by stripping his dialogue of any substantive content and then by turning what few remarks he does make into meaningless, comedic prattle.

On the opposing page of the scene depicting the doctor's office, the surgeon's assistant takes the "before" photos of the mother (Figure 2.2). Dr. Michael is present in the exam room for these photos, as is the young narrator. Even more tellingly, she is not standing near her mother during this process but is on the side of the room with the medical personnel. In so doing, the young girl is being trained in or, at least, invited to join the process of inspecting a woman's physical appearance and diagnosing its "problems." Seeing the mother standing before a full-length mirror—with her slim waist, long legs, and proportional bosom—causes not only many adult but surely also some child readers to wonder what surgical proce-dures are needed. As Kathy Davis has noted about one of the diagnostic peculiarities of plastic surgery, "In most medical specialties, patients don't know what their problem is, and leave it to the specialist to figure out. Not so with cosmetic surgery. Here, it is the patient who knows what's wrong and the surgeon who often has a hard time seeing it" (2). Indeed, throughout her experience interviewing cosmetic surgery candidates in the Netherlands, Davis made the following discovery: "Not only did I rarely see what the applicants were coming in to have done, but once I knew what the problem was, I found myself feeling astounded that anyone could be willing to undergo such drastic measures for what seemed to me such a minor imperfection" (72).

For some men and women, this personal discomfort becomes a type of pathological fixation, a condition known as body dysmorphic disorder (BDD). As Victoria Pitts-Taylor has written, BDD is defined as "a mental disorder characterized by a person's obsession about a slight or imagined flaw in his or her appearance to the point of clinically significant distress or dysfunction" (2). Individuals who are diagnosed with BDD are not

Then Laura took
pictures of Mommy in a
funny gown.

Figure 2.2 From *My Beautiful Mommy*, written by Michael Salzhauer and
illustrated by Victor Guiza. Reprinted with permission.

candidates for cosmetic surgery and, in an effort to help surgeons identify
those who suffer from it, the American Society for Aesthetic Plastic Surgery
developed guidelines during the 1990s for how much cosmetic surgery is too
much for an individual. Not surprisingly, the list of acceptable procedures is
rather lengthy, "establishing a regimen over one's adult lifetime that, if one
took the advice to its maximum, would amount to approximately fifteen
surgical procedures, along with numerous laser treatments and dozens of
injections, sustained over a span of forty to fifty years" (Pitts-Taylor 29). In
the words of Pitts-Taylor once again: "Generally, they see women who get
cosmetic surgeries, even most that get multiple procedures, as people who
understand the social pressures surrounding youth and beauty and who
want to improve or maintain their good looks and their self-esteem" (116).
While it is unclear whether the mother in *My Beautiful Mommy* suffers
from body dysmorphic disorder—as readers do not know if she has had
cosmetic surgery before and are also unaware how much she fixates on her
body image—many will likely agree that her perceived flaws are just that:
merely perceived. Indeed, as one customer review on Amazon pointed out
about the character of the mother, "she is already thin, and complains about
not being able to fit into her clothes after having children. But again she is
already thin!" ("Ugh," par. 2).

The mother's justification for wanting the mommy makeover only enhances this perspective. As Anthony Elliott, Sander Gilman, and Elizabeth Haiken have all written, plastic surgery has historically been viewed in a negative light. Women who have had facelifts, tummy tucks, and breast augmentations are commonly seen as victims of a patriarchal Western beauty system that imposes strict, limited, and even oppressive standards about how the female body should look. Deborah Sullivan aptly summarizes this perspective in a comment from a recent book: "cosmetic surgery inscribes our gendered beliefs about appearance, physical fitness, and age in our flesh. It personifies the social, psychological, and economic value we place on an attractive appearance, regardless of gender. ... It incarnates the image-obsessed consumerism and competitive free-market economy of the late twentieth century" (x). Women who succumb to societal pressures about their appearance by going under the knife are seen as possessing a whole host of psycho-social problems, ranging from narcissistic vanity and patriarchal brainwashing to pathological illness and even a masochistic longing for self-mutilation. Indeed, women's desire for cosmetic surgery is often viewed, especially by feminist critics, as little more than an outward manifestation of "internalized oppression" (Pitts-Taylor 9).

The popularization of cosmetic surgery during the past few decades has challenged this viewpoint. Rather than viewing women as "brain-washed victims of media hype" or "cultural dupes" of the patriarchal beauty culture, psychologists, sociologists, and even feminists have sought to "explore how women actually experience and negotiate their bodies in the context of many promises and few options" (Davis 49). This approach resists discounting or discrediting women's desire to have cosmetic surgery and instead strives to listen to their rationale, acknowledge their reasons, and respect their choices. Kathy Davis has documented how, for many women who have elective cosmetic procedures, the desire to have a tummy tuck, breast lift, or liposuction does not arise from a longing to possess a perfect physique, but rather to correct a long-disliked personal trait and thus have a body that is "ordinary" (12). After conducting interviews with dozens of women who were candidates for cosmetic procedures, she discovered the extreme amount of psychological suffering that they had experienced: self-consciousness over small breasts, embarrassment because of a crooked nose, and even self-loathing as a result of protruding ears. In an acute reversal of the victimization model, after decades of having their self-image hampered by a disliked physical feature, they decided to be a victim no more. Ironically, many of these women drew on the language of feminist empowerment to explain this decision, describing their cosmetic surgery as an act that finally allowed them to "take control" of their body and "be in charge" of their life. In this way, as Davis notes, cosmetic surgery is reframed not as a symptom of pathology or the product of patriarchal brainwashing, but "as a strategy for interrupting the downward spiral of suffering which can accompany a woman's problematic relationship to her body" (12).

This alternative way of viewing cosmetic surgery, however, is neither this simple nor one-sided. Even if we see tummy tucks and breast augmentations as a form of female empowerment, this rationale does not eradicate the problems associated with our contemporary beauty culture. After all, a woman's new, surgically modified body may liberate her from feelings of inadequacy, but it creates a standard by which other women are judged. As a result, as Davis notes, cosmetic surgery participates in the oppression of women while it paradoxically helps them to escape it. For this reason, cosmetic surgery remains a site of intense cultural controversy. Deborah A. Sullivan encapsulates this dilemma, writing: "Respect for the right of competent adults to make decisions about their own bodies should not blind us to the larger cultural and social context in which personal choices occur" (5).

My Beautiful Mommy reflects this binary. On the whole, the book presents the mother's decision to have a mommy makeover as the result of personal suffering and the decision to "take control" of her body. When the young narrator asks her mother why she is having an operation to make "her tummy smaller," she gives the following reply: "You see, as I got older, my body stretched and I couldn't fit into my clothes anymore." As the mother kneels down while explaining this rationale to her daughter, a thought bubble shows her struggling to button her

Figure 2.3 From *My Beautiful Mommy*, written by Michael Salzhauer and illustrated by Victor Guiza. Reprinted with permission.

jeans (Figure 2.3). In an effort to convey both the physical frustration and psychological discomfort associated with this situation, her cheeks are puffed out, her eyes are crossed, and her knees are knocked. In language that echoes the sentiments of many women about how cosmetic surgery allows them to "take charge" and "regain control," the mother informs her daughter: "'Dr. Michael is going to *help fix that* and *make me feel better*'" (emphasis added).

In these and other passages, *My Beautiful Mommy* participates in the growing societal distinction of health versus wellness. Victoria Pitts-Taylor delineates the important semantic difference between these seemingly synonymous terms: "Whereas the sick body was once the primary territory of medicine, appearance and beauty are now increasingly seen as occasions for medical consumerism, and healthy bodies are regularly tuned up both inside and out" (28). While health has traditionally been defined as the absence of disease or sickness, wellness refers to a state of satisfaction, contentment, and happiness (both physical and psychological) with a body that is more than simply free from pathogens. For this reason, "the trend toward lifestyle medicine has 'massively expanded' the subjects of health care from sick bodies to the whole population" (Pitts-Taylor 28). Under the auspices of "wellness," women as well as men "take more elective medicines, from those to improve our sex lives to those that limit menstruation, or help us sleep, concentrate, relax, perform athletically, or look better" (Pitts-Taylor 28). As a result of the ascendency of a wellness approach to living, "The body is no longer simply a dysfunctional object requiring medical intervention, but a commodity—not unlike 'a car, a refrigerator, a house—which can be continuously upgraded and modified in accordance with new interests and greater resources.' It can be endlessly manipulated—reshaped, restyled, and reconstructed to meet prevailing fashions and cultural values" (Davis 17).

The mother's desire for cosmetic surgery in *My Beautiful Mommy* can be located within discourses of wellness and not simply health. After all, her presurgical body is a medically healthy one, but one in which she does not experience personal, physical, and psychological wellness. That said, the mother's initial explanation for seeking Dr. Michael's services is far less noble. "'Why are you going to look different?'" the daughter innocently asks about the aftermath of the cosmetic procedure. In what forms the most vehemently criticized passage in the book, the mother gives the following response: "'Not just different, my dear—prettier!'" (Figure 2.4). Even more problematic, a thought bubble above the mother's head shows her wearing an evening gown and the burly Dr. Michael placing a crown on her head. A sash draped across her body reads, "The Prettiest Mom." This detail alters the overall message in *My Beautiful Mommy* about elective aesthetic procedures. As Linda Lowen laments, "instead of looking at plastic surgery as part of the spectrum of self-improvement inside and out," it offers "the 'mommy wants to be prettier' cliché" (par. 7). Julie

"Not just different, my dear—prettier!" Mommy said.
"But you're already the prettiest Mommy in
the whole wide world!"

Figure 2.4 From *My Beautiful Mommy,* written by Michael Salzhauer and
illustrated by Victor Guiza. Reprinted with permission.

Deardoff concurs, commenting on the implications of this message to
young readers:

> Although many parents strive to teach their children that beauty begins
> from within, many do not and the book reflects that. Parents who
> choose plastic surgery for non-medical reasons are going to emphasize
> the importance of physical appearance whether they have a book to
> read to their children or not. Kids ape everything we say and do; if
> you're unhappy with how you look, chances are your kid will be ques-
> tioning her own appearance too. (par. 7)

Of course, societal pressures about appearance are highly gendered. Commenting on Salzhauer's text, child psychiatrist Elizabeth Bergen "worries that
kids will think their own body parts must need 'fixing' too. The surgery on
a nose, for example, may 'convey to the child that the child's nose, which
always seemed OK, might be perceived by Mommy or somebody as unacceptable'" (qtd. in Springen, par. 14). This implication has been noticed by figures beyond child development experts and medical professionals. Journalist
Tom Barlow made the following remark about the message of *My Beautiful
Mommy*: "What's the lesson here? I can just hear the child saying, 'I can't
wait until I can pay to have someone make me pretty!'" (par. 12). Likewise,

a customer on Amazon echoed this sentiment, writing in a review of the book: "In Dr. Salzhauer's world it is okay to teach young girls that the only path to self-esteem is to have potentially life-threatening surgery" ("I Can't Recognize," par. 5). Meanwhile, another comment posted on the same site reiterated this observation: "this book delivers the message to children that people are not beautiful without plastic surgery" ("Ugh," par. 2). Finally, a third customer review on Amazon offered an even grimmer suggestion about the possible take-away message of Salzhauer's book for young readers: "What if, after the bandages comes off and [you are] showing off your new face, your adorable little daughter comes up to you and says, 'Mommy, I'm ugly'" and expresses a desire to have plastic surgery (Juniper J, par. 1).

Far from mere speculation, the number of young people having cosmetic procedures is on the rise. According to Diana Zuckerman, "In 2003, more than 223,000 cosmetic procedures were performed on patients 18 years of age or younger, and almost 39,000 were surgical procedures such as nose reshaping, breast lifts, breast augmentation, liposuction, and tummy tucks" (par. 1). Especially among the upper- and upper-middle classes, it is becoming increasingly more common for parents to give their daughter a breast augmentation, some liposuction, or an ear pinning as a sixteenth birthday present. In *Flesh Wounds*, for example, Virginia Blum recalls being taken for a nose job when she was a teenager: "my mother considered it parentally irresponsible not to do what she could to make me more 'marketable'" (9). The number of young people having elective aesthetic procedures has increased so much in recent years that a small but growing subgenre of nonfiction books discusses the subject. Texts such as *Cosmetic Surgery for Teens: Choices and Consequences* (2003), *Can I Change the Way I Look?: A Teen's Guide to the Health Implications of Cosmetic Surgery and Beyond* (2005) and *Everything You Need to Know about the Dangers of Cosmetic Surgery* (2002) weigh the pros and cons involved in getting cosmetic surgery as well as the various procedures that are available, how much they cost, and the medical risks associated with them.[6]

If readers of Salzhauer's book feel uneasy with the mother's reason for visiting a cosmetic surgeon, then they are likely to experience even more discomfort with how the book helps the young girl cope with the resulting procedures and their disruption to her family life. As the narrator leaves Dr. Michael's office with her mother, she notes: "A nice lady in the office gave me two lollipops and a cookie." (See Figure 2.5.) These treats are featured prominently in the illustration that accompanies these lines. The foreground of the drawing shows the administrative assistant smiling broadly while holding out a plate filled with treats to the protagonist. The young girl reaches toward the candy and cookies with a look of surprise, delight, and even joy on her face. In the background, both Dr. Michael and the girl's mother look on happily: the mother is smiling warmly and the surgeon is either laughing or—given that his mouth is open in a wide grin—saying something jovial.

Figure 2.5 From *My Beautiful Mommy*, written by Michael Salzhauer and illustrated by Victor Guiza. Reprinted with permission.

The use of sugary sweets to console the child continues throughout the remainder of the story. On the day of her mother's surgery, the youngster's grandmother takes her—and her alone, her brother is not present—for a double-scoop ice cream cone. Once again, the sweets serve as the focal point in the illustration. The two ice cream cones—one being held by the young girl and other by her grandmother—occupy the foreground of the drawing. Moreover, they are centered in the composition. Finally, on the closing page, after the mother's bandages have been removed, she is rewarded with candy once again: "Mommy took out two big lollipops shaped like butterflies. Mommy gave me the pink one, which is my favorite color."

The "mommy makeover" is not the only type of cosmetic surgery that the mother in Salzhauer's book receives. She also has rhinoplasty. As Elizabeth Haiken, Virginia Blum, and Sander Gilman have all written, nose jobs are one of the first but also most culturally fraught aesthetic procedures. In *Making the Body Beautiful: A Cultural History of Aesthetic Surgery*, Sander Gilman discusses the longstanding practice of cosmetic surgery being used to alter the appearance of members of racial and ethnic minority groups and allow them to "pass" in white American culture. She explains: "Race- and ethnicity-based surgery has always focused on the most identifiable, and most caricatured features: for Jews, noses; for Asians, eyes; for African Americans, noses and lips" (Haiken 176). In the 1920s, for instance, Fanny Brice became famous for having a nose job to alter her "Jewish" appearance (Haiken 1–2).

Such practices continue to this day. Kathy Davis recounts attending a conference in the early 1990s where a cosmetic surgeon gave a lecture about successful techniques for making the eyes of Asian women appear Western (2). Finally, many sociologists, psychologists, and cultural commentators have discussed entertainer Michael Jackson as "only one among hundreds of thousands of Americans who have attempted, through plastic surgery, to minimize or eradicate physical signs of race or ethnicity that they believe mark them as 'other' (which in this context has always meant 'other' than white)" (Haiken 175–6). The use of cosmetic surgery to eliminate physical markers of ethnicity has become so pervasive that Gilman devotes an entire chapter to just what he calls "the racial nose."

The mother in *My Beautiful Mommy* is presented with a visage that could be placed in dialogue with this phenomenon. In the illustrations by Guiza, she possesses a noticeable bump and downward-sloping "hook" to her nose, traits that Gilman, Blum, and Haiken have all written are historically coded as markers for Jewishness. Even if the mother in *My Beautiful Mommy* is not trying to eradicate a real or imagined sign of ethnicity through rhinoplasty, she is nonetheless perpetuating homogenized notions of what it means to be attractive. In the words of Haiken, "by recognizing 'ugliness,' diagnosing inferiority complexes, and prescribing surgery, plastic surgeons reproduced and replicated a definition of beauty that clearly derived from and relied on Caucasian, even Anglo-Saxon, traditions and standards" (10).

The conclusion to *My Beautiful Mommy* amplifies this theme. The text reads: "One afternoon, Mommy came home from her appointment with Dr. Michael—and all of her bandages were off. She was smiling. She looked different. 'Your cocoon fell off,' I said. 'Yes, I feel much better,' Mommy answered." The illustration that accompanies these remarks nearly replicates the one that appears on the book's cover and title page. The mother is shown in a full-length pose against a fuchsia background. She is smiling and her arms are open and extended up in a "Ta-dah!" style gesture. As on the cover, the mother is wearing a light pink half-shirt and a pair of darker pink form-fitting pants. Indeed, as Catherine Price has written, although slim and shapely before, she now possesses "the sort of waist-to-hip ratio that's the stuff of Barbie's dreams" (par. 1). Finally, in a detail that presents surgical makeovers as not simply a medical marvel but nothing less than magical, streams of sparkly fairy dust, bright laser beams, cartoon stars, and rays of sunlight emanate from her body.

The following page shifts the perspective to show the daughter's reaction to her mother's new physique. Amazed and astounded, the youth asserts: "'Mommy your eyes are sparking like diamonds. You're the most beautiful butterfly in the whole world.'" A huge smile adorns the daughter's face, her eyes are open wide in awe and her hands are clasped in front of her face in adoration (Figure 2.6). A thought bubble beside the young girl's head depicts the mother as a beautiful, colorful butterfly. On the closing page, the pair is cuddled on the couch, the girl's head resting on her mother's lap. Brightly colored butterflies dot the page and the caption reads: "We snuggled on the sofa and Mommy hugged me tight. I fell asleep dreaming of butterflies." The butterflies mentioned in this passage can be read in at least two different ways. On one hand, of course, they refer to the narrative's present situation: the young girl is thinking about butterflies while she sleeps because she is thinking about her mother and her recent physical metamorphosis. On the other hand, though, the daughter's dream about butterflies can be read as an expression of her own future hope, wish, and even prophecy: she is dreaming about butterflies because she is dreaming of the day when she too will undergo cosmetic surgery and be transformed into "the most beautiful butterfly in the whole world." Far from either an overly academic or an overly cynical reading, it echoes events that appeared earlier in the book. Right after the mother's surgery, the protagonist sits at the kitchen table with her mother and mentions "We are learning about butterflies and watching cocoons hatch" for a school project (Figure 2.7). In response to this news, the mother "laughed and said she felt like a cocoon herself with all her bandages." In the illustration that appears below these lines, the young girl is wearing a t-shirt that has a butterfly on it. While this detail links the protagonist to her schoolwork, it also links her to her mother's plastic surgery. The drawing literally marks her as cosmetic surgery's next "butterfly."

Figure 2.6 From *My Beautiful Mommy*, written by Michael Salzhauer and illustrated by Victor Guiza. Reprinted with permission.

Figure 2.7 From *My Beautiful Mommy*, written by Michael Salzhauer and illustrated by Victor Guiza. Reprinted with permission.

Diagnosis: A Severe Case of Motherhood

Of course, the problematic physical features being treated in *My Beautiful Mommy* do not appear on merely any bodily form but a postreproductive one. The loose skin, extra fat, and sagging breasts that the mother wants the cosmetic surgeon to alter are the direct result of pregnancy and childbirth. In so doing, Salzhauer's picture book adds a new component to the long-standing medicalization of motherhood in the West.

Feminist critics have frequently discussed the way in which the largely male medical establishment—especially the specialties of obstetrics and gynecology—have cast women's reproductive processes as medical "problems." As Iris Marion Young has written, "Medicine's self-identification as the curing profession encourages others as well as the woman to think of her pregnancy as a condition that deviates from normal health" (408). Instead of viewing pregnancy, childbirth, and even menstruation as part of wom-en's natural biological processes, they see them as debilitating "conditions" requiring the interventionist treatment of (mostly male) physicians. As Phyllis L. Brodsky, Amanda Carson Banks, and Charlotte G. Borst have all discussed, the professionalization of medicine during the nineteenth century—with the advent of compulsory attendance at medical training, the rise of allopathic as opposed to homeopathic approaches to health and the formation of the American Medical Association—transformed the stages of reproduction from being handled by women in the home to being managed by male medical professionals in a hospital setting. For generations, menstruating women were encouraged by male doctors to refrain from strenuous activity and, afterward, to douche thoroughly. Meanwhile, those who became pregnant were subjected to an array of medical tests, advice, and procedures, many of which encroached on their privacy, placed unnecessary restrictions on their movement, and reduced their body to a mere vessel. These phenomena only increased during childbirth. While delivering a baby, women have been subjected to everything from epidurals, enemas, and episiotomies to having to lie prostrate in stirrups, being subjected to vacuum extractions, and the removal, through shaving, of their pubic hair.

In this way, the male medical establishment largely framed women's reproductive functions as health problems or at least "infirmities" rather than as natural bodily processes. In the words of Young once again, there is a "tendency within gynecological and obstetrical practice to approach menstruation, pregnancy, and menopause as 'conditions' with 'symptoms' that require 'treatment'" (415). Moreover, some of the practices prescribed by medical professionals were not simply unhelpful but actually harmful. Douching, for instance, which was once commonly recommended by physicians to ensure feminine health and hygiene after menstruation, is now discouraged for the way that it interferes with the body's natural levels of bacteria and its attendant ability to regulate itself (L. Jones, "Douching," par. 3). Likewise, midline episiotomies, which had been routinely performed on women in labor, are now decreasing, given the way in which they can cause nerve damage and interfere with both sexual and urinary function. In a vivid demonstration of the gendered divide between the realm of male doctors and the largely female realm of midwives and doulas, the latter have equated episiotomies with female circumcision (Cameron and Anderson 53). In a recent book, in fact, Caroline Sweetman groups episiotomies among various societal practices that constitute "violence against women."

My Beautiful Mommy extends the medicalization of the female reproductive body. The narrative, written by a male surgeon, goes beyond simply casting menstruation, pregnancy, and childbirth as conditions requiring medical intervention, but motherhood itself. *My Beautiful Mommy* presents the mother's postpregnancy body as a medical problem or, at least, condition that needs treatment. Instead of viewing her changed breasts and altered shape as the natural by-product of pregnancy, childbirth, and breastfeeding, it views these elements as physical deformities that can be corrected by the male medical establishment. Far from being limited to the perspective of one fictional picture book, this viewpoint has been expressed by many factual physicians. Dr. David A. Stoker, a plastic surgeon in Marina Del Rey, California, who specializes in mommy makeovers, has remarked: "'The *severe physical trauma* of pregnancy, childbirth, and breast-feeding can have *profound negative effects* that cause women to lose their hourglass figures,' he said" (qtd. in Singer, par. 3; *my emphasis*). His practice, Marina Plastic Surgery Associates, maintains a website, amommymakeover.com, that describes the surgeries *"required to overhaul* a postpregnancy body" (qtd. in Singer, par. 3; *my emphasis*).

Such attitudes exacerbate the pressures placed on wives and mothers by society's already powerful beauty culture. As Natasha Singer has written, "Many women struggle with the impact of aging and pregnancy on their bodies. But the marketing of the 'mommy makeover' seeks to pathologize the postpartum body, characterizing pregnancy and childbirth as maladies with disfiguring aftereffects that can be repaired with the help of scalpels and cannulae" (par. 7). This attitude stands in sharp contrast to the way in which women's postchildbirth bodies have historically been viewed. The first edition of *Our Bodies, Ourselves* (1970), for example, "described cosmetic changes that can happen during and after pregnancy simply as phenomena. But now narrowing beauty norms are recasting the transformations of motherhood as stigma" (Singer, par. 5). With marketing materials for mommy makeovers detailing how pregnancy, childbirth, and breastfeeding "deforms" breasts and "disfigures" a woman's stomach, they turn "the postpregnancy body 'into a socially unacceptable thing'"—a condition to be diagnosed, treated, and cured (Singer, par. 8). As Karen Murphy, a mother of four and author of the blog *StrollerDerby* aptly noted, "Those badges of motherhood have turned into badges of shame" (qtd. in Singer, par. 30).

* * *

Even women in the United States who do not have children have likely heard of the "Supermom." A mythic and even larger-than-life figure, Supermom is not simply a skilled wife, mother, and homemaker, but a perfect one. Her home is always clean, her husband is always chipper, and—perhaps most important—her children are always nutritiously well-fed, socially well-adjusted, and publicly well-behaved. Shari Green provides a more detailed portrait of this powerful female persona:

> Supermom is amazing. She's always got her act together and is never frazzled and unorganized. She never goes out with her blouse misbuttoned, and she certainly never smells like baby barf. There are no runs in her stockings. Her hair is shiny and soft, and her skin glows. There are no bags under her eyes.
>
> Supermom's home is tastefully decorated, spotlessly clean, and smells of freshly-baked bread (think *Martha Stewart*). She lovingly prepares tasty, well-balanced meals for her family. Her baby is always beautifully dressed and never screams in the supermarket. Supermom is always patient and gentle, and every night she sings her baby to sleep with the voice of an angel.

As Supermom's baby grows up, Supermom efficiently and cheerfully juggles a successful career, volunteer work, carpooling, gym workouts, and domestic duties. She does it all, and she does it all *well*. (pars. 1–3; emphasis in original)

As these comments indicate, akin to the comic book figures from which Supermom draws her name, there is no childrearing crisis that she can't handle, no domestic challenge that she can't overcome, and no parenting obstacle that she can't proverbially leap in a single bound. As a consequence, in the words of Shari Green once again, "Supermom is set up as the ideal after which mothers everywhere strive to model themselves" (par. 4).

My Beautiful Mommy adds another trait to the already dauntingly long—and, of course, impossibly unobtainable—standard of the Supermom. Now, in addition to having the perfect house, the perfect children and the perfect husband, women also need to have the perfect postpregnancy body. Natasha Singer has observed: "There is more pressure on mothers today to look young and sexy than on previous generations" (par. 20). For individuals whose bodies do not naturally return to their prechildbirth form, *My Beautiful Mommy* relays that they can—and possibly even should—obtain it via a surgical intervention. Viewed from this perspective, perhaps it is no longer surprising or even vain that Michael Salzhauer presents his picture book persona with the physique of a comic book hero, for it seems fitting that only a "Supersurgeon" can create a "Supermom."

Between the stresses of a successful career and the demands of home life, the pressures that twenty-first century American society places on women in general and mothers in particular have perhaps never been greater. Salzhauer raises these expectations even more in his picture book. Although the surgeon-author claims to have penned the narrative to alleviate the fears that young children experience when a parent undergoes cosmetic surgery, his text tacitly addresses another, far different anxiety: the one experienced by many young mothers that they will not be seen as a "Supermom" who "has it all." Ultimately, this message about possessing the perfect house, husband, children, and even body is the one that *My Beautiful Mommy* conveys via its young female narrator to a presumably young female audience, a group who embodies—conveniently and not coincidentally—the nation's next generation of wives and mothers.

Doctored: The Myth of Childhood Innocence

In spite of the Salzhauer's oft-stated commitment to produce "quality informational books to communicate effectively with children" ("About"), *My Beautiful Mommy* does not present an entirely accurate, honest, or even realistic portrait of cosmetic surgery. His narrative ignores important aspects of abdominoplasty, liposuction, breast augmentation, and rhinoplasty while it minimizes others.

The most significant and perhaps most noticeable omission is the level of pain and discomfort that patients experience. Near the middle of Salzhauer's picture book, the young girl asks her mother about her rhinoplasty, "'Mommy is it going to hurt?'" to which she gives the decorous reply: "'Maybe a little ... but only for a few days.'" The truth is that nose jobs are exceedingly painful, as surgeons often need to break the nasal bone and/or chisel it down. In addition, many rhinoplasties necessitate having skin grafted, removed, or reconstructed. Several patients quoted on an informational message board for those contemplating rhinoplasty likened their nose job to being punched in the face ("Making," par. 5). They described the tremendous pain that they experienced whenever they moved any part of their face and which routinely left them unable to lie down, chew, and, at times, even talk. In addition, nose jobs involve extensive facial bruising and swelling, often with double black eyes and blood oozing from the nasal cavity—symptoms that can persist for several weeks or even a month ("Making," par. 5).

Abdominoplasty and liposuction are even more debilitating. In spite of its playful name, a tummy tuck is major abdominal surgery. First, two large incisions are made in the skin, from hip bone to hip bone, one above the belly button and one below it. Then, the large crescent-shaped piece of flesh that is located between the two cuts is removed. Afterward, the muscles are realigned and the belly button is reattached and repositioned. The wound is then sutured closed. Recovery time is lengthy: the procedure requires at least an overnight stay at the hospital, one week with surgical drains in the wound, around two weeks before the stitches can be removed, and roughly six weeks until the patient is able to get around without assistance or significant discomfort ("Tummy Tuck Recovery," par. 6).

The healing period for liposuction varies, depending on the size of the area targeted. However, as Dr. Jim Greene noted on an informational website for potential patients, some medical benchmarks exist: "For the first 3 to 14 days following the liposuction surgery you can expect some pain. This pain can range from mild all the way up to severe depending on the technique that was used during the procedure as well as the type of liposuction procedure that was performed" (Greene, par. 2). He continues: "For the first 2 weeks all the way to more than 2 months you can expect swelling associated with your liposuction procedure. ... Furthermore along with this swelling you will also need to expect some bruising for at least the first 2 weeks" (Greene, par. 3). Loss of sensation and drainage of fluid from the incision are also common side effects. In the words of Greene once again: "Numbness in the treatment area will be limited to the actual skin and can last several weeks after having undergone the liposuction procedure" (Greene, par. 4). To help combat all of these symptoms—pain, swelling, numbness, and fluid—liposuction patients don a compression garment. The item is worn for at least the first few weeks after surgery and, in the days following the procedure, it must be changed daily (Greene, par. 5).

The presentation of the mother's postsurgery appearance, her experience with pain, and the time needed for recovery in *My Beautiful Mommy* is markedly different. When the mother comes home from the hospital, she is shown with only one thin bandage across the bridge of her nose. In reality, most individuals receiving rhinoplasty have multiple bandages: one spanning across the bridge of the nose, one running vertically down the length of it, and one extending horizontally beneath the nostrils. For at least the first few days, these items are routinely bloodied. Not so with Salzhauer's mommy. Not only does her face show no sign of bruising, blood, or swelling, but her solitary bandage is pristinely white.

Salzhauer's presentation of the mother's liposuction and tummy tuck is even more unrealistic—and misleading. As Karen Springen notes, the mother has only a "demure" dressing around her waist, not the compression garment that, because of oozing fluid, needs to be changed frequently (par. 7). In addition, as Sandra G. Boodman humorously observes, "she's up and around a few days after her tummy tuck, not lying in bed in a haze of pain waiting for her next Percocet" (HE05). On her first day home from the hospital, for example, the girl narrator says of her mother: "She was sitting up in bed and eating chicken soup." Her only symptom is that "[s]he looked sleepy." The next day, the mother is out of bed. The young girl comes home to find her mom dressed and downstairs "sitting in her chair watching television." On the following morning—which, in the timeline created by the book, is only four days after the surgery—she has returned to almost her normal routine. The text reads: "The next day, Mommy was up in the kitchen helping Daddy make breakfast. I ran over and gave Mommy the biggest hug in the world. I passed her the milk because Daddy told me she couldn't lift heavy things."

These misrepresentations stand in direct contrast to Salzhauer's stated purpose for writing the narrative. In numerous articles, interviews, and even on his own jacket flap, the surgeon-turned-author has said that he wrote *My Beautiful Mommy* out of a desire to break the silence regarding cosmetic surgery and be more open and honest with children. Drawing on events that he had witnessed in his own practice, when a parent undergoes an elective cosmetic procedure but does not discuss this process with their children, young people "fill in the blanks in their imagination" (qtd. in Springen par. 6). This process is both frightening and detrimental, the surgeon explains, as young people tend to conjure up scenarios that are far more terrifying than the actual truth (qtd. in Springen, par. 6). Salzhauer wrote *My Beautiful Mommy* to combat this phenomenon. The "About the Author" section on the website for Barnes & Noble explains: "As a father of four young children—and an avid bed-time storyteller—he recognizes the importance and value of using quality informational books to communicate effectively with children" ("About"). Accordingly, the jacket flap to *My Beautiful Mommy* promises parents that by reading the narrative with their children and talking about the issues addressed in it, "you will be able to calm your children's fears, address their concerns, and help your family sail easily through the plastic surgery experience."

My Beautiful Mommy, however, has the exact opposite effect in many ways. The book does not provide an accurate, honest, and realistic portrayal of what young people will experience when their mother undergoes cosmetic surgery, but a highly sanitized one. Especially with regard to recovery period after surgery—which is the phase of the process to which young people have the most contact and exposure—the text glosses over essential details, omits crucial specifics, and neglects to mention a variety of important, if graphic and gruesome, particulars. In so doing, the picture book arguably—and quite ironically, given Salzhauer's intent—harms rather than helps. Through the narrative's words and especially via the images that he had commissioned and approved, the narrative informs child readers that their mother's recovery period will be free of any visible blood, serious pain, and noticeable bruising—not to mention oozing fluids, weeping drains, and multiple weeks' worth of serious swelling—which Salzhauer, as a trained cosmetic surgeon, surely knows will not be the case for most if not all patients. In so doing, *My Beautiful Mommy* gives young people false expectations; the book lulls its child readers into a fraudulent and even perilous sense of knowledge. Indeed, as the surgeon himself concedes on the jacket flap to the book, "children are very perceptive." Unfortunately, he does not extend this awareness to his own text. After seeing the mommy in Salzhauer's text sitting up in bed with a solitary and pristine white bandage across the bridge of her nose, for example, it will be a shock for them to see their own mother with multiple blood-soaked gauze pads, dark bruises under her eyes, and a noticeably swollen face. Likewise, after reading about the mother in the book helping to make breakfast only a few days after surgery and gleefully receiving "the biggest hug in the world" without the slightest wince of discomfort, it will come as an unsettling surprise when their own mother remains bedridden and in profound pain, fluid oozing into drains.

Of course, this disjunction between what Salzhauer says will happen postsurgery and what actually transpires can be seen as part of the public relations and even advertising campaign operating in his book. But, I would argue, they also emanate from another, unrelated phenomenon: his view of children. Salzhauer subscribes to a long-established conception about childhood in the United States as a happy, innocent, and carefree period. As James Kincaid, Henry Jenkins, and Steve Mintz have all articulated, this viewpoint frames boys and girls as being blissfully ignorant of any serious problems, upsetting issues, or "adult" worries. Instead, they spend their time doing what all children not only were "born" to do, but—as James Kincaid has discussed—are often seen as having the "right" to do: play and have fun (79–80). So powerful is this belief that adults are routinely cast as needing to protect young people "from the harsh realities of the adult world" (Jenkins 2). Men and women have a responsibility to shield children from information and events that are upsetting (Kincaid 60–71). In examples ranging from the Victorian-era rebuke "not in front of the children" to the millennial admonition that a certain movie, television show, or video game is "not 'appropriate' for children," Western society has long been typified by the desire to preserve childhood innocence.

Michael Salzhauer subscribes to this viewpoint. His portrayal of the daughter in *My Beautiful Mommy* demonstrates his adherence to the maxim that young people are—and ought to remain—happy, innocent, and blissfully unaware of any upsetting information about themselves, their families, and the world in which they live. The young girl's consternation about her mother's dissatisfaction with the changes to her aging, postpregnancy body, for example, suggests that she has been wholly sheltered from media messages about feminine appearance and remains gleefully ignorant about Western standards of female beauty.

A problem arises when Salzhauer's view of children as doe-eyed innocents comes into contact with his desire to create a didactic picture book about cosmetic surgery. The surgeon-turned-author cannot continue to protect young people from the unpleasant and even unsavory elements of life while also writing a narrative about the realities of undergoing multiple elective aesthetic procedures. These two desires are incompatible. A young person whose mother has a tummy tuck, breast lift, liposuction, and/or rhinoplasty will not be able to remain blissfully ignorant to the often unpleasant and even gruesome facets of cosmetic surgery. On the contrary, especially if their mother convalesces at home, they will witness these details firsthand.

James Kincaid, in *Child-Loving: The Erotic Child and Victorian Culture*, challenges both the biological naturalness and the socio-cultural beneficence of Western society's belief in childhood innocence. Calling this longstanding viewpoint a cultural myth rather than an empirical reality, he argues that the contention that boys and girls are inherently happy, consistently carefree, and blissfully ignorant about the "evils" of the adult world was "constructed and not discovered" (Kincaid 72). For this reason, the trait of innocence that young people are purported to possess "was not only 'protected' but inculcated and enforced" (Kincaid 72). Attaching what he calls "the burden of innocence" (Kincaid 73) to childhood "empties" young people of political agency and even basic individuality. "The child's innocence, then, becomes a vulnerability" (Kincaid 73). It disempowers young people rather than empowers them. The notion that children are delightfully naïve and enviably "unsullied" gives license for adults to exert authority over young people while it also assigns boys and girls a subordinated status. Adults use arguments about children's "innocence" to curtail their rights, curb their freedoms, and restrict their autonomy. For this reason, Kincaid asserts, "innocence is a faculty needed not at all by the child but very badly by the adult who put it there in the first place. Giving this innocence to a child, then, may satisfy our own needs but possibly not the child's" (73).

My Beautiful Mommy makes visible both the socially constructed nature of childhood innocence and the way in which this belief routinely serves adult needs and desires far more than those of young people. Rather than providing his child readers with an accurate and honest account of what they can expect when a parent undergoes cosmetic surgery, Salzhauer opts to protect what he sees as their blissful ignorance and carefree innocence. As a consequence, his picture book does not give the children of plastic surgery patients the written or visual information that they need to be prepared for this experience. If anything, in fact, *My Beautiful Mommy* has the opposite effect: by painting a portrait that ranges from overly rosy to patently incorrect, it sets up a false expectation that is going to be even more jarring when it is debunked than the truth would have been in the first place.

This observation applies not only to the written text of Salzhauer's book but also to its visual images. As Perry Nodelman has commented, "Pictures in picturebooks also do sometimes seem to be trying to be childlike—to be in simple cartoon styles ...; but they always imply an exterior view of their child or childlike characters—a view, I believe that is both adult and meant to be adopted by child-readers at the same time as they relate to, identify with, or in fact adopt the text's childlike view of the child protagonist" ("Words" 18). Salzhauer explained that the Disney-fied style for the illustrations was ostensibly chosen to serve children's needs: they give the picture book a "familiar" appearance. But, this aesthetic choice can also be read as serving the needs of adults: the cartoon-looking illustrations perpetuate adult views that children are cutesy, adorable, and innocent. To be sure, of the fifteen pages in the book where readers can see the young protagonist's face, twelve show her with a big smile. Meanwhile, her three visages that are not happy grins are equally cartoonish exaggerations of human emotion: expressions of childlike confusion (as the young girl wonders what her mother's new nose will look like), inquisitiveness (when she asks her mother if the surgery will hurt), and tenacity (when she insists that her mother is "already the prettiest Mommy in the whole wide world!").

In so doing, *My Beautiful Mommy* highlights the impossibility of presenting a different and even daring new subject for children's literature without employing a similarly different and even daring new viewpoint about children and childhood. The real pitfall in Salzhauer's narrative is not that he was unable to overcome his own professional self-interest by presenting the cosmetic surgery industry in such a positive light, but that he could not overcome his own view about children and childhood to disclose its more negative qualities. Ironically, for all of the surgeon-author's stated desires to "help" kids, this more realistic discussion is what young people who are facing this situation actually need and, I would argue, would also want. As Roderick McGillis has commented, "Rather than trying to shield children from the world they live in, we ought to be trying to give them the tools to read this world carefully and critically" (130).

Young adult author Sherman Alexie, in an article that appeared in *The Wall Street Journal* in 2011, discussed the gulf that exists for many young people in general and especially those who hail from the non-white and non-middle class backgrounds between popular conceptions about child-hood and their own lived experiences of it. While growing up on the Spo-kane Indian Reservation, Alexie was not blissfully unaware about a variety of serious and some would say "adult" problems. On the contrary, he had extensive firsthand knowledge about issues like poverty, alcoholism, domes-tic violence, sexual abuse, parental neglect, and child mistreatment. Yet, in newspaper articles, on radio reports, and especially in television inter-views, conservative politicians and cultural arbiters of the day repeatedly proclaimed about how "they wanted to protect me": from the sexuality inherent in rock 'n' roll music, from the violence contained in video games, and from the gritty social underbelly of drugs, crime, and poverty being depicted in many popular movies. "But, even then, I could only laugh at their platitudes," Alexie recalls (par. 12). Given his personal circumstances and resulting childhood experiences, he did not need to be "protected" from these issues; he was already exceedingly familiar with them. "What was my immature, childish response to those would-be saviors? Wow, you are way, way too late," Alexie writes (par. 14). The future author—and countless past and present young people like him—would have been far better served if the adults in his life would have helped him to better understand and more effectively deal with these issues, rather than engaging in the futile task of trying to "shelter" or "protect" him. As a consequence, Alexie offers the fol-lowing indictment not only of media lamentations that young adult litera-ture has become "too gritty," but also of lingering beliefs in the "innocence" of children on which such assertions rest:

> When some cultural critics fret about the "ever more appalling" YA [young adult] books, they aren't trying to protect African-American teens forced to walk through metal detectors on their way into school. Or Mexican-American teens enduring the cultural schizophrenic life of being American citizens and the children of illegal immigrants. ... No, they are simply trying to protect their privileged notions of what literature is and should be. They are trying to protect privileged chil-dren. Or the seemingly privileged. (pars. 16–17)

My Beautiful Mommy echoes while it extends this debate about what children should and should not know, as well as what information young people already have and what information adults wish to believe remains restricted and thus unavailable to them.[7] The narrative demonstrates that the gap between knowledge and innocence can be just as powerfully present in picture books as it is in the more often-discussed realm of YA literature. *My Beautifully Mommy* reveals how false perceptions about the innocence of youth can apply even to children who have historically been seen as its ideal embodiment: young white girls from the middle- and upper-middle classes, like Salzhauer's narrator-protagonist.

Ultimately, *My Beautiful Mommy* suggests that the actual individuals who occupy a state of "blissful ignorance" are not boys and girls but, ironically, men and women. Their firm, and usually faulty, belief in childhood innocence allows adults to remain "gleefully naïve" about the real lives and factual circumstances of young people from a wide range of socio-economic backgrounds who are facing an equally wide array of different personal challenges. Salzhauer's text ostensibly concerns one woman's quest to preserve her ideal of feminine beauty. But, the picture book is equally concerned with preserving a certain adult ideal about children and childhood. Although the surgeon-turned-author decided to call his book *My Beautiful Mommy*, he could have just as accurately deemed it—from his perspective, though doubtfully from that of its first-person narrator—*Her Beautiful Childhood*.

Notes

1. Theresa Agovino, writing for the Associated Press, has reported that men constituted 9.7% of the recipients of cosmetic surgery procedures performed in the United States in 1998, 11.7% in 2002, and 13% in 2007 (pars. 5–6).

2. *My Beautiful Mommy* is not paginated.

3. The first instance occurs when the mother explains to her daughter that she is going to have an operation; the young girl asks if it will be anything like her brother's game called *Operation*. Later, when the mother discusses the period of recovery from her procedure, her daughter asks: "'Are you going to have a cast like when Billy broke his arm playing baseball?'" A thought bubble above her head shows the young boy in his baseball uniform with his arm in a sling. It is only after the mother has returned home from the hospital that Billy returns. The caption reads, "Daddy told Billy and me that we had to play quietly downstairs while Mommy was resting." In the illustration that accompanies this text, Billy's back faces the reader. Finally, near the end of the book, the young man gets one page to himself. While the mother is recuperating, the narrator notes: "Billy even picked up his clothes and put them in the hamper without being told. Mommy was so proud." The page shows Billy in his bedroom loading his laundry into the hamper. Appropriately boyish toys and decorations surround him: a fire truck, a baseball, and a fielder's mitt are scattered on the floor. Meanwhile, the walls are adorned with posters of professional athletes and sports stadiums. Finally, and in a detail that further suggests that that pink color palette used throughout the book targets a readership of young girls rather than boys and girls equally, Billy's bedroom is painted blue.

4. The illustration of this scene is equally problematic, for it reinforces long-held stereotypes of cosmetic surgery as the realm of wealthy white women: the double-page image shows the young Caucasian girl walking hand-in-hand with her equally fair-skinned mother on a palm tree-lined street with perfectly manicured landscaping. In the background is a pristine high-rise building, presumably the locale of Dr. Michael's office. Many additional accouterments of wealth and privilege appear at various points throughout the remainder of the book. On the page where the mother and daughter return home from the consultation, a large, silver SUV is parked in the driveway and a spacious, modern

suburban home—designed in the style that is sometimes pejoratively called a "McMansion"—can be seen across the street.

5. I want to thank Karly Marie Grice for this closing insight.

6. To a lesser extent, cosmetic surgery has also been discussed in works of fiction. Laura and Tom McNeal's novel *Crooked* (1999), for example, explores the life of teenager Clara Wilson. Coupled with troubles with friends, homework, and the recent separation of her parents, the young girl struggles with an additional hardship: as the title of the YA novel implies, she has a crooked nose. The opening paragraph of the novel demonstrates the extent to which the self-conscious young girl fixates on this trait. The language recalls the discourse of suffering that Kathy Davis discusses in *Reshaping the Female Body*:

> Before everything stopped being normal, the thing that Clara Wilson worried most about was her nose. It wasn't straight. The bridge began in a good downwardly vertical line, and then it just swooped off to the left. It was crooked even in her baby pictures. It looked as if someone—a doctor? A nurse? God in a mean mood?—had laid a finger at the side of her nose and pushed the straightness out of it. The problem was, a crooked nose could make a whole face look crooked. Even when she was in a good mood and smiling, some little part of Clara was observing herself. *She smiled a crooked smile. She grinned a crooked grin. She walked a crooked mile.*
>
> Her best friend, Gerri, whose nose was perfect, said Clara's nose wasn't that bad, but if it bothered her that much, why didn't she just get a nose job and forget about it? (McNeal and McNeal 1; italics in original)

Clara ultimately decides not to get a nose job, realizing that in light of life's myriad other difficulties her crooked nose is not really a problem. *Crooked* was the recipient of the California Book Award in Juvenile Literature.

7. I am indebted to an earlier anonymous reviewer of my manuscript for this insight.

3   Good Things Come in Small Packages

Little Zizi, Schoolyard Bullying, and the Sexualization of Boys

Perhaps no other topic within the American educational system experienced such a massive uptick in attention during the opening years of the twenty-first century as that of bullying. In school districts around the nation, the problem of peer harassment became the subject of intense discussion among teachers, new policy initiatives by administrators, and prevention programs for students. The sheer number of new books about bullying that were released during this period provides a powerful indication of the heightened interest in the issue. According to WorldCat, a global catalog of library holdings, in the hundred years spanning 1900 to 1999, a little over 1,200 books had been published on this subject. By contrast, in just the opening decade of the twenty-first century, more than 4,700 were released.

As many of these texts discussed, the reason why a young person is bullied varies tremendously. Joanne Mattern has noted, for example, that "[s]ome victims are chosen because of their physical appearance. Victims might look different than others. They might wear glasses or have a disability or an illness" (14). That said, the modus operandi for bullying is not consistent. In the words of Mattern once again: "Victims may be heavier or thinner than their peers, or much taller or shorter" (14). Some young people are bullied because they are high achievers in school, while others are harassed because they struggle academically. As even this brief overview reveals, virtually any personal trait or behavioral quality can become the subject of ridicule. For this reason, Mattern emphatically reminds her readers: "Anyone can be a victim of bullying!" (14).

In 2008, French author Thierry Lenain added to the growing body of materials on the subject of bullying when an English-language version of his picture book, *Little Zizi*, was released to American audiences.[1] Translated by Daniel Zolinsky and published by the independent imprint Cinco Puntos Press, the narrative offers a very specialized take on the issue of peer harassment. *Little Zizi* spotlights a prepubescent boy who is being ridiculed by his classmates for a specific and somewhat unusual reason: having a small penis. Martin's classmates see his penis—or "zizi"—when the school bully Adrian bursts into his dressing room while he is changing out of swim trunks. Together with mocking Martin for his diminutive genitalia, Adrian also taunts him by declaring that, because of his small penis, he will never be able to father children. This pronouncement proves worrisome, for Martin has a crush on Anais, the prettiest girl in school. Of course, Adrian is also vying for Anais's attentions and a rivalry ensues. Adrian proposes that they settle the dispute via a literal pissing contest: the boy who can urinate the farthest wins not only the right to woo Anais but also—and perhaps more importantly—the prestige of having the superior penis.

Given the focus of *Little Zizi*, both the niche audience and the didactic intent of the book is clear. As a reviewer for Kirkus remarked, Lenain's narrative "provides direct reassurance to worried readers (of the male persuasion, at least) that Size Doesn't Matter" ("Little Zizi," par. 1). In so doing, the picture book adds to the ongoing millennial interest in examining children and childhood in relation to discourses of victimization. Echoing recent discussions about marginalized, oppressed, and "othered" youth by Judith Butler, Kathryn Bond Stockton, and Steven Bruhm and Natasha Hurley *Little Zizi* explores questions of ostracism, powerlessness, and resiliency.

Akin to all of the other specialty texts presented in this project, however, *Little Zizi* has significance that extends far beyond either its specific subject or target audience. As this chapter will discuss, the picture book spotlights an especially pernicious form of peer harassment, what is known as sexual bullying. Encompassing behaviors ranging from snapping a girl's bra strap or calling her a slut to forcing a classmate to engage in unwanted erotic activity and labeling a boy a faggot, sexual bullying is one of the most hurtful types of schoolyard harassment. *Little Zizi* engages with while it expands upon contemporary conversations about sexual bullying. Through its presentation of male anxiety about penis size, masculine virility, and sexual potency, the picture book calls attention to an even more serious but widely overlooked topic: the eroticization of boys. While young girls are commonly seen as the targets of socio-culture pressures to act, dress, and view themselves in highly sexualized ways, *Little Zizi* demonstrates that such pressures, along with the personal problems and bodily anxieties that they produce, are also powerfully present among their male peers. This message disrupts the seemingly singular focus in Lenain's narrative on heterosexual procreation and opens the book to explorations of male homoeroticism and the nonheteronormative child.

"A Great Roar of Laughter Echoed Through the Locker Room": Peer Harassment Among Elementary-Aged Children

For generations, the phenomenon of young people being teased by their classmates was seen as a common and even inevitable part of growing up. As Sandra Harris and Garth F. Petrie have written, such behavior was often "dismissed via comments such as 'boys will be boys'" or addressed in a purely perfunctory way with "admonitions 'just to tough it out'" (viii). Either way, bullying was considered an unpleasant but nonetheless unavoidable "rite of passage," a facet of adolescent life that must be endured, like acne, pop quizzes, and curfews.

The bland normality and, thus, presumed unimportance of bullying was reflected in scholarly discussions of the subject. As Neil Duncan has written, "bullying was surprisingly late in attracting academic attention. Only in the last three decades has the problem been the focus of serious research, and only since the late 1980s have academic studies in the English language appeared in significant number" (144). The first study that focused on the issue, *Mobbing: Group Violence Among Children*, was released in 1972 by Swedish physician Peter-Paul Heinemann. As Ian Rivers, Neil Duncan, and Valerie E. Besag discuss, "Heinemann recorded his observations of aggression among a group of children in a school playground" and, as a result, "educators and researchers began to question the acceptability of such behavior" (3).

While Heinemann may have conducted the first analysis of bullying, "it was a fellow countryman, Dan Olweus, who systematically investigated the nature, frequency, and long-term effects of mobbing in Scandinavian schools, which culminated in a national study he conducted in Norway in 1983" (Rivers, Duncan, and Besag 3). As a result, Olweus is "generally recognized today as the foremost authority on bullying" (Harris and Petrie 1). In fact, he is the first scholar who "began using the terms 'bully/victim' ... in his early studies" (Harris and Petrie 1).

Since most young people have frequent disagreements with their peers— over toys, friends, treats, etc.—a central concern of both past and present research has been differentiating between peer conflicts that are simply routine disputes and those that are instances of bullying. Opinions on this issue vary widely, but scholars agree on an array of hallmarks of bullying. In the words of Anne G. Garrett: "The word 'bully' is used to describe many different types of behavior ranging from teasing or deliberately leaving an individual out of a school gathering or ignoring them to serious assaults and abuse" (6). She elaborates: "Bullying can also be defined as something that someone repeatedly does or says to gain power over or to dominate another individual. Bullying is where a child or group of children keep taking advantage of the power they have to hurt or reject someone else" (Garrett 6).

Of course, the specific methods by which one child may bully another vary widely. Some of the most common means include "calling them names, saying or writing nasty comments about them, leaving them out of activities or not talking to them, threatening them, or making them feel uncomfortable or scared, stealing or damaging their belongings, hitting or kicking them, or making them do things they don't want to do" (Garrett 6). The unifying factor in all of these actions is that they are deliberate, recurring, and hurtful. Harris and Petrie identify the following four defining characteristics of bullying:

- It is aggressive and intentionally harmful.
- It is carried out repeatedly.
- It occurs in a relationship where there is an imbalance of power.
- It occurs with no provocation from the victim. (2)

Ultimately, all forms of peer harassment emanate from one simple fact: "It is an issue of power" (Garrett 10). The more powerful bully is seeking control over a vulnerable victim. As Harris and Petrie discuss, because of the malicious intent, extended duration, and coercive goal of bullying, this behavior is sometimes deemed not simply "peer harassment" but "peer abuse" (1).

However bullying is defined or conducted, it occurs at alarmingly high rates. Writing in 2002, Jane Middleton-Moz and Mary Lee Zawadski revealed, "in a study sponsored by the Centers for Disease Control and Prevention, 81 percent of student surveyed *admitted* to bullying their classmates in one form or another" (5; italics in original). These abstract percentages translate into alarmingly high concrete numbers: "Students receive an average of 213 verbal put-downs per week, or 30 per day" (Garrett 36). The toll that such experiences take on both personal well-being and academic achievement is immense. The National Educators Association, for example, "estimates that 160,000 students miss school every day, totaling 28 million missed days per year due to fear of attack or intimidation by a bully" (qtd. in Garrett 36). Given these statistics, the National School Safety Center called bullying "the most enduring and under-rated problem in American schools" (qtd. in Midleton-Moz and Zawadski 10).

While bullying can occur among children of any educational grade, it is most prevalent among students in middle and high school. "Studies show that more than 30 percent of teens are involved in bullying, either as a victim or a bully. Some studies say up to 90 percent of middle-school students have been victims of bullies at one time or another" (Mattern 7). Many other reports confirm this data. For example, "[t]he National Institute of Child Health and Human Development (NICHD) reported in 2001 that 17 percent of students in grades six through ten had been bullied 'sometimes' or 'weekly,' 19 percent had bullied others, and 6 percent had both bullied and been bullied" (Harris and Petrie ix). For this reason, bullying is largely seen as a problem of adolescence. As Norah Piehl writes, "Many people tend to associate bullying with late elementary and middle school years" (17).

Little Zizi engages with ongoing cultural conversations about bullying while it simultaneously expands on them. The book demonstrates that even though incidents of bullying may be more common during puberty, they are certainly not absent from the years prior. As a recent study by Education Equity Concepts and the Wellesley College Center for Research on Women revealed, "Teasing and bullying are part of daily life for students in kindergarten through third grade" (qtd. in Garrett 64).

Little Zizi is acutely aware of this phenomenon. Maria Nikolajeva and Carole Scott have made the following observation about picture books: "If we consider what images and words do best, it is clear that physical description belongs in the realm of the illustrator, who can, in an instant, communicate information about appearance that would take many words and much reading time" (83). While Thierry Lenain never directly states either the age of his characters or their grade level in the written text of his picture book, the illustrations by Stéphane Poulin indicate that they are preadolescent.

The physical height, facial features, and body proportions that Martin and his classmates possess suggest that they may be as young as six or seven. In any event, the characters are clearly prepubescent, occupying one of the earlier grades in elementary school.

In the same way that bullying is associated with certain developmental ages, it also tends to occur in predictable locales. According to Harris and Petrie, "The four most common ... places/times that elementary students observed bullying at school were at recess (78 percent), in the hallways (52 percent), in the restroom (50 percent), and in the classroom (43 percent)" (17). The reason that these settings are such common sites for bullying is simple: They are gathering places for "large numbers of students ... without a lot of adult supervision" (Mattern 10).

That said, even in cases where adults are present to witness the harassment, they often do not stop it. In a survey conducted by Education Equity Concepts and the Wellesley College Center for Research on Women, "[s]tudents reported that 71 percent of the teachers or other adults in the classroom ignored bullying incidents" (Garrett 14). The rationale for this behavior varies. Sometimes, the adult does not wish to expend the time or energy that would be required to deal with the problem. Meanwhile, in other instances, they fail to intervene because they actually condone the bullying behavior in some way: they personally dislike the child who is being targeted, or they see being teased as an unavoidable part of growing up.

Little Zizi reflects these facts. Martin's experience of being bullied commences in a venue where a large number of students congregate without the benefit of much adult supervision: the locker room. As the narrator relays, the harassment begins suddenly and without provocation: "He was taking off his swimsuit when suddenly Adrian opened the door of Martin's dressing room."[2] This aggressive invasion of privacy ceases when the swimming instructor enters: "Suddenly the teacher appeared. All of the spectators scattered." Reflecting research findings about the apathy of many adults when it comes to bullying, the swim instructor's arrival may stop the immediate harassment, but it does nothing to solve the larger problem. If anything, in fact, the teacher's response seems to confirm the bully's choice of victim: "'All right, Martin, hurry up and get dressed,' he shouted *in a mocking tone as if he agreed with the others*" (my emphasis).

While one might imagine that a bully would prefer to operate alone—isolating his or her victim from the presence and thus possible assistance of others—this is usually not the case. Harris and Petrie report that "frequently the bully's behavior is sustained by a supporting group" (5). These individuals may act as active fellow participants in the bullying, adding taunts, throwing punches, or uttering insults. But, more commonly, they become passive participants, by serving as an audience. As Garrett reveals about onlookers, "In 54 percent of cases, they reinforced the bullying by watching but not joining in" (15). Either way, observers form a crucial component to the initiation and the perpetuation of peer harassment, providing the audience for what is often called the "theatre of bullying" (Garrett 77).

Once again, *Little Zizi* replicates this dynamic. While Adrian may be the one who consistently utters the taunts, he does not operate alone. Almost immediately after the bully bursts into Martin's changing room, "All the boys gathered around." Perry Nodelman, in *Words about Pictures*, has commented about how the illustrations in picture books "often fill in the details of emotions ... that the words leave out" (69). The illustrations by Stéphane Poulin repeatedly highlight the humiliation that Martin feels. The double-page image that accompanies this particular passage, for instance, gives a bird's eye view of Martin standing naked inside his pool-side dressing stall, his classmates surrounding him (Figure 3.1). As Nikolajeva and Scott have discussed, the perspective or point of view employed in an illustration is often used to convey the power dynamics among and between characters (117–24), and this is certainly the case with Poulin's depiction of Martin on this page. By presenting an aerial or overhead view, Poulin not only maps the physical topography of the scene but he also relays the lack of control that the protagonist experiences. A cluster of boys are standing in the open door pointing and staring at Martin. Meanwhile, another is peering over the wall at the protagonist while a third has crawled under the divider from the stall next door. In a detail that further underscores the main character's feelings of being singled out and shamed, no one else's zizi is visible. While the two boys who occupy the stalls beside Martin appear undressed, their genitals are not in view: one boy is lying chest-down on the floor, while the torso of the other is concealed behind the partition.[3] Whatever their specific vantage point, the boys' response to seeing Martin naked is the same: "A great roar of laughter echoed through the locker room."

Figure 3.1 From *Little Zizi*, written by Thierry Lenain, illustrated by Stéphane Poulin, and translated by Daniel Zolinsky. Reprinted with permission.

Throughout the remainder of the book, this group of boys play a central role both in the public perpetuation and in the hurtful power of the bullying. For instance, as soon as Martin finishes changing and emerges from his dressing stall, "Adrian crowed, 'Little zizi, little zizi!' And the others joined in with him." However, as Lenain points out: "the story doesn't end there. The next day Adrian gathered all the boys in the class to the park [*sic*]." Almost immediately, Adrian once again begins ridiculing Martin for his little zizi. As before, the group of onlookers enhances the humiliation that the protagonist feels: "Everyone burst out laughing. The hecklers started again. 'Little zizi, little zizi!' Martin ran away." Poulin's accompanying illustration, drawn once again from a bird's eye view to accentuate Martin's sense of powerlessness, shows the group of boys pointing, staring, and laughing at the protagonist; one boy is even chasing Martin as he runs away. Indicating the urgency with which the central character wishes to leave this situation, Martin has knocked over a few folding chairs in his haste.

However bullying is orchestrated or conducted, it is always a hurtful experience for the victim. As Anne G. Garrett has discussed, "The effects of school bullying can be devastating. Students who are bullied suffer from low self-esteem, often have poor concentration and may refuse to continue in school. Bullied students tend to feel stupid, ashamed, unattractive, and gradually begin to view themselves as failures" (65). In some cases, the impact can be more serious. Victimized youngsters may suffer from depression and express hopelessness because they "feel that they are unable to defend themselves effectively" (Harris and Petrie 15) and, as a result, have "impaired social relationships" (Harris and Petrie x). Finally, for some individuals, these sentiments "can become overwhelming [and] children can begin to see suicide as the only possible option" (Garrett 65).

Little Zizi accurately portrays the harmful personal, social, and psychological effects that a victim experiences. Over the course of the narrative, Martin exhibits fear, low-self esteem, and social isolation as a result of Adrian's taunts. These reactions begin immediately. In the opening scene, after Martin is humiliated in front of all of the boys in the locker room, he withdraws: "Once he was dressed, Martin didn't dare go out of his dressing room." When the young boy finally does emerge and the taunting begins again, feelings of shame and dread become even stronger. "Martin held back his tears," readers learn. Later that day, after Martin has arrived home and gotten in bed, he is still haunted by this encounter. The text reports: "That night Martin had a lot of trouble getting to sleep." The young boy keeps reliving the harassment and this experience steadily erodes his self worth: "He kept a flashlight under the covers to look at his zizi. He thought it looked even smaller than before, even downright rinky-dink." As before, the illustration by Stéphane Poulin accentuate these sentiments. The drawing shows Martin sitting up in his bed, hesitantly peeking at his lap under the covers and holding what appears to be a ruler in his right hand. A magnifying glass is sitting atop his quilt and an alarm clock has been knocked off the chair at his bedside so that a lamp could be placed there. The shade is angled to form a spotlight. Martin's room is filled with various items that can be seen as phallic. For instance, a gun hangs in a holster from the headboard to his bed. Meanwhile, a figure wearing a pointed hat that is suggestively droopy adorns the wall beside his bed. Indicating the significance of this image, the portrait of the person with the flaccid-looking hat occupies the exact center of the page, serving as the illustration's focal point.

Throughout the book, Martin's appearance in the illustrations reveals his physical insecurity, emotional pain, and psychological anxiety. In the words of Nikolajeva and Scott once again: "though words can express emotion both obviously and subtly, their impact is challenged by the speed and efficacy of illustrations' potential to communicate emotion" (83). This trait or quality about picture books is powerfully evident in *Little Zizi*. While Lenain's words routinely state the hurt that Martin feels as a result of being bullied, the illustrations by Poulin convey these feelings in a much more vivid and immediate way. The protagonist is almost always shown slouching, his eyes downcast and his face bearing a look of acute embarrassment. On one page, for example, the young boy is depicted hiding behind a tree during recess. Meanwhile, in another drawing that also serves as the book's cover, he is standing with his feet pigeon-toed, his knees angled in, and his shoes untied. In many of these images, Martin's dog—who is never mentioned in the written text of the book—serves as a further barometer of the boy's emotional state. The pet is frequently cowering, running away, or—in one particularly poignant image—using his paw to cover his eyes in shame.

Not surprisingly, when the day of the peeing contest finally arrives, Martin's anxiety overwhelms him. The young boy becomes so nervous that he is unable to urinate. "He concentrated ... and concentrated. ... But nothing happened. It was a catastrophe," the text reads. Thoroughly humiliated, Martin slinks back home and literally cries himself to sleep. When Anais sees the protagonist the next day at recess, "She passed by Martin, who didn't dare look at her. Although she did notice his swollen eyes. He had cried all night." As even Anais can plainly detect, being bullied has had a significant damaging impact on Martin's well-being.

In spite of the pain that the bullying causes him, Martin engages in yet another common response by victims: he does not reach out to his parents, teachers, or other trusted adults for assistance. As Joanne Mattern has written, "Although family members can be supportive, victims are often too ashamed to tell their parents or siblings that something is wrong" (17). Instead, the action that Martin does take is unhealthy and even dysfunctional. In the days leading up to the peeing contest, the young boy regularly and somewhat compulsively practices how far he can urinate in his backyard. While this training regiment does help him to pee farther, it also, not surprisingly, causes him to be seen as unusual. As the narrator reflects "even ... his parents were wondering if he wasn't a little bit wacky." There is no indication in either the written text or in the visual images that the protagonist's mother or father ever asked him the reason why he is practicing peeing. Moreover, if they do ask him off-stage from the story, he does not tell them. The reason for such silence is both simple and typical. As Harris and Petrie have written, "Generally, bullied children, as well as bystanders, do not report incidents of bullying, because they fear retaliation or are not sure if teachers and administrators in their schools are even interested in trying to stop bullying" (8). Martin's swimming teacher certainly conveyed this message after Adrian first began to taunt him. And, unfortunately, this negative experience may have contributed to the young boy's decision not to tell any other adults—including his own parents—about the ongoing harassment.

"You Smell Like an Old Hen!": Victim Agency, Outside Intervention, and the Cessation of Peer Harassment

Lenain's book does an excellent job portraying the physical setting, social dynamics, and personal impact of bullying. However, it regrettably does not provide an equally productive portrait of ways for young people to handle peer harassment. First, and perhaps most noticeably the book never points out the folly of Martin's failure to report the bullying to an adult. Not once does either the protagonist or the narrator lament his decision to withhold news about the harassment from his mother, father, or trusted adult authority figure.

While this detail is undoubtedly meant to empower Martin and demonstrate that he—akin to all other children—possesses the ability to solve problems without adult intervention, it is not an accurate reflection of how bullying situations usually resolve. *Little Zizi* suggests that young people can and perhaps even should handle problems with bullies on their own. But, as Christine Oliver and Mano Candappa have discussed, they usually require adult intervention (71–72). Adults have the ability to punish a bully, monitor their behavior, and enforce codes of acceptable conduct in ways that young people typically do not. Thus, as Oliver and Candappa have noted, episodes of bullying routinely cease only when the bully moves on to a new victim or when an adult steps in and stops the situation; not when the victim attempts to get the bully to leave them alone (70–73).

In *Little Zizi*, Martin's decision to keep quiet and not enlist the assistance of an adult proves effective. In the end, the central character wins Anais's affections and, more astoundingly, this development immediately ends the harassment. The day after Martin's humiliation at the peeing contest, Anais sneaks back into the classroom during recess, scribbles a note on a piece of paper, and leaves it in his desk. While Lenain's readers can likely surmise the content of this missive, the narrator nonetheless makes it explicit: "After recess, Martin found the message. It was a heart, a big red heart signed by Anais." Lest any doubt remains that the two are now a couple, the text continues: "That evening, Anais and Martin gave each other a kiss."

When readers turn the page to see the finale to *Little Zizi*, they are like-wise assured of the couple's future procreative abilities. The final page to the picture book shows Martin's dog pulling a long string of small sausages—as he had done at numerous points throughout the narrative, including on the book's dedication page. But, this time, the pooch is assisted by three small puppies. Not only do all of the puppies roughly resemble in each other—both in breed and in coloration—but they also resemble Martin's dog, suggesting that they are his offspring. Of course, readers are encour-aged and even expected to extrapolate this scenario to that of Martin and Anais, given the recurring role that babies and procreation has played in their interaction. Indeed, in case readers are tempted to skip this page or to regard it merely as "bonus" or even extraneous paratextual material, right below the picture of the dog, sausage string, and puppies, it says in large print: "The End."

In a detail that is arguably even more satisfying than receiving Anais's affections, Martin also witnesses Adrian receive his richly deserved come-uppance. First, Anais publicly rebuffs Adrian's romantic advances. In the school play yard, where everyone can both see and hear, she tells Adrian: "'My boyfriend will be the boy that I choose. At any rate, it's not you.'" Then, adding verbal insult to amorous injury, she goes on to say: "'You smell like an old hen!'" The bully's response to such belittlement could not be more pleasing to Martin—or, undoubtedly, to the book's audience. As the narrator reports: "Adrian's mouth opened and then closed, a little bit like the mouth of a goldfish in a bowl. He looked really stupid." The illustration that accompanies this passage only enhances the humor and humiliation. Encompassing a double-page spread, it shows Anais plugging her nose while running swiftly away. The other children in the play yard look on as Adrian stands there shocked. The young boy is presented in a highly comedic way. His mouth is hanging open, his eyes are bulging from his sockets, and his hair is sticking up in a bizarre manner.

Such *Schadenfreude* recurs a few pages later. When Adrian sees Martin and Anais kiss, "he began to make fish faces again. He looked really stupid." Once again, the illustration augments this effect. Adrian is shown leaning on the side of a public fountain within sight of the lovebirds, his face puck-ered in a sulky pout and his hair is once again wildly out of place. The top of the fountain is appropriately adorned with a statue of Cupid who is, not coincidentally, urinating. Moreover, the stream emanating from his "zizi" is aimed directly at Adrian.

While this scenario may provide a satisfying ending to Lenain's story, it offers a dangerous message to its child audience about how to handle bullies. Even in the rare instances where young people are able to stop a bully from targeting them without the intervention of an adult, justice is not always served. In bullying, as in life, the "good guys" don't always win and the "bad guys" aren't always punished—and especially not in ways that are as satisfying as in *Little Zizi*. As Elizabeth Cooney has written, bullies, because they have more social power than their victims and also since they frequently have manipulative, assertive, and aggressive personalities, are often able to avoid blame (pars. 1–2). In some cases, they might even turn the tables, casting their victim as the "guilty party." As Cooney reports, a recent study conducted in Sweden revealed that 42 percent of ninth-grade students surveyed "said the victims brought their torment on themselves because they didn't fit in" (par. 2). In their mind, this person was "at fault for being different" (Cooney, par. 1)

In the end, bullying is always a complex problem that has no simple solution. As Anne G. Garrett aptly opined: "Bullying and being bullied appear to be important indicators that something is wrong. Children who experience either or both need help" (7). Constituting yet another disappointing omission in *Little Zizi*, there is no indication that either Martin or Adrian will have any lingering negative effects from this experience: that Martin won't continue to worry about the size of his zizi; or, conversely, that Adrian won't simply go on to bully another child. As Rivers, Duncan, and Besag have discussed, if bullies do not receive help in the form of behavior modification, psychological counseling, and/or more productive outlets for their energies, they tend to continue their harassing behavior (119–21). Similarly, as Susan M. Swearer, Amie E. Grills, Kisha M. Haye, and Paulette Tam Cary report, the damage done to young victims of schoolyard bullies can be especially serious because the harassment occurs during a time when their self-image is still forming (64–65). As a result, they may suffer from low self-esteem long after the teasing has stopped; for some, the incident becomes a painful memory that they carry with them throughout life.

These facts have a direct implication for *Little Zizi*. In spite of the many positive details that the picture book relays about bullying, its problematic finale undercuts them. *Little Zizi* does provide an illuminating portrayal of how peer harassment is initiated, conducted, and perpetuated, but its misleading presentation of how this problem is resolved jeopardizes such benefits. The model that *Little Zizi* offers for how to respond to being bullied will likely not result in empowering young people to free themselves from peer harassment. Instead, the example that the picture book sets can unwittingly leave its child reader trapped in a harmful situation.

"With Such a Little Zizi ... You Can't Make Babies!": Sexual Bullying, Male Anxiety Over Penis Size, and the Eroticization of Preadolescent Boys

The bullying that occurs in *Little Zizi*, of course, is not generic name-calling. Instead, it is a very specific type of harassment—what is known as sexual bullying. The UK-based National Society for the Prevention of Cruelty to Children (NSPCC) offers the following explanation of this phenomenon: "Any bullying behaviour, whether physical or non-physical, that is based on a person's sexuality or gender" (par. 1). As the NSPCC goes on to explain, sexual bullying "can be carried out to a person's face, behind their back or through the use of technology" (par. 1). Although this behavior can take a myriad of different forms, some of the most common examples include the following:

- Teasing or putting someone down because of:
  - their sex life (e.g., because they haven't had sex or if they've had sex with a number of people)
  - their sexuality (e.g., making fun of someone for being homosexual)
  - their body (e.g., the size of their breasts, bottom or muscles) (par. 3)

Sexual bullying, whether in these forms or others, is one of the most socially hurtful and psychologically harmful forms of peer harassment. As Ian Rivers, Neil Duncan, and Valerie E. Besag have written, "In an aggressive competition for position among peers, the most hurtful weaponry will be deployed to attain the gain—and such weaponry is often rooted in sexuality" (59). From the all-too-common occurrence of calling a girl a slut to the equally ubiquitous phenomenon of deriding a boy by deeming him a fag, these utterances make visible "the exceptionally high level of sexualized or gendered language used by young people to attack others" (Rivers, Duncan, and Besag 58).

The bullying that Martin faces in *Little Zizi* is both highly gendered and exceedingly sexual. In taunting the protagonist for having a small penis, Adrian and the other boys are not simply deriding an isolated physical trait; they are calling into question his masculinity. As Harrison Pope, Katherine A. Phillips, and Roberto Olivardia have discussed, "'Threatened masculinity' arises from the long-standing desire of boys and men to establish their 'maleness' within their societal group. Throughout most cultures in history, men who exhibited traditional 'male' behaviors and who succeeded at traditional 'male' pursuits have received approval and respect" (23). With Martin's skinny frame, nerdy glasses, and wardrobe comprised of ties and sweater vests, he is presented as not very macho. Adding to this quality, readers learn that the protagonist lacks athletic ability. Even his gym teacher "was always saying that Martin was a real dimwit, especially when he missed the ball playing soccer. Martin didn't like soccer!" The illustration that appears on the opposing page shows Martin tripping and falling on the soccer field, the laces of his cleats tangled together (Figure 3.2). Players from both his team and the opposing one laugh at him; a boy who appears to be Adrian is pointing and snickering. Finally, and in a detail that is surely not coincidental, this entire scene is seen through the legs of another, presumably male, soccer player. Readers peer between the sprinting legs of this faceless player in the extreme foreground of the image to see Martin tripping and falling in the middle ground. Not only is the soccer player whose legs frame this scene depicted only from the waist down, but— in a detail that calls further attention to the book's focus on male genitalia— the pose of his body mid-sprint calls attention to his groin area. As Rivers,

Duncan, and Besag have written about one of the most common causes of schoolyard bullying, "fights break out over issues of dominant forms of femininity and masculinity: what it means to be a male and female" (58). They go on to explain: "In a hypermasculine culture, the goal for boys is to belong to the elite ideal group of males who hold social power" (Rivers, Duncan, and Besag 62). Martin is clearly not a member of this fraternity, and his status as an outsider makes him the subject of a highly gendered form of ridicule. After the protagonist is initially bullied, for example, the narrator relays: "Martin held back his tears so that he wouldn't be called a girl."

Figure 3.2 From *Little Zizi*, written by Thierry Lenain, illustrated by Stéphane Poulin, and translated by Daniel Zolinsky. Reprinted with permission.

That said, Lenain's protagonist is bullied not simply because he fails to conform to conventional notions of masculinity but to those of conventional male heterosexuality. When Adrian first taunts Martin about his "little zizi," the protagonist asks emphatically "So what? Why should anyone care?" The bully, however, has a quick response: "Adrian stood right in front of him. His eyes beamed spitefully. 'With such a little zizi,' he said, 'you can't make babies.'" Adrian reads Martin's small penis as a sign of inferior male virility. Having diminutive male genitalia makes the protagonist both literally and figuratively unmanly: it means that he cannot measure up to the other boys physically and, even more important, he cannot participate in the ultimate "proof" of manhood by fathering children. This pronouncement devastates Martin. "He thought a lot about what Adrian had said." The protagonist is so troubled by this news that "after the swimming pool incident, out of the blue, Martin had asked Anais, 'When you grow up, will you want to have babies?'" Her reply alarms the young boy even more: "'Yes,' exclaimed Anais. 'Ten!' Ten babies! Ten! But how could Martin possibly make them with such a little zizi." The illustration that accompanies these lines highlights Martin's anxiety. The double-page spread shows the young boy envisioning ten little infants wrapped in blankets parachuting down from the sky.

Of course, the peeing contest that Adrian proposes is merely a displaced version of this same issue. While the boys may ostensibly be measuring who can urinate the farthest, they are really measuring who has the more powerful—and thus, presumably, more potent—penis. As Adrian tells Martin soon after announcing the competition: "Obviously ... With your little zizi, you can't pee very far at all." When Martin is unable to urinate in front of the boys at the contest, his failure assumes all sorts of sexual overtones, namely, male performance anxiety and, of course, impotence.

It has become commonplace in the twenty-first century to comment on the intense sexual pressures that Western society places on girls and women. As M. Gigi Durham has discussed, "The turn of the new millennium has spawned an intriguing phenomenon: the sexy little girl" (24). Diane E. Levin and Jean Kilbourne enumerate some of the many sites and sources of this phenomenon: "Mainstream national chains such as Target and J. C. Penny are selling padded bras and thong panties for young girls that feature cherries and slogans such as 'Wink Wink' and 'Eye Candy'" (42). In addition, "A T-shirt for four-year-old girls says 'Scratch and Sniff' across the chest" (Levin and Kilbourne 42). Likewise, "Gym shorts for ten-year-old girls have two handprints on the back—one on each cheek" (Levin and Kilbourne 42). As even this brief discussion indicates, "Increasingly, very young girls are becoming involved in a sphere of fashion, images, and activities that encourage them to flirt with a decidedly grown-up eroticism and sexuality—and the girls playing with these ideas are getting younger and younger every year" (Durham 21). Given the pressures placed on young girls to dress and act provocatively, Durham reports: "One angry mom calls these kids 'prosti-tots,' and another describes them as 'kinderwhores.' Others declare that corporate marketing machines are turning little girls into 'sex bait'" (23).

The increasing sexualization of girls contributes to the growing phenomenon of "age compression" or, as it is sometimes known, "kids getting older younger" in the twenty-first century. As Levin and Kilbourne explain, "'Age compression' is a term used by media professionals and marketers to describe how children at ever younger ages are doing what older children used to do" (69). From wearing makeup and reading heartthrob magazines to shaving their legs and dating, "The media, the toys, the behavior, the clothing once seen as appropriate for teens are now firmly ensconced in the lives of 'tweens and are rapidly encroaching on and influencing the lives of younger children" (Levin and Kilbourne 69–70). As Levin and Kilbourne argue, while age compression is alarming when it applies to toys, clothes, or leisure-time pursuits, it "is especially disturbing when it involves sexual behavior. Children become involved in and learn about sexual issues and behavior that they do not yet have the intellectual or emotional ability to understand and that can confuse and harm them" (70). Even those who escape this hazard often fall victim to another one. Sexualized media images encourage all girls "to judge themselves and other based on how they look; in essence they learn to see themselves as objects" (Levin and Kilbourne 63).

By 2005, this problem had become so pervasive that the American Psychological Association launched a Task Force on the Sexualization of Girls (American Psychological Association v). As the Executive Committee asserted in its report: "Ample evidence indicates that sexualization has negative effects in a variety of domains, including cognitive functioning, physical and mental health, sexuality, and attitudes and beliefs" (American Psychological Association 20–21).

In a message that extends far beyond the immediate target audience of *Little Zizi*, the picture book demonstrates that young girls are not the only demographic who experience the intense social pressures and damaging personal problems associated with early sexualization. This phenomenon is also present among boys. Even though Lenain's characters are preadolescent, they are all concerned with an array of "adult" issues: present and future romantic pairings, real or imagined virility, and their own still-developing genitalia.

While such concerns might seem like the fanciful obsessions of very young children, anxiety over penis size is a relatively common male concern. As Grace Paley has written, "Most men know what size penis they have because they've measured their erections. Some are happy with their size, but the majority would rather be bigger. Some of those who are not happy are actually bigger than average—they feel small anyway" (11). Linda Madaras and Area Madaras, who have authored several body books for boys, agree. In a comment that demonstrates how the topic of *Little Zizi* is not so niche after all, they inform the young male audience of their book *My Body, My Self for Boys*: "Surveys show that most men either think their penises are too small or at least wish theirs were larger. In the letters we get from male readers, the most common questions and concerns are about penis size. So if you've worried or wondered about penis size, you're not alone" (Madaras and Madaras 22).

The reason for such widespread unease is simple. As Harrison G. Pope, Katherine A. Phillips, and Roberto Olivardia explain: "Genitals symbolize virility, procreative potency, and power. As one man explained, 'Penis size is what makes you a man. Guys don't talk about it, but they think about it'" (165). For some men, akin to Martin in *Little Zizi*, unease over the size of their penis begins when they are very young. Pope, Phillips, and Olivardia discuss their research interviews with one man who was especially tormented by this issue:

> "It's been a problem for as long as I can remember, since I was seven or eight," he began, with much hesitation. "I remember noticing it when I

was in the locker room in junior high. I thought my penis was smaller than the other guys. I constantly compared myself with them in the shower. Then this girl told me I didn't have any bulge. That sent me over the edge. Ever since then, for the past fifteen years, I've constantly worried about whether people are noticing how small I am. I've asked girls about it, and they say I'm fine and shouldn't worry. I've seen three different urologists over the years, and they've all told me the same thing. But I was convinced that they were just trying to get me out of the office. They just tried to humor me, even though they were secretly laughing to themselves about how small it was." (166)

While not all of the men that Pope, Phillips, and Olivardia's interviewed expressed such high levels of anxiety, many reported being concerned about the size of their penis. One middle-aged man who confessed that he "had lived with the problem for years" described a childhood experience similar to that of Martin in *Little Zizi*: "When I was a kid, I always skipped gym class because of it, and now I won't work out at the gym because of it. I'm terrified people will make fun of my genital size" (Pope, Phillips, and Olivardia 167). Meanwhile, another man who was interviewed expressed similar sentiments: "I'm uncomfortable stripping down to my underwear in the locker room," he explained, "because the bulge doesn't look big enough. And a couple of times I've turned down chances to go away to sports competitions because I was afraid I'd be put in a situation where I might have to take a shower in a public place" (qtd. in Pope, Phillips, and Olivardia 167).

Echoing the pressures that the media places on young girls to dress, act, and present themselves in highly sexualized ways, many of the men in Pope, Phillips, and Olivardia's study "blamed advertisements for [their] worries" (167). As one gentleman reported: "Those guys in the magazine ads who model underwear. ... When I see those ads, I always feel a little insecure about the way I look. I always find myself thinking that they probably stuffed something in the underwear to make the bulge bigger for the advertisement. Maybe they don't, but it makes me feel more secure to think that they do" (Pope, Phillips, and Olivardia 167).

As a result of such sentiments, a large and very profitable penis-enlargement industry has emerged. From pills, weights, and creams to pumps, "stretchers," and surgery, the amount of time, money, and energy that men can spend in an attempt to lengthen their penis is astounding. Linda Madaras and Area Madaras describe one kit that contains "weights you attached to the penis or scrotum" (23). Meanwhile, Grace Paley describes another product, the "Yank Super Stretcher": "This is made of elastic and is advertised as something you can keep on discretely all day long. An elastic band fits around the corona and is attached by means of elastic to another band around the thigh so that it exerts a constant pull" (35). As she goes on to explain, however, this device is only one among many of its kind. "The Yank, which costs only $18.50, is the most elementary of stretcher. Upscale from the Yank are several makes with a ring that fits around the base of the penis, another ring that fits over the head, and rods of adjustable length running between the two rings to keep the penis in a state of constant anxiety. Stretchers can cost as much as $900" (Paley 35).

In 1991, cosmetic surgery to lengthen or widen the penis—or, in a combined procedure, to do both—"was introduced to the general public" (Paley 29). While such surgery generally yields better results than any of the stretchers, it also entails more risk and, of course, more expense. As Paley explains:

> The standard penis lengthening procedure entails cutting the suspensory ligament that holds the penis at a particular angle to the pubic bone. Freed of this ligament, the logic goes, the penis can dangle farther down out of the body. Surgeons promise one to two and a half inches of increased length, and then prescribe the wearing of weights a few hours each day for several months, to keep the extra piece of penis from retreating back inside. (30)

An array of alternative procedures exist. "Some penile augmentation techniques use Gore-Tex or collagen," Pope, Phillips, and Olivardia explain (166). Moreover, another and even more drastic "technique augments penis size by removing fat from the buttocks or thighs and grafting it onto the penis" (Pope, Phillips, and Olivardia 166).[4]

Regardless of the specific procedure used, "penis enlargement surgery is not perfected" and thus "both the American Urological Association and the American Society of Plastic and Reconstructive Surgeon refuse to endorse it" (Paley 30). In fact, as Paley relays: "Medical schools don't teach it and textbooks don't describe it" (30). Nonetheless, there is a sizable—and steadily increasing—market for it. "In mid-1997 one surgeon estimated that at least fifteen thousand in the U.S. had already had their penises surgically enlarged" (Paley 29). One of the most notable individuals "was the comic Flip Wilson, who claimed his penis needed enlargement because he'd worn it down with overuse. In August of 1997 Wilson gave the surgery its first celebrity endorsement when he pulled it out and showed it off to the people in the control booth on Howard Stern's radio show" (Paley 29). Dr. Jed Kaminetsky, a urologist who was the first surgeon to perform the procedure in New York, describes the results in a way that would likely assuage Martin's anxieties in *Little Zizi*: "You can add length, but not that much erect length, so basically it makes guys look better in the shower" (qtd. in Paley 32).

That said, very few men who either worry about the size of their penis or who have enlargement surgery actually have undersized genitals. Dr. Kaminetsky reveals: "Most of the people who came to me for this surgery had average-size penises. I measured all of them, flaccid and erect, before the surgery, and I photographed them" (qtd. in Paley 29). The questionable necessity of the surgery for most patients, and the ethical issues that arise as a result of it, prompted the urologist to no longer perform the procedure. As he reported, "That was one reason I stopped doing the surgery—the patients had too much emotional baggage" (qtd. in Paley 30).

In light of the common disjunction between a man's perceived penis size and his actual one, Pope, Phillips, and Olivardia locate these worries within a larger phenomenon of male anxiety over body image. As they write, "There's a widespread crisis among today's boys and men—a crisis that few people have noticed. Men of all ages, in unprecedented numbers, are preoccupied with the appearance of their bodies" (Pope, Phillips, Olivardia xiii). Especially over the past two decades, they explain, the United States has witnessed "a huge rise in compulsive exercising, soaring rates of anabolic steroid use, exploding sales of nutritional supplements, proliferating cosmetic treatments for men, and the birth of dozens of magazines and other publications devoted to male 'fitness' and 'health'" (Pope, Phillips, and Olivardia xiv). Deeming this phenomenon the "Adonis Complex," it is fueled in large part by media images of masculinity. Ironically, at a time when girls and women have never been more aware of the impossibility and thus the harmfulness of the "beauty myths" directed at them, young boys and men are increasingly buying into analogous messages concerning manhood. As countless movies, advertisements, and television shows assert, "real men" are strong, brave, and powerful; they have big muscles and, of course, big penises.

For boys and men who try to live up to the impossible standards of male perfection promulgated by the media, the negative impact on their physical, personal, and psychological health is immense. As Pope, Phillips, and Olivardia discuss, some "go on in adolescence to take anabolic steroids," others "develop serious eating disorders," and still others "experience other psychiatric conditions involving body image" (xiii–xiv). Exacerbating this situation, most of these men suffer in silence. "Both scientific researchers and the popular press have assumed for decades that body image problems and eating disorders were women's illnesses. Men have been overlooked" (Pope, Phillips, Olivardia xiv). In addition, men are socialized not to discuss their troubles. "Parents, teachers, and coaches are usually unaware of these problems because boys, like adult men, don't spontaneously talk about their appearance concerns," Pope, Phillips, and Olivardia report (xiv). On the contrary, "[i]n our society, 'real boys' aren't supposed to worry about such things. Parents don't ask, and boys don't tell" (Pope, Phillips, and Olivardia xiv).

Little Zizi brings the underdiscussed issue of male anxiety over body image in general and penis size in particular to light. The book gives a much-needed voice and visibility to a widely experienced but also widely neglected socio-cultural issue. Indeed, this observation was articulated both in official reviews of the picture book and in comments posted about it around the Internet. Jyotsna Sreenivasan, for example, began her customer review of *Little Zizi* on Amazon with the following statement: "This funny picture book is about a subject that many little boys think about, but that is rarely written about in children's books" (par. 1). The *Midwest Book Review* made a similar observation, asserting: "*Little Zizi* is a unique children's picture-book that dares to address a part of growing up that virtually no other children's literature will touch" ("Little Zizi," par. 1). As these comments indicate, *Little Zizi* pushes the potential subjects for picture books into a new and necessary area.[5]

While Lenain's written text in *Little Zizi* may break the silence about male anxiety over penis size for children in the twenty-first century, Poulin's visual illustrations suggest that such concerns are not anything new. The artistic medium, aesthetic appearance, and visual style of the images harken back to an earlier historical era and, in so doing, suggest that these fears have troubled boys for many generations. Poulin's illustrations are not created using highly contemporaneous methods such as computer animation, photoshopped graphics, or postmodern pastiche. Rather, they appear to be made using the very traditional medium of oil paint. Moreover, these compositions have a warm, soft, and almost gauzy look. There are no sharp edges or 90-degree angles; instead, everything has a rounded appearance, giving the book both a nonthreatening feel and an Old World look. From the clothing worn, buildings shown, and furniture depicted to the fact that none of the characters have cell phones, their classroom does not possess any computers, and the town does not have signals or even streetlights, the story could be set in the early twentieth century. Indeed, the most modern—and, I might add, the only—electric appliance that appears anywhere in the book is the lamp on Martin's bedside table.

While *Little Zizi* rightfully suggests that male anxiety over penis size is a common and longstanding issue, the book's treatment of this subject is not all worthy of praise. The picture book may be commended for breaking the social and literary silence that many boys worry about the size of their genitals, but it does little to address the generally unwarranted nature of such concerns. Akin to the narrative's problematic portrayal of how bullying situations can be resolved, Lenain's text presents some inaccurate or at least incomplete information about male genitalia, especially during puberty. First and foremost, as Linda Madaras and Area Madaras inform the adolescent male readers of their nonfiction book, *My Body, My Self For Boys*: "For starters, you should know that the size of your penis has nothing to do with how macho, brave, or attractive you are. It has nothing to do with the kind of lover, husband, or father you'll be. Your penis size is a reflection of one and only one thing: the size of your penis" (22). Equally important, and thus even more conspicuously absent from *Little Zizi*, is the reassurance that penis size has no bearing on male fertility. As Karen Gravelle flatly asserts: "Penis size ... has nothing to do with how many children a man can have or how easily he can make a woman pregnant" (15). While the closing lines of Lenain's text does reveal that when Anais and Martin grow up "they will have lots of children. At least ten. Because love isn't a question of a zizi—large or small," it does not unequivocally refute the earlier equation of virility with penis size.

Similarly, and perhaps even more surprising, *Little Zizi* makes no mention of the fact that changes in temperature, environment, or mood can affect penis size. As Madaras and Madaras remind their young male audience, "Besides, as you well know, your penis changes size, and not just during erections, either. Being afraid, cold, or nervous reduces the blood inside the penis, making it smaller in size. If you've ever waded into cold water, you know what we mean!" (23). Given that Adrian first begins taunting Martin about the size of his zizi while he is changing after having been swimming—and, thus, is presumably cold and wet—this seems like an important detail.

Equally useful information is the lack of correspondence between the size of a flaccid penis and an erect one. As Paley points out, "Penises are unpredictable. You can't tell from the size of a flaccid penis what it will look like when it's erect. Some of those that look biggest when flaccid enlarge the least upon erection" (15). The converse is also true. In the words of Gravelle: "smaller penises tend to increase more in size than larger ones. That means that differences in penis size generally even out when men have sex" (15). Thus, while Martin's penis may be smaller than Adrian's when it is flaccid, it may be larger or, at least, of comparable size, when erect—facts that are once again not mentioned during the course of Lenain's text.

Finally, and of equal importance, *Little Zizi* also omits any information about the process of puberty and the fact that boys' bodies undergo change at varying rates. Jonathan Mar and Grace Norwich highlight this fact on one of the opening pages of *The Body Book for Boys*: "Every boy's body is different, so some may start the process [of going through puberty] earlier, while some may start it later" (5). In a subsequent chapter, they go on to explain in more detail: "For some boys, this process starts as early as the age of nine. For others, it doesn't begin until they're fourteen or fifteen" (Mar and Norwich 61). Thus, the size disparity between Martin's zizi and the one belonging to Adrian might be more accurately attributable to a disparity in their developmental stages, with the bullying boy having already begun the process of puberty while Martin has not. Given the varying ages at which boys can begin puberty, Madaras and Madaras remind their readers when discussing average penis size: "don't get all flustered if your measurements don't match these numbers. ... you're still growing" (22).

This lack of discussion about changes in penis size as a boy matures is especially surprising given that *Little Zizi* begins by informing readers that Martin has seen his father's penis.[6] "He wondered if one day his zizi would look like his dad's. But that's normal. All boys wonder about that," writes Lenain on the book's opening page. The drawing that accompanies these lines accentuates this point about size (Figure 3.3). The illustration is a double-page spread that shows Martin strolling down a street in town. In his line of sight as he gazes over his shoulder is a large, phallic-looking sausage hanging from a wooden bracket above the entrance to the butcher's shop. Lest readers miss the fact that Martin appears to be looking, if not directly at the big plump sausage, then at least in its general direction, the item appears in the center of the double-page spread, where its presence cannot be missed.

Until this morning everything was going along very well. Like all boys, Martin had a zizi, and this zizi didn't cause him any problems. Of course, from time to time, Martin worried a little. He wondered if one day his zizi would look like his dad's. But that's normal. All boys wonder about that. So everything was going along quite well.

Figure 3.3   From *Little Zizi*, written by Thierry Lenain, illustrated by Stéphane
    Poulin, and translated by Daniel Zolinsky. Reprinted with permission.

The protagonist is already aware that the zizis of little boys like himself are smaller than those of grown men, such as his father. But, Martin does not extrapolate that this same situation may also apply to boys who are closer to his own age. Martin's failure to make this connection also suggests that his father has not discussed such issues with him or, if he has, this discussion has not been as thorough or detailed as he needed. What's more, *Little Zizi* ends without returning to this issue. Not only does it never encourage Martin—and, by extension, the book's presumably young male readers—to talk with their fathers about their developing bodies, but it also does not include any reproach of Martin's dad for failing to do this in the first place. For all of the emphasis in *Little Zizi* about giving voice to formerly silenced issues, this omission embodies a missed educational moment in a book that presents itself as having a primarily didactic purpose.

"This Was Adrian's Favorite Game. He Was Always Talking About Such Things": Phallomania, Male Homoeroticism, and the Nonheternormative Child

In spite of the focus in *Little Zizi* on heterosexual courtship and male reproductive virility, this is not the only niche issue and accompanying target audience that the narrative can be seen as addressing. The picture book also possesses a powerful subtext of male homoeroticism and engagement with the nonheteronormative child.

These issues emerge within the first few pages of *Little Zizi*. Given the eager interest with which the boys in the locker room clamor to view Martin's zizi, it is difficult to attribute their behavior to mere bodily curiosity. On the contrary, Poulin's illustration—which shows boys crawling under dividers, climbing over partitions, and jostling classmates for a better view of the naked protagonist—imbues this homosocial scene with a powerful homoerotic quality. In so doing, it introduces an alternative way of reading *Little Zizi*: as a narrative that addresses the anxieties that boys experience about compulsory heterosexuality. As Jeffrey Fishberger has written, while all young people struggle "to understand the changes in their bodies and their new and different feelings," this process is even more difficult for a queer young person "as negative things he [or she] has heard or read about gay people can affect his journey of self-discovery. Such negative messages can also hinder [a youth's] acceptance of their sexuality and their comfort with being open with others" (pars. 12, 13). For this reason, when Lenain writes that "[a] great roar of laughter echoed through the locker room" upon seeing Martin naked, the cause for at least some of this reaction can be called into question. Surely, for some of the young boys in the locker room— as well as, undoubtedly, a segment of those reading the picture book—this laughter is not cruelly directed outward at Martin but nervously inward by uneasiness over their own nascent and perhaps nonconformist sexuality.

Nowhere perhaps is this possibility more powerfully apparent than with the bully Adrian. For all of his stated romantic interest in the girl Anais, he is obsessed with penises. The young boy spends what seems like an excessive amount of time thinking about male genitalia; looking at them; comparing them; arguing about them; and arranging contests to display, use, and evaluate them. In a comment that suggests Adrian possesses if not phallomania then, at least, a male form of penis envy, the narrator comments about the boy's decision to have a peeing contest: "This was Adrian's favorite game." Lest any doubts remain about Adrian's longstanding fixation on male genitalia, the very next sentence asserts: "He was always talking about such things."

Such suggestive elements return near the end of the book, conveyed this time via Poulin's illustrations rather than Lenian's text. When Anais chooses Martin over Adrian in the story's finale, the vanquished bully is depicted sulking off to the side behind a public fountain that has, as mentioned previously, a Cupid statue in the center (Figure 3.4). While this object obviously resonates with the book's central theme of heterosexual romance, both Adrian's physical location in relation to the figure and his behavior while standing beneath it imbue the scene with homoerotic overtones. The antagonist is not only standing on the side of the fountain where he has an unobstructed view of the naked Cupid's penis, but he is looking up at it, watching the stream of water that is shooting from its zizi. Going beyond simply providing further evidence of Adrian's obsession with male genitalia, this closing image evokes Eve Kosofsky Sedgwick's well-known argument in *Between Men* about triangulated desire. She asserts that many seemingly heterosexual contests in Victorian British literature where two male suitors compete over the same female love interest can actually be read as homosexual in nature. Rather than being genuinely interested in the woman, the two men have simply projected or displaced their feelings for each other onto her. In these narratives, women emerge "as exchangeable objects, as counters of value, for the primary purpose of cementing relationships with other men" (Sedgwick 123). The presence of the female love interest and the ruse of the love triangle shields the men from homophobia while it also provides a means for them to cope with their own homosexual panic (Sedgwick 83, 86–89).

Figure 3.4 From *Little Zizi*, written by Thierry Lenain, illustrated by Stéphane
Poulin, and translated by Daniel Zolinsky. Reprinted with permission.

The triangulated relationship that Adrian creates with Martin over Anais can be read in an analogous way. The romantic rivalry that he initiates over a girl can be seen as a means for the bully to cope with his own repressed or, at least, displaced erotic feelings for a boy. To be sure, Adrian's reaction to the resolution of the love triangle—placing himself in front of the naked Cupid and looking up at the water provocatively spouting from his zizi—suggests that his frustration and disappointment may not be related to losing Anais. Rather, it may have more to do with losing Martin and the penis-focused interactions that he has with him.

The specter of nonheteronormative male sexuality appears in additional sites and sources throughout *Little Zizi*. When the boys initially gather in the park to hear Adrian's announcement about the peeing contest, a grown man appears in the illustration. The individual, whose presence is not mentioned in Lenain's words to the text, is sleeping in the shadows on the side of the giant lion statue, out of view of most of the boys. His dirty overcoat suggests that he is homeless; meanwhile, the empty wine bottle standing on the step below him indicates that he is inebriated. Poulin's inclusion of this figure provides a physical manifestation of the adult male sexuality for which Adrian and the other boys are so desirous while it also undercuts it: after all, the man, who is the only adult depicted in any of the illustrations to the book, is a seeming "failure" as a man. He is indigent, intoxicated, and alone, hardly an emblem of male virility in any sense of that word.

At the same time, though, the homeless man sleeping on the steps of the statue introduces another tacit element to *Little Zizi*: the possibility of child endangerment and even predation. The group of young boys who are all alone in the park while an unkempt, inebriated male stranger lies prostrate just around the corner evokes erotic peril and, possibly, pedophilia.[7] On the following page, Martin flees the taunting laughs of the group, knocking over some of the folding chairs as he runs away and a couple of boys ardently pursue him (Figure 3.5). The commotion rouses the man, who has slid down a few steps from where he was sleeping; Poulin now shows him with his legs splayed awkwardly in the air and his arms on the ground supporting his torso. As Barbara Kiefer has commented about picture books, "young children pick out small details in illustrations" (8). She goes on to explain: "In fact, they seem to scan pictures differently than adults" (Kiefer 8). Because early elementary-aged boys and girls have not been fully "trained" in how to "properly" view and "effectively" decode an image, they often privilege visual elements that adults miss or minimize. As Kiefer asserts: "One of the first things I noted was that children picked up the smallest details that many illustrators include in their pictures and that we adults often overlook" (35).

Figure 3.5 From *Little Zizi*, written by Thierry Lenain, illustrated by Stéphane
    Poulin, and translated by Daniel Zolinsky. Reprinted with permission.

Sandra L. Beckett makes the same point but for an alternative reason. As she discusses, some young people read picture books differently from adults not because they lack literary training, but because they are more comfortable and accustomed to reading visual images than older generations. In comments that have been uttered by a variety of critics, "modern children often have better visual literacy skills than adults. In addition to being more skilled at reading graphic details, they are often more receptive to untraditional visual and verbal narratives then adults" (Beckett 2).

Whichever phenomenon is at play, the end result is the same: a potential alternative interpretation of picture books like *Little Zizi*. Especially for a boy or girl who is being read Lenain's narrative aloud or who is only browsing through the book looking at the images, small and seemingly "insignificant" visual details like the inebriated man assume added significance. Indeed, for young people who notice this figure rather than ignore or discount him as an unimportant background element, they may regard the scenario on this page in a wholly different way. To them, it may appear that Martin is not fleeing the taunts of his peers, but that the unkempt man is frightening the protagonist and the other boys away. Looking at the illustration from this perspective, it is unclear whether the man is trying to stop himself from falling further down the monument's steps or whether he is trying to stand up to chase the youngsters deeper into the park with its thickly trunked, phallic-looking trees. Barbara Kiefer has commented about the tendency of children to notice tiny details in picture books: "The rewards of looking carefully at illustrations to find what one teacher called 'secrets' may in turn help children become more sensitive to the artistic qualities in picturebooks" (36). This practice may also help them to form alternative interpretations or, at least, readings that go against the grain of adult authorial intent. As Maria Nikolajeva and Carole Scott have written about picture books, "The verbal text has gaps, and the visual text has its own gaps. Words and images can fill each other's gaps, wholly or partially. But they can also leave gaps for the reader/viewer to fill" (2). As a result, they go on to conclude, "readers are required to bring their own answers, their own resolutions to the works, and to join forces with the author/illustrator in creating the scenario, the story, and the interpretation" (Nikolajeva and Scott 259). Either consciously or unconsciously, *Little Zizi* offers the same invitation to its readers.

Ironically, even the seemingly most heteronormative facet of *Little Zizi*—Martin's quest to win the affections of Anais and father children with her—also embeds queer elements. In *No Future: Queer Theory and the Death Drive*, Lee Edelman articulates the way in which children have long been used as a material argument against homosexuals and homosexuality in the United States. Not only are young people routinely co-opted by conservative forces in their portrayal of the traditional, normative, heterosexual family, but LGBTQ (lesbian, gay, bisexual, transgender, and queer) couples are also positioned as existing outside the "cycles of reproduction" given their inability to biologically procreate (Edelman 97). Edelman encourages LGBTQ individuals to push back against both the ubiquity of the child in American culture and the "reproductive futurism" that it engenders. After all, as he points out, these practices only work to perpetuate a heterocentrist society (2). This position stands in marked contradistinction to the politics of assimilation that have typified the LGBTQ movement in the United States over the past few decades with the increased emphasis on marriage and adoption rights for same-sex couples. In a stance that runs contrary to this trend, Edelman argues: "Abjuring fidelity to a futurism that's always purchased at our expense ... to the necessary contradiction of trying to turn its intelligibility against itself, we might rather, figuratively, cast our vote for 'none of the above,' for the primacy of a constant *no* in response to the law of the Symbolic, which would echo that law's foundation act, its self-constituting negation" (4–5).

Little Zizi, for all of its privileging of heteronormative procreation, evokes this phenomenon. Throughout the book, the protagonist expresses his anxiety and even ambivalence about participating in reproductive futurism. When Adrian informs him that his small zizi will be unable to sire babies, he does not argue otherwise, cite facts to the contrary, or fight back in any way. Instead, as the narrator relays, "Martin ran away." Later, the protagonist blanches when Anais tells him that she wants "'Ten!' Ten babies! Ten!" In the privacy of his bedroom, in fact, he seems to resign himself to the "no future" that Edelman advocates: "now it all seemed hopeless for him. Finished." Moreover, in the double-page spread that shows Martin sitting on the park bench imagining ten infants dropping from the sky in parachutes, the presentation of these figures is telling (Figure 3.6). None of the babies are depicted in cute, adorable, or romantic ways. Instead, nearly all of them are engaged in some type of mischief or being subjected to some form of mishap. In almost the exact center of the right side of the page, for example, one baby has crashed into another baby's parachute, causing it to crumple and, presumably, the baby to soon drop rapidly to the ground. Likewise, another infant, who is depicted just above this scene, is shown upended and struggling inside the blanket bundle in which they are all being delivered: a clenched fist and a bare foot stick out from the top near the knot. Meanwhile, on the left side of the page, another baby looks like he plans to crash into Martin, kamikaze-style. He is peering out of his blanket in a way that suggests he might be deliberately steering his parachute bundle directly for the protagonist. Finally, the two babies who have already reached the ground are certainly not acting in any cute or adorable way: one has a mean-looking grimace on his face while he pulls the tail of Martin's dog; meanwhile, the other one is trying to tug the pup's treat—which is, quite symbolically, a small sausage—from his mouth. Clearly, as Martin imagines it, the thought of fatherhood in general and heterosexual procreation in particular does not conjure happy scenarios.

Figure 3.6 From *Little Zizi*, written by Thierry Lenain, illustrated by
      Stéphane Poulin, and translated by Daniel Zolinsky. Reprinted
      with permission.

Not surprisingly, Martin himself can be placed on a spectrum of queerness. In *Curioser: On the Queerness of Children* (2004), Steven Bruhm and
Natasha Hurley discuss a powerful paradox in American conceptions of
children and childhood: "There is currently a dominant narrative about
children: children are (and should stay) innocent of sexual desires and intentions. At the same time, however, children are also officially, tacitly, assumed
to be heterosexual" (ix). From clothing for infant boys with sayings like
"Ladies, I Have Arrived!" "Lock Up Your Daughters," and "That's Mr. Stud
to You" emblazoned across the chest to greeting cards depicting a little girl
in a dress receiving a rose from a little boy in an oversized suit, evidence
abounds that "we accept the teleology of the child (and narrative itself) as
heterosexually determined" (Bruhm and Hurley xiv).

That said, prevailing beliefs in the presumed heteronormativity of children are far from this simplistic or straightforward. As Bruhm and Hurley go
on to point out, childhood is routinely framed as a liminal state of alterity;
it is a time of flux, uncertainty, evolution, nonconformity, experimentation,
and even otherness (xiv). As a result, it can be seen as possessing a variety
of queer qualities. "The very effort to flatten the narrative of the child into a
story of innocence has some queer effects," Bruhm and Hurley observe (xiv).
For this reason, they go on to assert: "Childhood itself is afforded a mod-
icum of queerness when the people worry more about how the child turns
out than about how the child exists as a child" (Bruhm and Hurley xiv).

Kathryn Bond Stockton has expanded on this concept. As she provocatively claims on the opening page of her book *The Queer Child: Or Growing*

Sideways in the Twentieth Century (2009): "If you scratch a child, you will find a queer, in the sense of someone 'gay' or just plain strange" (1). She explains the basis for this argument: "What a child 'is' is a darkening question. The question of the child makes us climb inside a cloud—'a shadowy spot on a field of light'—leading us, in moments, to cloudiness and ghostliness surrounding children as figures in time" (2). That said, Stockton makes a case that "[o]ne kind of child brings these matters into view. And, to my mind, it is the means, the fine-grained lens, by which to see any and every child as queer, even though the troubles of this specific child seem to be unique" (2). Given the ways in which children are constantly morphing and shape-shifting—imagining themselves during play as fantastical creatures, newfangled beings, and even inanimate objects—combined with the fact that many social manners and mores are unknown and even alien to them, such as when they try to wear their pants as a shirt or cut their meat with a spoon, they routinely embody elements of queerness. "Estranging, broadening, darkening forms of the child-as-idea are my pursuit, with a keen eye on the ghostly gay child (emblem of children's queerness) … and a figure braiding with other forms of children who are broadly strange," Stockton explains (3).

Little Zizi's Martin, both via the text by Thierry Lenain and especially via the illustrations by Stéphane Poulin, is a multivalent queer child. His small penis causes him to be cast as physically aberrant, sexually suspect, and socially outcast. In addition, his nerdy eyeglasses, spindly legs, fussy sweater vests, and prim neckties imbue him with a variety of physical and sartorial traits that are stereotypically associated with sissies. Moreover, his sensitivity, shyness, and lack of athletic ability causes him to mirror an array of behavioral characteristics commonly read as indices of current or future queerness in children. In this way, although the conclusion to *Little Zizi* presents Martin happily paired off with Anais, he embodies a powerful point of concentration for what Stockton calls the "ghostly gayness in the figure of the child" (4).

Finally, but far from insignificantly the very process by which Martin wins the affections of Anais locates him within what Judith Halberstam has called "the queer art of failure." As Halberstam argues in her book by the same name, LGBTQ individuals have a unique relationship with disappointment. Building on the work of Lee Edelman, Heather Love, and José E. Muñoz, she explains that because notions of success with regard to sexual activity are commonly defined not simply in heteronormative terms concerning the interplay between male and female sexual organs but also from the reproductive standpoint of impregnation and procreation, queer erotic interactions are always acts of failure. In the words of Halberstam: "Failing is something queers do and have always done exceptionally well" (3). That said, failure for the LGBTQ community is not simply a dour state of perpetual frustration; it can also have distinct advantages and even important rewards. As Halberstam points out, "while failure certainly comes accompanied by a host of negative affects, such as disappointment, disillusionment, and despair, it also provides the opportunity to use these negative affects to poke holes in the toxic positivity of contemporary life" (3). In this way, "failure allows us to escape the punishing norms that discipline behavior and manage human development" (Halberstam 3). Failing to conform both to gender and to sexual norms has allowed LGBTQ individuals to imagine new, and often more liberatory, ways of being. It has permitted them to escape the traps, pitfalls, and limitations associated with mainstream heteronormative American life. For this reason, Halberstam asserts, "there are definite advantages to failing" (4).

While Martin is not explicitly ascribed an LGBTQ identity in *Little Zizi*, he nonetheless embodies "the queer art of failure." The young boy fails repeatedly and consistently. In the opening pages of the book, he falls down while playing soccer. Then, he runs away when a bully insults and challenges him. Finally, he is unable to perform during the peeing contest. However, these disappointing actions and embarrassing events paradoxically yield success. Martin wins the affections of Anais in spite of having botched every chance to prove his manhood. In some ways, in fact, Martin's lack of machismo—his failure to conform to conventional notions of masculinity—has helped rather than hurt his case. Anais's impassioned rebuke when Adrian dons his father's cologne, slicks down his hair, and attempts to "claim her" as his girlfriend in the schoolyard suggests that she is repelled, not attracted, by male sexual assertiveness and pompous displays of normative masculinity.

* * *

As M. Gigi Durham accurately observes about American culture in the twenty-first century, "we have a tendency to be scandalized by the idea of children and sexuality" (45). In keeping with the persistence of Enlightenment-era views of young people as pure and innocent, children are seen as existing outside of not simply erotic activity but even erotic awareness.

Given the ubiquity of sex and sexuality in popular culture, this attitude is untenable. As Durham says flatly: "We've got to wake up. To imagine that childhood is a pure and innocent state, closed off from the rest of the world, is to live in a fantasy of denial" (46). Rather than naively seeing young people as unaware of or uninterested in erotic activities, adults need to recognize that "[k]ids have complicated, multilayered, and profound associations with sex that need to be explored and brought to the surface in order to develop any kind of effective intervention strategies" (Durham 55). In light of this fact, she asserts: "It is pointless to wonder whether children who are in grade school or middle school *should* be thinking about sex—the reality is that sex pervades their world" (Durham 68; emphasis in original). As a consequence, Durham declares, "instead of wringing our hands or shrugging our shoulders hopelessly, we should be thinking about how best to enable kids to develop healthy, sensible, and responsible understandings of sexuality at appropriate stages of their development" (46).

Little Zizi heeds this advice. The picture book breaks the silence surrounding an array of vital but long-neglected issues concerning prevailing notions about masculinity, the eroticization of boys, and even the queerness of children and childhood. Although *Little Zizi* may not always offer the most thorough treatment of these subjects, it does perform the important task of beginning a conversation with children, parents, and educators about them. Given that nothing less than the long-term physical health, emotional welfare, and sexual well-being of boys are at stake, this discussion is far from niche—and also, hopefully, far from finished.

Notes

1. The book was originally published in France and Montreal in 1997 as *Petit Zizi*.
2. *Little Zizi* is not paginated.
3. I am indebted to an earlier anonymous reviewer of the manuscript for pointing out this detail.
4. In *The Book of the Penis*, Paley also discusses various penis-widening techniques. "Extra girth—up to 50 percent more, some surgeons say—can be added in one of two ways. A few years ago surgeons favored liposuction. They would suction fat out of the patient's abdomen and insert it into the penis. This is the same method that is used to add pout to women's lips, and it was invented by the same man who invented lip liposuction. It has the same drawback, too—eventually all of the fat gets reabsorbed and the procedure needs to be repeated" (Paley 31). As a result, a newer and seemingly more effective method has been introduced: the dermal fat graft. In this procedure, the "surgeon removes a strip of dermis, or skin layer, from the buttocks or thigh, and sews it onto the penis. This is more permanent, but it is also a more complicated operation. Still, it's now the only widening procedure some surgeons will do. Too often when liposuctioned fat is injected into the penis it distributes itself unevenly, forming lumps. Imagine a man who used to worry that his penis was too thin. He has the surgery and now it's fatter, but lumpy" (Paley 31). As Paley goes on to discuss, however, a "[l]umpy penis is only one of the surgery's possible side effects … Either surgery can cause scarring, numbness, blood vessel damage, and impotence" (31). Finally, Pope, Philips, and Olivardia point out that "[s]ome critics maintain" that any surgical attempt at lengthening or widening "is an unsafe procedure that can result in permanent erectile dysfunction, and others maintain that the penis can end up looking like a tired balloon" (166).
5. As Sandra Beckett notes in *Crossover Picturebooks: A Genre for All Ages*, this comment is especially true for children's literature in the United States. "Nudity and sexuality do not have the same taboo status in many European countries as they do in the English-speaking markets" (240). As mentioned earlier, *Little Zizi* was originally written in French and released in Canada and France as *Petit Zizi* (1997) before being translated into English and published in the United States. Moreover, it is not the only book to discuss the issue of male genitalia. Francois Braud's *À quoi sert le zizi garçons* (What's a boy's willy for?), which was released in France in 2002, engages with a similar subject. For more

on the differing treatment of nudity and sexuality in American picture books versus those released in Europe, see pages 238 to 240 in Beckett's *Crossover Picturebooks*.

6. I am indebted to an earlier anonymous reader of the manuscript for calling my attention to this detail.

7. I would like to thank an anonymous reader of an earlier version of this manuscript for pointing me in the direction of this possible interpretation, as well as the one that appears in the previous paragraph.

4 Will Power

Maggie Goes on a Diet, the Fully Autonomous Child, and the Hazards of Unsupervised Adults

In October 2011, Hawaii-based children's author Paul M. Kramer released *Maggie Goes on a Diet*. The narrative featured the eponymous fourteen-year-old character who, as the title of the book suggests, decides to alter her eating habits after being teased by peers and hindered on the athletic field because she is overweight.

Maggie embodied many of the hallmarks of niche marketing and production. In a remark that was echoed by many other reviewers, Leanne Italie noted that the book's illustrations, which were drawn by Mari Kuwayama, and especially its writing style were "amateurish" (par. 5). The images that appear throughout the text are not only cartoonish-looking with characters rendered in thick black outline, but the color palette used to pigment them is so bright that, at times, it seems garish. Meanwhile, *Maggie* is told via rhyming couplets where the meter is often inconsistent, the grammar is frequently awkward, and the end rhyme is sometimes forced. A representative passage, for example, reads: "Maggie moved around very slowly, but oh could she kick that soccer ball. / Maggie agreed to play but whenever she tried to run fast she would fall."[1] Akin to the bulk of writers profiled in this project, Kramer was not a professional author: after working for many years as a travel agent, he discovered a calling to compose narratives for young people. *Maggie Goes on a Diet* was his first book. In a final point of similarity with the niche ethos, Kramer's narrative was released by Aloha Publishers, a small independent imprint that the author founded himself and that issues only his books.

Even before *Maggie Goes on a Diet* was officially published, it ignited a firestorm of controversy. In newspaper articles, online reviews, and especially blog posts, commentators were alarmed by the book's message. As Karen Kaplan pointed out about the author, "Paul M. Kramer has no expertise in child health" (par. 8). As a consequence, his narrative offers some uninformed and even irresponsible views about pediatric nutrition. For example, the protagonist loses weight at an alarmingly high and unhealthy rate. As the text reports: "After the first week, Maggie lost seven and a half pounds." Then, about midway through the narrative, Kramer writes: "Four months had passed and Maggie was over thirty pounds lighter." By the close of *Maggie Goes on a Diet*, ten months have elapsed and the title character has shed a total of fifty-one pounds. These figures far exceed medical recommendations for pediatric weight reduction. As the Centers for Disease Control has asserted: "Weight loss in children should be recommended with caution and should generally be no more than one pound per month" ("Overweight Children and Adolescents," sec. 5, par. 4).

Just as problematic as the presentation of pediatric weight loss in *Maggie Goes on a Diet* are the reasons that the eponymous character gives for wanting to slim down, along with the impact that her newly trim physique has on her life. Numerous passages present thinness as a solution to all of Maggie's previous personal, social, and psychological problems. Rather than emphasizing improved health, Kramer's book calls attention to improved physical appearance: "Maggie missed her treats but imagined how she would look in smaller sized jeans." The young girl's weight loss results in increased academic achievement, newfound social acceptance, and her first-ever romantic overtures. As lines from one of the closing pages relay: "Maggie was getting more and more attention from the guys. / Maggie's reputation was slowly increasing and on the rise." By the end of the book, the now-slim protagonist has become a star althete and school role model. "Every time Maggie scored a goal, her cheering section would scream. ... Playing soccer gave Maggie popularity and fame."

Kramer's target audience exacerbated concerns over the equation of thinness with happiness in *Maggie Goes on a Diet*. Although the title character in the book is a teenager, Barnes & Noble lists the age range for the text as six through twelve. Meanwhile, Amazon.com identifies the readership as being even younger, from four through eight years old. As one blogger asserted about this demographic, "Little girls shouldn't even know what a diet is, much less be encouraged to lose weight!" (qtd. in Kaplan, par. 7).

These issues propelled this self-published picture book by a novice children's author into the national spotlight. Months before *Maggie Goes on a Diet* officially appeared on bookstore shelves, it was the subject of extensive discussion in publications ranging from *Time* magazine, *The Washington Post*, and the *Los Angeles Times* to *The New York Daily Post*, the *Chicago Sun-Times*, and *The Huffington Post*. In addition, the text was the topic of heated debate on the Internet: in customer comments on Amazon.com, on social media sites like Facebook, and around the blogosphere. As Leanne Italie documented in September 2011, "There is ... a 'Say No to Maggie Goes on a Diet' Facebook page, [which] calls for a boycott and demands that Amazon and Barnes & Noble pull the book" (par. 6).

In response to such viewpoints, Paul M. Kramer appeared on *Fox News*, *Good Morning America*, and CNN to defend both himself and his text. During an appearance on *Good Morning America* in August 2011, for instance, he asserted: "My intentions were just to write a story to entice and to have children feel better about themselves, discover a new way of eating, learn to do exercise, try to emulate Maggie, and learn from Maggie's experience" (qtd. in Hopper and Allen, par. 2). The author even issued a revised version of his book—*Maggie Eats Healthier* in late 2011—which removed any references to "dieting" and also reduced the number of pounds the title character loses. But, the damage was done. Joanne Ikeda, the cofounding director of the University of California at Berkeley's Center on Weight and Health "described Kramer's response to the public health peril's of pediatric obesity as 'well-intentioned but very misguided'" (Hopper and Allen, par. 22). In light of the intense societal pressures that young women already face to look a certain way, especially with regard to their weight, a large and vocal cadre of critics asserted that *Maggie* did far more harm than good.

Given the fervor with which *Maggie Goes on a Diet* has been condemned for privileging certain body types, emphasizing outward appearance over inner worth, and equating thinness with happiness, this chapter has no interest in reiterating such remarks. Such ground has not only been well-trod in previous discussions, but comments of this nature have become predictable, typically uttered within the first few minutes of conversation about Kramer's book, even by individuals who have not read it.

Instead, I seek to change the conversation regarding *Maggie Goes on a Diet*, pushing discussion of the narrative beyond the realm of self-evident analysis and simple surface reading. In the pages that follow, I make a case that Kramer's picture book not only merits further consideration but also rewards such efforts with new interpretive insights. While *Maggie Goes on a Diet* fails miserably at presenting a positive portrait of pediatric health, it succeeds in accomplishing another and, one might argue, far more elusive task in the realm of books for young readers: the presentation of a wholly autonomous child character. Echoing a feature that critics like Perry Nodelman, Roberta Seelinger Trites, and Maria Nikolajeva have identified as a hallmark of books for young readers, Maggie's parents are absent from the narrative, as are any other adult influences. As a result, the protagonist exists in a state of empowered independence. Unencumbered by adult restrictions, Maggie has the authority to make decisions about her life as well as the agency to implement them.

While *Maggie Goes on a Diet* may possess this common trait of narratives for young readers, it does not present the same equally common resolution: children being returned to adult control and placed back under parental authority in the end of the story. Although Kramer's book may seem to reaffirm the need for young people to remain under adult supervision—given the young girl's unhealthy rate of weight loss and her often misguided reasons for changing her eating habits—I contend that the text points to the opposite conclusion: that there are instances when adults are the ones who need to be supervised, monitored, and controlled, such as when they decide to write a book on a subject about which they are not well informed and have not properly researched. The shortfalls in *Maggie* are the result of the adult author's failings, rather than those of the youthful protagonist. In so doing, the picture book inverts conventional distinctions between adult and child, especially with regard to their social subject position and power relation. Children are routinely relegated to a subjugated status because they are seen as lacking important knowledge, wisdom, and experience. But, in *Maggie*, these traits are ultimately, if inadvertently, ascribed to adults. Previous critics of Kramer's picture book have lamented how his young protagonist was unable to escape the cult of thinness; but, in their singular focus on this issue, they have overlooked how she was able to elude an even more powerful cultural force: adult control. Maggie may not be a role model for pediatric nutrition, but she is a daring new type of unfettered child protagonist.

"And It Was Still Hot": The Myth of Child Empowerment in Literature for Young Readers

Robert Hurley, in remarks that have been echoed by numerous teachers, parents, and librarians, discusses the pleasure that countless young people receive from literature: "What adolescent has not lingered over a novel, drinking in every word, smelling every syllable, not wanting to finish too quickly, fearing that once the last page was turned the tones of those book-bound friends would fade forever into oblivion" (1173). Younger readers routinely experience this same thrill, as they beg their parents to read a favorite picture book, fairy tale, or nursery rhyme "again and again" (Hurley 1173). For this reason, Hurley asserts that "the experience of literature is often liberating; at its best, transcendent" (1173). Reading allows boys and girls to meet new people, embark on fantastic adventures, and experience different ways of life. In this way, books are emotionally, intellectually, socially, and psychologically transformative. "Things which we formerly accepted as incontrovertible facts, historically and scientifically established," Hurley observes, "prove to be malleable and open to amendment" (1173).

While few would contest the assertion that literature delights young readers, challenges their assumptions about the world, and permits them to transcend their own worldview, many would debate the extent to which these narratives are, in fact, liberating. For all of their ostensible interest in enlightening and, by extension, empowering children, most books for young people actually serve the opposite function: they demonstrate the importance of children remaining safely within the realm of adult control and authority. Karen Coats has commented on this phenomenon, asking: "Why is it ... that no matter how much power a child character gains over the course of a book, he or she still returns to a disempowered state at the end?" (338). She goes on to lament: "Worlds could be saved, enemies slaughtered, any number of problems cunningly solved—but in the end, the protagonist, if a child, must necessarily go back to a parent lecture or explanation that diminishes the experience, an existence hemmed in by rules, or simply the same oppressive situation left behind during the adventure" (Coats 338).

Even a cursory examination of some of the most commercially successful as well as critically acclaimed books for young readers demonstrate the veracity of this claim. In Maurice Sendak's *Where the Wild Things Are* (1963), for example, the main character, Max, travels to a fantastical world of the Wild Things. While there, he has a myriad of exciting adventures: romping with the creatures, leading the wild rumpus, and even being crowned king. But, at the end of the book, Max's newfound agency, freedom, and even sovereign power are eliminated. The child character leaves the land of the Wild Things and returns home. Far from being framed as a lamentable decision, Max's choice is presented as laudatory. The closing lines of the book reveal that upon reentering his room, "he found his supper waiting for him / and it was still hot"—a passage that suggests that while the child protagonist may have abdicated his material throne as king of the wild things, he has gained nonmaterial items that are even more valuable: parental care, maternal love, and familial belonging.

A variation on this phenomenon occurs in Chris Van Allsburg's *Jumanji* (1981). When their parents are away one afternoon, protagonists Judy and Peter Shepard grow bored and venture to a nearby park. While there, they discover an abandoned board game, *Jumanji*. They take the game home and begin playing it, only to discover that it possesses magical powers: whatever events transpire during the course of the game also transpire in real life. Together, Judy and Peter use their wits to survive such harrowing experiences as the appearance of a ferocious lion, the outbreak of a flooding monsoon, and the sudden entrance of a thundering stampede. But, in the end of the story, these accomplishments are eradicated. The final roll of the dice returns their disheveled house back to normal. "Everything was just as it had been before the game. No monkeys, no guide, no water, no broken furniture, no snake, no lion roaring upstairs, no rhinos," the text reads. Moreover, Judy and Peter return the game to the park before their parents arrive back home. Mrs. Shepard asks them about their day, but their attempt to recount all of the exciting events is thwarted: "Peter was interrupted by the adults' laughter." As a result, the parents in the book remain unaware of the incredible experiences that their children had as well as the bravery, skill, and pluck they exhibited in the face of these challenges.

This phenomenon of a child protagonist being stripped of whatever agency and autonomy they have achieved over the course of the narrative is not merely limited to picture books; it also appears in numerous novels. In Lewis Carroll's *Alice's Adventures in Wonderland* (1865), the title character embarks on a fantastical adventure after declaring her ennui with her current mundane circumstances. While in Wonderland, Alice exerts a great deal of courageous authority: she rebukes a judge, challenges the competency of a jury, and argues with a king. However, the exact moment when the child protagonist reaches the apogee of her power—defiantly telling the dictatorial Queen of Hearts "Who cares for *you*? ... You're nothing but a pack of cards!" (124)—is also the exact moment when the whole adventure comes to an abrupt end: upon uttering these remarks, Wonderland is revealed to be merely a dream. Alice awakes "with her head in the lap of her sister, who was gently brushing away some dead leaves that had fluttered down from the trees upon her face" (124).

A comparable pattern of disempowerment occurs in C. S. Lewis's beloved *The Lion, the Witch and the Wardrobe* (1950) as well as the bulk of the wildly popular novels in J. K. Rowling's *Harry Potter* series. The four protagonists in Lewis's well-known story step through an enchanted piece of furniture and into the world of Narnia where they successfully face a number of challenges: from shrewdly spoiling the sinister machinations of the White Witch to courageously aiding the rightful ruler, the lion Aslan. Indeed, for their valiant efforts, the now-grown Lucy, Edmund, Susan, and Peter are crowned the kings and queens of Narnia. But, in the finale to the novel, they all leave this realm. After stepping back through the wardrobe and into their bedroom, the group not only abdicates their sovereign power but they also become mere children once again.

The narrative arc for many of the books in the *Harry Potter* series likewise depicts the title character being removed from a realm in which he exerts tremendous power to one where he is exceedingly disempowered. Jack Zipes, in his book *Sticks and Stones: The Troublesome Success of Children's Literature from Slovenly Peter to Harry Potter* (2002), argues that the books follow a formula: most begin by presenting Harry within a prison environment, usually the home of his aunt and uncle, Vernon and Petunia Dursley; then, they progress to his series of "Noble Adventures" while at Hogwarts; finally, the books conclude by reluctantly returning Harry home once again (Zipes 176–7). In so doing, whatever agency and autonomy the main character obtains over the course of the narrative—bravely battling the Dark Arts; ingeniously foiling Voldemort's schemes; and valiantly saving teachers, friends, and classmates from danger—are effectively eliminated.

This particular plot pattern appears so often in books for young readers that it is has been given a name: "home–away–home." As Perry Nodelman has discussed, many works of children's literature—including all of the books discussed in the previous paragraphs—begin with their child protagonist at home, then have him or her embark on an adventure in a real or imagined world outside of this realm, only to return the character to the safety and security of their home again at the end of the story (*Hidden* 61). The home–away–home pattern forms such a common and important element in books for young readers that Nodelman identifies it as one of the genre's defining hallmarks (*Hidden* 66–67, 226). However, it is also a key tactic by which young people are stripped of agency and autonomy in the finale of these narratives. By returning a child protagonist to his or her home, the authors are returning them to a state of dependence. As Nodelman explains, in texts that follow this pattern, "home represents above all a place where change is unlikely or even impossible, a safely static enclosure designed to keep uncertainty and flux outside" (*Hidden* 66). While this arrangement is intended to protect children and keep them safe, it also keeps them subordinated and disempowered. Home is a place where adults—and not children—make the rules and are in charge. Consequently, whatever achievements, insights, and powers child protagonists obtained during the course of their adventures—be it braving the dangers of *Jumanji* or eluding the White Witch in Narnia—are dismissed, erased, or ignored when they enter back into domestic space.

While many young adult novels do not follow the home–away–home pattern, they nonetheless deny their juvenile protagonists any real agency. As Roberta Seelinger Trites has written, these narratives may appear to challenge norms and break taboos, but most are "carefully constructed to perpetuate the status quo" (xii). In examples ranging from early classics like Richard Cormier's *The Chocolate War* (1974) and Judy Blume's *Forever* (1975) to more contemporaneous favorites such as Lois Lowry's *The Giver* (1993) and Karen Hesse's *Out of the Dust* (1997), Trites documents how young adult (YA) literature ultimately "directs power away from adolescents and towards adults" (81).

This trend has not gone unnoticed by either past or present critics. Jacqueline Rose, in her groundbreaking book *The Case of Peter Pan: Or, The Impossibility of Children's Literature* (1984), lamented how child characters in books for young readers are presented as "artless beings devoid of agency" (32). Likewise, Marah Gubar, in her examination of the Golden Era of children's literature, draws a poignant parallel between the condition of fictional children in books with factual ones in the outside world, asking in a question that is equal parts indictment and lament: "given their status as dependent, acculturated beings, how much power and autonomy can young people actually have?" (4–5). Finally, Maria Nikolajeva offers one of the most recent and extensive explorations of this issue in her book *Power, Voice and Subjectivity in Literature for Young Readers* (2011). She argues that even more than the commonly identified themes of "rebellion and obedience, growth and change, dreams and imagination" (Gruner, par. 4), power is a key concept in books for young readers. From ABC books through young adult novels, "the main thrust of the literary work is the examination of power positions, the affirmation or interrogation of the existing order of power" (Nikolajeva, *Power* 7). This quality makes children's literature "conspicuously similar to other literatures dealing with powerless social groups, women's literature, indigenous literature, or gay [*sic*] literature" (Nikolajeva, *Power* 7). However, one central difference remains. Whereas other minority literatures question the existing status quo and seek to change it, children's literature does the opposite: these narratives ultimately reaffirm the established power structure. Nikolajeva argues that the reason for this condition is simple: adults are the ones who routinely write, edit, publish, purchase, and endorse books for young readers. These men and women have a vested interest in preserving their power over young people, not dismantling it. For this reason, "[a]dults can never fully interrogate their own power position, and the overwhelming majority of children's books do not even attempt at [*sic*] such interrogation, either by ignoring the issue altogether or by unconditionally affirming adult norms" (Nikolajeva, *Power* 203).

"Maggie Knew That Now Was the Time for Her": Child Agency and Autonomy in *Maggie Goes on a Diet*

Maggie Goes on a Diet adheres to many longstanding stereotypes about the appearance, content, and message of books for young readers. From the author's decision to compose his narrative in Dr. Seuess-esque rhyming couplets to the predictably happy ending that he gives his story, *Maggie Goes on a Diet* epitomizes many public perceptions, especially by novices, about picture books. In fact, the way Kramer's narrative conforms to popular impressions about children's literature has contributed to the text being deemed "amateurish." As numerous reviews indicate, *Maggie* embodies many of the traits associated with "bad" children's books: clunky writing, cartoonish illustrations, and a didactic message that is both overly simplistic and exceedingly heavy-handed. Even the reason that Kramer himself has given in articles and interviews for why he became a children's author smacks of naiveté. As he explains on his website, he has a desire to pen narratives about "issues that children face today" (Aloha Publishers). Perry Nodelman has commented about remarks of this general nature: "It is revealing, for instance, that even those who want to write *for* children often express the lack of awareness" about the past origins, ongoing evolution, and current state of books for young readers (*Hidden* 135; emphasis in original). He goes on to provide an example: "The pop star Madonna echoes many newcomers to writing for children when she blithely announces that she has taken up her new pursuit after reading a few books to her son: 'I couldn't believe how vapid and vacant and empty all the stories were. ... There's like no books about anything'" (qtd. in Nodelman, *Hidden* 135). Paul M. Kramer penned *Maggie Goes on a Diet* to address the important problem of pediatric obesity. But, contrary to the author's perception, this issue had long been the subject of national conversation. From First Lady Michelle Obama's much-publicized "Let's Move" program—which debuted in early 2010—to the growing number of public school districts that have banned junk food both from the meals being served in their cafeteria as well as the vending machines in their hallways,[2] it was far from an overlooked issue. By late 2011 when Kramer's narrative was released, dozens of fiction and nonfiction books for both parents and their children had been released on the subject.

Although *Maggie Goes on a Diet* may contain an array of limiting stereotypes about books for children, it resists another equally common one: the phenomenon of adult authors maintaining the established power structure by denying their child characters true agency. Kramer's title character possesses both the authority to make decisions about her life and the ability to act on them. Maggie is the one who decides to lose weight; she is the one who implements changes to her eating and exercise habits; and she is also the one who has the drive, motivation, and will power to keep to her new health regiment. Finally, and most significantly, Maggie's agency, accomplishments, and autonomy are not eradicated in the end of the book. On the contrary, these traits are preserved. In this way, Kramer's picture book disrupts the formerly stable and even sacrosanct binaries of knowledge/ignorance, wisdom/naiveté, and experience/inexperience that have long been used to differentiate adults and children—and to justify young people's continued subordination. *Maggie Goes on a Diet* is ostensibly about a young girl's quest to lose weight, but the narrative participates in a second, more radical endeavor: shedding longstanding maxims about child incompetence and adult competence.

* * *

The presentation of Maggie as a determined, independent, and proactive protagonist emerges from the opening lines of Kramer's text. The title character is introduced to readers as a highly motivated individual: "Maggie Magee did not have much athletic skill. / She wanted to learn, she had the desire and also the will." The double-page spread on which these lines appear depicts the protagonist playing on a baseball team. Maggie is batting at the plate and she has seemingly just struck out: the baseball is sitting snugly in the center of the catcher's mitt, the umpire is holding up one arm while shouting something inaudible, and Maggie is clutching her wooden bat in a half-swing with a surprised look on her face. In both the written text and the visual illustration, the young girl's poor performance is largely attributed to her weight. This detail, however, only solidifies her resolve. "Disappointed in herself for she was the worst on the team. / Maggie was determined to one day be fit and be lean," a couplet on this page reads.

A few pages later, Maggie is invited to play in a practice soccer game and her strong drive and powerful will are reiterated. Although the out-of-shape protagonist finds running up and down the field laborious—"She was huffing and puffing and sometimes found it difficult to breathe"—she is not disheartened: "Maggie was so tired and sweaty and dirty, it was hard to believe. / But she was also having so much fun; Maggie *absolutely* did not want to leave" (my emphasis). Far from mere empty rhetoric, the title character acts on these sentiments. Kramer writes: "It took Maggie awhile to finally make up her mind. / She promised herself she was going to reduce her stomach as well as her big behind." While Kramer's language is less than elegant, the details of his character's vow are significant. Maggie "promised *herself*" that she was going to lose weight—not her parents, her teachers, or her pediatrician. In so doing, she demonstrates her autonomy: she is the one making this decision. Moreover, Maggie is doing so by herself and for herself. Indeed, in a statement that not only relays her resolve, but serves as a powerful testament to her autonomy and agency, the next line of the book reads: "Maggie knew that now was the time *for her* and that it was not too late" (my emphasis).

In keeping with this proclamation, Maggie wastes little time putting such words into action: "when was this new way of eating supposed to begin? / 'Tomorrow morning,' said Maggie, displaying a great big grin." The illustration that accompanies this passage emphasizes both the title character's tenacity and her sense of empowerment: her arms are pumped in front of her chest, her eyes are cast slightly upward, and she has a powerful look of determination on her face. A thought bubble on the left side of the page reveals her state of mind: it contains a silhouette of a slimmer Maggie running in long, confident strides while kicking a soccer ball. Moreover, the background to the image is a solid yellow color. There are no details to distract the reader or even indicate her setting; all of the reader's attention is focused squarely on Maggie and her action in this scene.

Calling further attention to the significance of this narrative moment, the drawing of Maggie on this page is larger than in any of the other illustrations. The spatial distance separating the reader from the title character has been reduced, and the protagonist is shown far more close-up than anywhere else in the book. As Maria Nikolajeva and Carole Scott have written, size routinely conveys importance and even relative power in picture book illustrations. As they posit, "We assume that a character depicted as large has more significance (and maybe more power) than the character who is small and crammed in the corner of a page" (Nikolajeva and Scott 83). I would argue that it is not a mere coincidence that the page where Maggie announces her resolve to change her eating habits is also the page where she is presented as the largest.

In the same way that Maggie has the autonomy to make decisions about her life, she also possesses the agency to implement these changes. As Kramer's text reveals: "The very next morning Maggie's new diet had begun." As the narrator goes on to explain, the child character is the one who selects her food and prepares her meals. "Breakfast consisted of oatmeal with yogurt and fruit. … For lunch, a turkey sandwich with mustard and lettuce greens. / For dinner, there were vegetables with various proteins," the story reads. Moreover, the young girl also keeps herself motivated and on task: "Maggie made a smiley face in the bowl which was actually quite cute." Of course, there are moments when the young girl finds changing her old habits difficult. But, even in the face of such challenges, she maintains her resolve: "The thought of cutting out junk food sometimes made Maggie sad. / She was pleasantly surprised that many healthy foods were actually quite tasty and for that she was glad."

In this scene—as in the rest of the narrative—adults are entirely absent. At no point do readers see either of Maggie's parents, one of her teachers, or any of her coaches. Moreover, there are no adults when Maggie goes to the house of one of her new friends for a slumber party, when she is walking the halls or eating lunch in the cafeteria of her high school, or when she tries on new clothes at a store. Finally, and perhaps most conspicuously, the fans in the crowd at Maggie's soccer and baseball games appear to be comprised exclusively of other young people. To be sure, the written text of Kramer's narrative never mentions adults. Moreover, there are only a few moments in the illustrations that depict grown-ups: the umpires at Maggie's two baseball games—and, based on the illustrations by Mari Kuwayama, both could be older teen boys rather than grown men—and the balding teacher who gives Maggie the "High School Soccer Award." However, these figures play no substantive part in the narrative; they are not given any lines of dialogue, and they are not shown interacting with the title character in any direct or meaningful way. Instead, they are literally background characters.

Children's literature has a long history of omitting adults in general and parents in particular. In examples ranging from the aforementioned titles like *The Lion, The Witch and the Wardrobe*, the *Harry Potter* series, and *Where the Wild Things Are* to other well-known books such as *The Cat in the Hat*, *A Series of Unfortunate Events*, and *James and the Giant Peach*, many of the most commercially successful and critically acclaimed narratives for young readers present child characters whose parents are recently deceased, psychologically distracted, or physically off-stage for most of the action. This phenomenon gives young people more freedom and autonomy. As Nathan Branford has written, it allows for the creation of "stories about children having adventures on their own" (par. 13). Away from the watchful eye and controlling influence of parents, young people are able to do things that they would not normally be permitted to do. In the words of Kenneth L. Donelson and Alleen Pace Nilsen, they can go to places that would otherwise be off-limits and they can likewise make decisions on their own "without the help of their parents" (29). For this reason, children's authors "get rid of the parents so that the young person is free to take credit for his or her own accomplishments" (Donelson and Nilsen 29).

Maggie Goes on a Diet participates in this longstanding tradition while it simultaneously expands on it. Even though many books for young readers find a way to remove parents from the action of the story so that their child characters can take center stage, they also typically introduce them—however briefly and sometimes only as a verbal rather than physical presence—at the start of the story. Max has an argument with his mother before he escapes to the land of the Wild Things in Sendak's picture book. Likewise, Mr. and Mrs. Shepard appear at both the start and the end of *Jumanji*. Finally, the first book in *Lemony Snicket's Series of Unfortunate Events* begins with the Baudelaire children being informed that their parents have perished in a fire.

By contrast, readers know absolutely nothing about Maggie's mother or father: if they are still together, whether the title character lives with one or both of them, or even if they are living. Maggie's parents are never depicted and, even more surprisingly, they are never discussed. Maggie has no interactions with them at any point in the story, and the narrator likewise does not mention them. In this way, the protagonist's parents are not simply moved off-stage, they are wholly erased.

While the complete omission of any parental presence would be daring for a children's narrative published during any historical era, it is especially bold given the socio-historical backdrop for *Maggie*. Kramer's picture book was written and released during a time of unprecedented levels of parental control over the lives of young people in general and white, middle-class, suburban children like Maggie in particular. As Hara Estroff Marano, Bella English, and Alyson Shafer have all discussed, children in the United States are being monitored, supervised, and even micromanaged by adults with greater frequency and intensity than at any other time in the nation's history. Whereas young people were formerly allowed to have unsupervised and unstructured time—to romp outside in their backyards, ride their bikes through the neighborhood, or enjoy the swings and slides of a local playground—such experiences have drastically decreased if not disappeared altogether. Beginning in the 1970s and accelerating rapidly in the 1980s, growing media coverage about "child predators"—ranging from cult members kidnapping young people for Satanic practices, crazed lunatics putting razor blades in Halloween candy, and babysitters and daycare workers physically abusing and/or sexually molesting youngsters—caused many parents in general and mothers in particular to be more watchful and, in many cases, even vigilant. Telling youngsters to "go out and play" shifted from being the childrearing norm to being regarded as dangerous, irresponsible, and even neglectful (Douglas and Michaels 90–103). Instead of playing a pickup game of baseball in the empty lot at the end of the street, kids needed to be on an organized team in an official league, at least in part to ensure their safety (Douglas and Michaels 90–103). This same maxim held true for seemingly every facet of a child's life. As Susan J. Douglas and Meredith Michaels have written about the mainstream media message to parents and especially mothers during the 1980s, "No place was safe ... you just never, ever know" (98).

This phenomenon increased exponentially during the final decade of the twentieth century and the opening years of the new millennium. Throughout this period, fears over children's physical well-being were amplified by newfound anxieties about their future emotional health as well as socioeconomic standing. Unlike previous eras where children were viewed as "robust and capable" (Schafer 6), they were now increasingly regarded as delicate and easily scarred. As a result, parents sought to do everything possible to protect their child's self-esteem and to ensure their future social position in an increasingly competitive global economy. The end result was that parents became hyperinvolved in nearly every facet of their children's lives and, in turn, the lives of children became hyperscheduled and übercontrolled.[3] Alyson Shafer has written about how this condition influences both millennial motherhood and millennial childhood: "So ... it's off to soccer practice, Kumon Math, piano lessons (which they hate, but playing an instrument is vital), and don't forget to stop at the Montessori school to drop off the pre-registration for the baby (yes, he's only three months old now, but you *know* how long those waiting lists are for good schools)" (5; emphasis in original). This desire to give one's child every possible advantage in an increasingly cutthroat world but simultaneously spare them from the setbacks and disappointments in life engendered some powerful paradoxes. As Judith Warner has observed, "Children play soccer at semiprofessional training levels before they start kindergarten. Nine- and ten-year olds are trained for national basketball championships" (215). But, at the same time, every child on most of these teams receives a trophy for merely participating.

Such parental control and even hypervigilance does not dissipate as the child grows up. Often, it extends even into the college years. As Bella English has discussed, "At Boston University, one father was so upset over his daughter's A-minus final grade that he called the professor to complain, and then the department chair, and then the academic dean" (par. 1). Meanwhile, at nearby Simmons College, "school officials have fielded parental concerns about noise, gluten-free diets, and food allergies. One mother called to request more variety on the salad bar" (English, par. 2). As even these few examples suggest, far from embodying isolated incidents, such behavior can more accurately be viewed as evidence of a new trend. According to Sarah Neill, the dean of students at Simmons, "there has been a real shift in the extent to which parents are involved and invested in the lives of their students" (qtd. in English, par. 3). Going off to college used to be a milestone that marked the transition from adolescence to adulthood. It was a time when mothers and fathers happily stepped back from their parental responsibilities and let their son or daughter experience both the successes and failures that came with independence. Especially for young people living away from home for the first time, college was a time when they became wholly responsible for issues like doing their laundry, getting themselves up for classes, handling their conflicts with friends and roommates, keeping track of due dates for their class assignments, and managing their time. This situation has changed, however. Now, many parents remain just as involved, vigilant, and controlling during their son or daughter's college years as when they were in grammar school. As Bella English explains about this phenomenon, "Everyone has heard of parents who do their grade schooler's science project or are overly involved in their kids' social lives. But the infamous helicopter parents, hovering over their young children, are now transitioning into so-called snowplow parents, trying to smooth a path for their kids even after they've started college" (par. 4).

Kramer's portrayal of Maggie stands in marked contrast to this trend. The central character does not rely on, turn to, or even expect her parents to assist her with any of life's difficulties, big or small. As discussed earlier, Maggie is the one who decides to make changes to her life. In addition, she is the one who decides on and then implements her new menu choices. Likewise, the protagonist sets, schedules, and adheres to her exercise regiment. Finally, and perhaps most significantly, Maggie navigates the social and psychological difficulties that arise from being overweight. In one of the opening pages of the book, the protagonist is ridiculed by a group of boys while walking home from school: "Maggie was teased and made fun of just about every day at school. / She was called fatty and chubby and other names that were very cruel." The illustration that accompanies these lines shows the forlorn-looking girl walking alone down a residential street. Her melancholy expression suggests that her solitary state is not chosen, but forced; Maggie is alone because she does not have any friends. Meanwhile, in the foreground on the right corner of the page, a group of boys are pointing, laughing, and snickering. The cruel expressions on their faces, coupled with Maggie's own mournful countenance, convey the sadness that she experiences.

Even so, the young girl does not seek outside help or adult assistance. Instead, in keeping with the agency that she displays throughout the book, she takes matters into her own hands, turning to the boys who are taunting her and telling them: "'Is your life so boring that you have nothing else better to do?' / 'How would you like it and how would you feel if everyone picked on you?' / 'So lose your stinger and make like a bee and buzz on through.'" Even if these remarks are not effective in ending the peer harassment—and, as discussed in the previous chapter on *Little Zizi*, research on bullying suggests that they would not be—it is significant that Maggie stands up for herself. Her decision to rebuke the boys who are bullying her took courage, daring, and even moxie. In this scene, as in vignettes throughout Kramer's narrative, Maggie is anything but a passive figure. On the contrary, she is an active figure who takes charge of her life.

There's No Place Like (Away from) Home: A Child Protagonist Who Is Not "Housebroken"

In the same way that *Maggie Goes on a Diet* does not echo previous children's books by presenting a protagonist whose power is contained within carefully circumscribed limits, the book also does not follow the same common plot structure. Instead of the typical home–away–home trajectory, Kramer's book can be characterized by the inverse: it maps an away–home–away pattern. Given the way in which the return home at the end of children's books signals the juvenile character's forced or chosen abdication of power, this narrative arc demonstrates what can happen when a child character is not redomesticated, in any sense of that word.

Maggie Goes on a Diet commences not with the expected trope of presenting the protagonist within the safety and security of her house but outdoors at a baseball diamond. Kramer quickly establishes that, far from a child-friendly space that is carefully controlled by adult supervision and thus the rules of polite conduct, it is an unsafe venue where young people often experience harm. Maggie is ridiculed by the spectators at the baseball field: "Most everyone chuckled as Maggie got up to bat. / Maggie was not only clumsy, she was also quite fat." In the closing line on the page, the narrator informs readers that this hurtful behavior has emanated from Maggie's peers. Moreover, it causes the protagonist to feel not merely personally defeated but psychologically disillusioned: "She could not understand why *some kids could be so mean*" (my emphasis).

The following page depicts Maggie at home. But, Kramer does not imbue this domestic space with the same stereotypical attributes as numerous other children's books. As Perry Nodelman reminds us, the common narrative purpose of home in narratives for young readers "is above all to defy time, to prevent change from happening or at least from affecting those held within it, to keep children from the effects of change and time, to keep them safely now as they are for as long as possible" (*Hidden* 66–67). The exact opposite situation occurs in *Maggie*. Home is a place where the title character is not sheltered and protected from the difficulties of the outside world but experiences their impact. Instead of being comforted by loving parents who soothe her and help her to feel better from the cruel bullying that she has just experienced on the baseball field, the protagonist remains deeply upset. "After the game Maggie was really quite sad. / It was certainly one of the worst days that Maggie ever had," Kramer writes. In marked contrast to the common portrayal of home as a safe, secure, and loving space, the protagonist has a profoundly different experience: "Maggie was anxious and depressed and not thinking clearly. / She was holding on to her dignity but only just barely." In fact, the title character is so upset by the peer ridicule that she experienced earlier that day that she comforts herself with food. "Searching the refrigerator in hopes she would feel better, / eating lots of bread and cheeses, including some cheddar," the text reveals. The illustration that accompanies these lines—and which embodies one of the most heavily criticized images in the book—shows the young girl in her pajamas, presumably late at night, squatting in front of the open refrigerator, eating items from a low shelf with both hands. In an indication of both the fast pace and the large quantity of food that Maggie is consuming during this binging episode, her cheeks are plumped out chipmunk-style.

In the same way that Maggie does not experience home as a happy refuge of safety and security, she also does not experience it as a place of stasis and atemporality. On the contrary, the title character makes some of her most profound personal, physical, and psychological changes while in this space. Home is the venue in which Maggie first alters her eating habits, where she charts her progress, and where she engages in her regiment of physical exercise. In this way, home serves as the seedbed or, at least, staging ground for change, not a refuge from it.

This alternative presentation of domestic space begins from the moment that Maggie vows to alter her eating habits. As discussed earlier, while the precise setting where she initially made the decision "that now was the time for her" is unclear—given the nonspecific solid-color background—the place where she first acts upon it is not. The following page shows the title character sitting at her kitchen table eating her healthy new breakfast of oatmeal, yogurt, and fruit. The lines that accompany this image call attention to the fact that Maggie wasted no time implementing changes to her life. "The very next morning Maggie's new diet had begun," Kramer writes.

Barbara Bader has said about the picture book genre: "As an art form, it hinges on the interdependence of pictures and words, on the simultaneous display of two facing pages and on the drama of turning the page" (1). *Maggie Goes on a Diet* makes effective use of all of these elements, but it especially capitalizes on the final feature—"the drama of turning the page"—during the remaining portion of its story. As readers encounter each subsequent double-page spread, they witness the profound personal and physical changes that the eponymous character has undergone. The first scene that follows Maggie's declaration that she is going on a diet begins this process. The double-page image presents the title character still within the confines of her home; this time, though, she is in the bathroom, stepping onto a scale. The text relays the amount of weight that she has lost and the impact that it has had on her physical well-being: "After the first week Maggie shed a few pounds. / It was already easier for Maggie to move and bend up and down." While these figures do not align with medical recommendations for healthy weight loss in children, they nonetheless indicate the significant changes that the title character has experienced. Indeed, precisely because this rate far exceeds the pediatric guidelines, it underscores Maggie's dramatic transformation.

Maggie does more than simply "go on a diet" within the domestic space of her home by eating healthier. She also uses this arena to further her program of physical fitness by adopting an exercise regimen. Near the middle of the book, Kramer depicts Maggie walking on a treadmill in the living room of her house. In the illustration that appears on the right side of the page, the young girl is shown wearing a tracksuit, holding a small free weight in each hand, and taking big confident strides while pumping her arms. As the narrative makes clear, this workout session is not an isolated occurrence; it is a key part of her strategy for fitness: "Maggie was exercising regularly just about everyday [*sic*]." As before, Kramer calls explicit attention to the tremendous physical, psychological, and personal changes that this home workout routine has helped to precipitate: "Four months had passed and Maggie was over thirty pounds lighter. / Maggie was looking better and better and her future looked brighter." In this way, the title character's dramatic public transformation—"Maggie looked like a different person in her brand new dress," Kramer writes while she tries on clothes at a store—is only possible because of the activities that have taken place in private at home. Far from being typified by stasis and the suspension of time, Maggie's domestic life is marked by the passage of time and the changes that have taken place during it.

The final pages of *Maggie Goes on a Diet* likewise do not return the title character to domestic space. Instead, they take place outside of her home: the penultimate double-page spread is set on the soccer field while the final one transpires in the high school auditorium. Instead of seeing Maggie stripped of her power by being returned to the private space of home, both of these scenes showcase her agency and accomplishments in the public realm. While at the soccer field, Maggie encounters a young girl who reminds her of her former herself: "There were several smaller girls kicking their ball back and forth. / One of them could hardly move but her kick was strong like a horse." Although the girl has brown hair instead of Maggie's orange locks, she looks strikingly similar to the formerly plump protagonist in every other way: she is roughly the same weight and has the same general body shape. Moreover, she is wearing the same jersey number as Maggie: 12. Whereas the bulk of other children's books strip their juvenile protagonists of their power in the closing pages, Kramer's text does the opposite: he depicts his main character passing lessons about personal agency and autonomy to another young person. "Maggie said to herself, if I could help this girl, wouldn't that be great. / Do you suppose that this day for both of them was fate?" the text asks. The implication is that Maggie will mentor this girl, helping her to make changes and take charge of her life. In so doing, the ultimate message of *Maggie Goes on a Diet* is to disseminate child agency rather than curtail it.

Perry Nodelman has written about the prevalence of repetition and variation in children's narratives: "Their plots tend to consist of a series of discrete episodes, each of which represents a different version of the same or similar actions and a development of the same basic themes" (*Hidden* 69). This observation certainly holds true for Maggie. But, at the same time, the plot repetition that appears in the closing pages of the book also serves a different function. Nodelman argues that instances of replication or duplication in children's books work to reinforce the narrative's main message, which reaffirms the status quo, especially when it comes to the power relationship between adults and children. To illustrate, he discusses six different texts, which address different subject matter, were released in different historical eras, and use different literary formats. But, Nodelman contends, this pattern could apply to any narrative for young readers: "despite any claims they might make as didactic texts for their protagonists having changed— learned to be better—the ... texts all apparently leave space for a similar story to be told again—for a child or childlike being to err in similar ways again, and to learn the same or a similar lesson again and again" (*Hidden* 76). The message being conveyed through this practice is simple: "The texts often insist that children continue to need adult protection even though, or even because, they have been wise enough to acknowledge and accept adult interpretations of their behavior" (Nodelman, *Hidden* 78). This situation persists, Nodelman postulates, even amid the paradox that the child protagonists' "acceptance of [their need for adult protection] ... makes them less childlike and therefore less in need of the protection they now are wise enough to acknowledge their need of" (*Hidden* 78). As a consequence, children's narratives—for all of their seeming interest in empowering young people—undercut this message at the end. The ultimate goal is to justify parental control and affirm adult authority, not call such practices into question.

This phenomenon does not occur in *Maggie Goes on a Diet*. The final page of the picture book celebrates Maggie's agency and autonomy, rather than eradicating or even diminishing these elements. The double-page spread presents the title character standing on the stage of the high school auditorium, receiving the annual soccer award. Her classmates cheer enthusiastically and the gray-haired teacher conferring the award has an avuncular look of pleased satisfaction. The closing lines of the text read: "Just think of all the benefits that came to Maggie because of her sacrifice. / There were some very difficult times but it was worth the price. / Especially being that the end turned out so nice." Kramer himself repeatedly stated his hope that the picture book would empower children and encourage them to take charge of their lives. As he explained during an appearance on *Good Morning America*, "Maggie is accepting that kids are mean and kids can be mean and *she has decided to do something about it, to take things in her own hands, try to change her own life, try to make herself healthy* by exercising" (qtd. in Hopper and Allen, par. 6; my emphasis). Meanwhile, when Kramer released the revised edition of his book in mid-October, he was even more explicit about this purpose. In an e-mail that the author sent to CTV, he issued the following press announcement: "I am hoping you will agree, as so many others have after reading this book, that it is both entertaining and inspirational for children to begin to eat healthier and begin exercising and most importantly, *to believe that they have the ability* to become healthier *if they choose to*" (qtd. in Favaro, par. 7; my emphasis). For this reason, Bonnie Rochman, in one of the few defenses of *Maggie Goes on a Diet*, asserted that Kramer's protagonist should be commended "for 'taking charge of her nutritional status, her weight and her life'" (par. 13). Instead of passively acquiescing to her situation, she defiantly acted.

Michel Foucault, in *Discipline and Punish*, sought to change the common public perception and, by extension, socio-political conversation about power. As he asserted, "We must cease once and for all to describe the effects of power in negative terms: it 'excludes,' it 'represses,' it 'censors,' it 'masks,' it 'conceals.' In fact, power produces: it produces reality; it produces domains of objects and rituals of truth" (194). Judith Butler, in *The Psychic Life of Power*, elaborated on this assertion: "power not only *acts on* a subject but, in a transitive sense, *enacts* the subject into being" (13; emphasis in original). Agency and autonomy permit individuals to construct their identity, shape their own belief system, and form their sense of self.

The dynamics at play in *Maggie Goes on a Diet* exemplify these observations. The way in which power is defined, deployed, and disseminated in the picture book is consistently concerned with the illumination of lived experience, the production of personal truth, and the creation of subjective identity rather than with the project of domination. The agency and auton-omy that Maggie wields throughout the narrative are used to enhance, enrich, and enliven her life; they are not used to defy, dominate, or suppress adults. The protagonist is not interested in using her agency to turn the proverbial tables and take revenge on adults who have long oppressed her. Instead, Maggie deploys power as a tool to authorize and actualize her own self. When power is viewed from this perspective and for these purposes, Kramer's picture book embeds an even more radical message for readers of all ages. When adults deny children power, they are not denying them the mere potential to rebel against authority, but the opportunity to learn, grow, and develop.

Please Do Not Leave Grown-Ups Unsupervised: The Limits of Adult Knowledge, Wisdom, and Expertise

The closing lines of *Maggie Goes on a Diet* aside, not everything can be said to have "turned out so nice" in Kramer's narrative. As media coverage about the book has repeatedly pointed out, the text is riddled with an array of problematic passages, inaccurate information, and misguided messages. These issues extend far beyond the unhealthy rate at which the title charac-ter loses weight that has been so-often discussed by critics. First and perhaps most obvious, *Maggie* offers an overly simplistic view of why young people are overweight. As Meghan L. Butryn and Thomas A. Wadden have written, a complex array of familial, social, psychological, economic, and dietary factors are usually at play in childhood obesity. For treatment of this condi-tion to be successful, it must address this constellation of issues, not just one of them, like the foods that a child eats or how much he or she exercises, as in *Maggie*.

In addition, the reason that Kramer's protagonist gives for changing her eating and exercise habits often stems from her longing to become more physically attractive than it does from her desire to become healthier. This rationale is showcased, in fact, via the image that appears on the cover to *Maggie Goes on a Diet*. In *How Picturebooks Work*, Maria Nikolejeva and Carole Scott have discussed the importance of paratextual material in these narratives, "such as titles, covers or endpapers" (241). As they assert, "These elements are … more important in picturebooks than in novels … the cover of a picturebook is often an integral part of the narrative, especially when the cover does not repeat any of the pictures inside the book" (Nikolejva and Scott 241). For this reason, "The narrative can indeed start on the cover, and it can go beyond the last page onto the back cover" (Nikolejeva and Scott 241). Although Paul M. Kramer may be an amateur author and *Maggie Goes on a Diet* may be his first text for young readers, he understands—and makes excellent use of—this aspect of picture books. The image on the cover presents the plump title character standing in front of a mirror and holding up a pink dress that is obviously too small for her. In the reflection, however,

Maggie sees a far slimmer version of herself—one who could clearly fit into the pretty gown. Lest this connection is not clear, the illustration on the back cover shows the now-thin Maggie wearing the Cinderella-style garment. These images suggest that the protagonist elects to "go on a diet" not because she seeks to take better care of herself, but so that she may wear pretty clothes.

The illustrations that appear on the book's front and back cover accurately foreshadow the plot. Near the end of *Maggie Goes on a Diet*, after the title character has lost a significant amount of weight, readers learn: "All of Maggie's clothes were falling to the floor. / They were so big on her; she could not wear them anymore." As a result, the narrator continues: "Maggie had no choice but to replace all her old clothes. / She had to buy everything new from her head to her toes." The drawing that surrounds these lines presents the now-slim title character standing in front of a long mirror in a store dressing room holding up a cute dress. Hanging on a series of pegs behind her is an array of other flattering feminine clothes: a formal gown, a short plaid skirt, and a form-fitting ballerina-style top with leggings. Significantly, one of the garments that Maggie has selected to try on is the pair of hip-hugging jeans that look very similar to the ones that she had fantasized about upon first starting her diet. Moreover, a passage from the text links the central character's new wardrobe back to another powerful force in the Western beauty industry that dictates standards about women's appearance, attire, and especially weight: "Maggie was so excited; it was like having her own *fashion show*" (my emphasis).

Of all the problematic messages in *Maggie Goes on a Diet*, by far the most disconcerting are the ones discussing the effects of the title character's weight loss. Numerous passages present losing weight and being thin as a solution to all of the title character's previous personal, social, and psychological problems. One of young girl's greatest sources of self-satisfaction comes from her newfound athletic prowess. As the narrator relays at Maggie's baseball game: "It was two out in the last inning and the game was tied one to one. / Maggie was batting and to everybody's surprise Maggie hit a home run." Maggie's sporting success extends to the soccer field. "Maggie was becoming one of the best players on her team. / Every time Maggie scored a goal, her cheering section would scream," the text relays. These events are puzzling in many ways, for they contradict the book's opening assertion that the young girl "did not have much athletic skill." Even more troubling, they present the erroneous message that losing weight increases one's athletic ability: that by becoming slimmer, a person also becomes better at skills like hand–eye coordination.

Newfound athletic success is not the only accolade that Maggie acquires from losing weight. Embodying another misguided and even dangerous message, it also brings an immediate end to peer harassment. In a comment that suggests that the way to end bullying is by "fixing" the victim, Kramer writes about his newly thin protagonist: "Maggie was now being teased less and less." Furthermore, the young girl's weight loss results in newfound social popularity. "Some of Maggie's classmates invited Maggie to sit with them during lunch break," Kramer writes. The success of this in-school social encounter leads to an invitation for an out-of-school one: "The following week Maggie was invited to her first sleepover get together. / She was going to Tina's house with Mary, Susan and Heather."[4] Even more important to the teenage girl, she begins receiving her first-ever romantic interest from the opposite sex: "Maggie was getting more and more attention from the guys." The illustration that accompanies these lines depicts the now-slim title character talking with one of her gal pals. The duo is just about to pass a group of three young men. All of the boys are smiling and looking excitedly at Maggie. Thus, when the narrator says at one point in the text, "She was so much happier now and was having a blast," it is clear that the benefits of her new life are far from merely health-related. If anything, the improvements to Maggie's physical health are secondary, or even tertiary, to the impact on her social, athletic, and romantic experiences.

These misguided messages may seem to undercut Maggie's accomplishments or, at least, detract from her status as a powerful, independent figure. To be sure, these passages could be seen as reinforcing the belief that Maggie needs adult supervision to help her understand the pressures that society places on women to look a certain way and to help her lose weight in a safe and healthy manner. But, there is an alternative way of viewing these elements. All of the problematic passages, inaccurate information, and even dangerous lessons in *Maggie Goes on a Diet* arise from the adult author's lack of knowledge, wisdom, and expertise, not that of its juvenile protagonist. Or, perhaps phrased more accurately, whatever mistakes Maggie makes in the book, they are attributable to the adult author, rather than this child character. While this claim could conceivably be made about any children's narrative that has been written by an adult, it has special resonance for *Maggie*. Unlike the bulk of other books for young readers, the mistakes, errors, and missteps that the child protagonist makes were wholly unintentional, unbeknownst to even the adult author until others pointed them out. As an article by Whitney Jefferson that appeared on the popular website Jezebel announced: "*Maggie Goes on a Diet* Author Was 'Amazed' By Backlash." During Kramer's appearance on *Good Morning America*, for example, he discussed his surprise and even bewilderment by the negative reactions and wanted the public to know that the problematic elements that they identify in his book were not deliberate, misogynistic, or mean-spirited. Kramer was not intentionally trying to send young girls unhealthy messages about their appearance, body, or health; on the contrary, his book sought to serve the opposite function. For this reason, any factual errors or negative viewpoints that the book contained were either entirely accidental or the result of simple misunderstandings. Such explanations applied even to the author's use of the word "diet": "Kramer says he believed the uproar was mainly due to people not using the word 'diet' the same way he does: 'Diet is kind of a misconstrued word, it has many many meanings'" (Jefferson, par. 5). In these and other instances, the author insists that aspects of his book that critics are finding objectionable can be attributed either to simple innocent obliviousness or to a mere difference in point of view, not to malice or callousness.

In *The Hidden Adult*, Perry Nodelman discusses a powerful underlying tenet not only of children's literature but of the cultural construction of childhood in the West: "a key question is whether children are capable of keeping themselves from danger. The usual answer is that they are not and that adults must therefore create safe havens for them" (*Hidden* 78). Young people are seen as lacking the knowledge, maturity, and life experience to stay safe and avoid problems. Without adult assistance and supervision, boys and girls would make poor decisions and get into trouble.

Maggie Goes on a Diet calls into question this longstanding and seemingly inviolable belief. If anyone is making poor choices and demonstrating the need for guidance to keep them out of trouble, it is Paul M. Kramer, not Maggie Magee. *Maggie Goes on a Diet* offers a rebuke to the maxim that adults are wiser, more informed, and more experienced. The picture book embodies a powerful cautionary tale to longstanding assertions that children require the presence of adults to keep them happy, healthy, and safe. As Kramer's narrative demonstrates, adults can be ignorant, naïve, and imprudent. As a result, their involvement can harm youngsters, not help them. *Maggie Goes on a Diet* serves as a testament not to the problems that arise when children lack supervision, but when adults do.

That said, the failure of Kramer's picture book paradoxically precipitates a different kind of success. The author's ignorance about pediatric nutrition and his misguided decision to write a book on the subject undercuts adult authority and destabilizes the existing power structure between children and adults. In so doing, it transforms *Maggie Goes on a Diet* from a book to unequivocally condemn to one to reservedly commend. As Perry Nodelman has commented about adult interactions with young people, "By and large, we encourage in children those values and behaviors that make children easier for us to handle: more passive, more docile, more obedient—and thus, more in need of our guidance and more willing to accept the need for it" ("Other" 30). Nodelman goes on to assert that this tendency also applies to the narratives that adults write for and about children: "we write books for children to provide them with values and images of themselves we approve of and feel comfortable with" ("Other" 30).

Maggie Goes on a Diet in spite of all of its problems and flaws, does not participate in this pattern. Kramer's picture book, rather than presenting a young person who is "appropriately" dependent, "adorably" inept, and therefore thoroughly nonthreatening, depicts one who is profoundly self-sufficient, unfailingly motivated, and exceedingly capable. Nodelman has written about young people's responses to the images of childhood that they encounter in literature: "Children do similarly submit to our ideas about what it means to be childish, and do show us the childish behavior we make it clear to them we wish to see, simply because they rarely have the power to do anything else" ("Other" 32). If this is the case, then *Maggie Goes on a Diet* offers a rare opportunity for young people to see an alternative model of how to "be children" and how they might experience or even "perform" their own childhood. Rather than presenting yet another model of how to be "less threatening to [adults]" (Nodelman, "Other" 32), Kramer's book offers an infrequent occasion for them to see how to be more true to themselves.

Roberta Seelinger Trites, in *Disturbing the Universe: Power and Repression in Adolescent Literature*, accounts for the disappointing ending to countless young adult novels: "adults hold the knowledge that represents the highest goal: truth. No adolescent is given the opportunity to be as wise" (79). While she was discussing the arena of young adult literature, this observation could apply to many other types of books for young readers. Frequently, not just inside of fictional stories but outside of them as well, young people remain locked in a dependent status because they are seen as lacking important knowledge. On those rare occasions when they do possess some necessary information, they are regarded as lacking the wisdom to put this knowledge to proper use.

Maria Nikolajeva, in *Power, Voice and Subjectivity in Literature for Young Readers*, affirms this viewpoint with regard to picture books. The opening sentence to her chapter that explores power structures in these narratives states flatly: "Picturebooks have great potential for subversion of adult power and interrogations of the existing order" (Nikolajeva 169). She explains, "The two narrative levels, the verbal and the visual, allow counterpoint and contradiction between the power structures presented by words and images" (Nikolajeva 169). But, none ultimately actualize this opportunity. As Nikolajeva laments midway through her analysis: "All confirm adult power, even though some are slightly subversive" (178). For this reason, she contends that texts for young readers—from board books through young adult novels—merely reinforce existing socio-political hierarchies with regard to age, a phenomenon that she terms "aetonormativity," with the prefix "aeto-" from Latin meaning "age" (Nikolajeva 8). "Children's literature has *the potential* to question the adults as a norm," Nikolajeva stresses (11; emphasis in original). But, the reality is that these narratives do not follow through on this promise. Even the most "genuinely subversive book is compelled to acknowledge adult authority" (Nikolajeva 183).

Maggie Goes on a Diet offers a rare defiance of this trend. Not only does the title character consistently demonstrate her autonomy and routinely exert her agency, but she is not robbed of these empowering qualities in the end of the narrative. The closing pages of Kramer's text showcase the changes that Maggie has made to her life, celebrate these accomplishments, and depict her passing along these insights to another young girl. Moreover, the problems that the book possesses spotlight the limits of adult knowledge and even competency. Thus, rather than affirming the authority of adults, *Maggie Goes on a Diet* makes a case for the aptitude of children.

Much has been written about the problematic representation of "the child" in children's literature. Beginning with Jacqueline Rose's ground-breaking discussion of this issue in *The Case of Peter Pan: Or, The Impossibility of Children's Literature* (1984), a myriad of books, essays, and articles have commented about how narratives for young readers do not present young people as they actually are, but as adults imagine, remember, or even wish them to be.[5] *Maggie Goes on a Diet* calls attention to the other side of this equation, demonstrating the equally problematic way in which adults have conceived and constructed themselves, not only inside the world of written narratives but outside of them as well.

Notes

1. *Maggie Goes on a Diet* is not paginated.
2. New Jersey became the first locale to do so in 2006, and, at the time of this writing, fifteen additional states have followed suit (Codey, par. 5).
3. Of course, this situation embodies the opposite end of the spectrum from the parental detachment and even aloofness that I discussed (and chastised) in the previous chapter on *Little Zizi*. When viewed in tandem, they demonstrate that either extreme form of parental behavior—either overinvolvement or lack of involvement—are harmful to young people.
4. This double-page spread featuring the slumber party goes on to include some even more troubling lines: "Susan yelled out, 'I am going to use the bathroom first.' / Twenty minutes later Maggie said, 'Hurry up or I am going to burst.' / Maggie was worried that she might leave a smell. / Maggie said to herself, 'There is nothing I can do about it, so oh well.' / But taking no chances, Maggie brought deodorant spray so no one could tell." Given the title character's high rate of weight loss, coupled with the fact that young people often read texts in unintended and even unauthorized ways, this passage raises the question of whether Maggie may suffer from an eating disorder in general and bulimia in particular. Indeed, the earlier scene showing Maggie's episode of binge eating while standing in front of the refrigerator may now be replaced with purging episodes—by inducing vomiting and/or taking laxatives—in order to lose such a dramatic amount of weight.
5. See, for example, Henry Jenkins's "Introduction: Childhood Innocence and Other Modern Myths" in *The Children's Culture Reader* (1998), James Kincaid's *Child-Loving: The Erotic Child and Victorian Culture* (1992), and Perry Nodelman's *The Hidden Adult: Defining Children's Literature* (2008).

5   Boys Gone Wild

Me Tarzan, You Jane; the Crusade to "Cure" Prehomosexual Children; and the New Face of the Ex-Gay Movement in the United States

In 2011, Janice Barrett Graham released her picture book *Me Tarzan, You Jane*. Illustrated by Lili Ribeira and Andrew S. Graham and released by the small Christian publisher Tidal Wave Books,[1] the text uses the central characters from Edgar Rice Burroughs's well-known narrative about the King of the Jungle to offer a Bible-based critique of nonheteronormative gender and sexuality identities. As the summary on the back cover promises, "Parents, leaders, teachers, here is a fun, gently-worded, nondenominational book for young children filled with God's timeless truths about male and female, romantic feelings, and marriage." Far from false advertising, the narrative contains passages such as the following: "Two men cannot mate with each other, nor can two women. Human mating involves both a male and a female."[2]

Me Tarzan, You Jane was certainly not the first picture book for young readers to offer a negative view of LGBTQ (lesbian, gay, bisexual, transgender, and queer) individuals and identity. On the contrary, by 2011, there was already a sizable and steadily growing body of such texts, including Richard A. Cohen's *Alfie's Home* (1993), Deborah Prihoda's *Mommy, Why Are They Holding Hands?* (1996), Sheila K. Butt's *Does God Love Michael's Two Daddies?* (2006), Christian YoungMiller's *Everybody Has Those Thoughts: So It Doesn't Mean You're Gay* (2010), and Amber Dee Parker's *God Made Mom and Dad* (2013). While *Me Tarzan, You Jane* can certainly be placed in dialogue with these titles, it also differs from them in significant ways. Whereas previous narratives that offered a negative viewpoint on LGBTQ individuals and identity addressed the presence of homosexuality in adults, teenagers, or adolescents, Graham's book is designed to address the possible existence of such behavior in prepubescent youth. More specifically, the book is directed at what has come to be known, within both the conservative Christian and secular scientific communities, as "prehomosexual" children: young people who have not yet reached the age of sexual maturity but who exhibit various behaviors, mannerisms, and social traits that are seen as indices of future LGBTQ identity. In boys, these qualities often take the form of a so-called sissy identity, which is typified by a penchant for playing with dolls, a fondness for the color pink, and a tendency to prefer female playmates (R. Green 274–319). By contrast, in girls, traits that are

coded as prehomosexual are those usually regarded as tomboyish: "a proclivity for outdoor play (especially athletics), a feisty independent spirit, and
a tendency to don masculine clothing and adopt a boyish nickname" (Abate,
Tomboys xvi).

Of course, the existence of pre-gay children and the identification of proto-
queer behaviors are not simply of interest to social and religious conservatives; they have also been the subject of attention within queer theory and
LGBTQ studies. Eve Kosofsky Sedgwick in her now-classic essay "How to
Bring Your Kids Up Gay" (1991) and, most recently, Kathryn Bond Stockton
in her book *The Queer Child, or Growing Sideways in the Twentieth Century*
(2009), have both discussed this issue. Stockton, for example, traces a teleology of what she calls the "ghostly" gay youngster, while she also articulates
the queerness inherent in all children. Because childhood is routinely framed
as a liminal state of alterity, she argues, it possesses its own set of queer qualities. For this reason, Stockton provocatively asserts on the opening page of
her discussion: "If you scratch a child, you will find a queer" (1).

Me Tarzan, You Jane shares this interest in the intersection of childhood
and queerness, but for different ideological reasons that have far different
socio-political ends. Janice Barrett Graham's picture book is not simply
another children's narrative that offers an anti-homosexual viewpoint; it
embodies a new type of such text. *Me Tarzan, You Jane* marks a significant shift in the strategies being used by faith-based entities to combat
the increasing cultural acceptance of the LGBTQ community in general
and the recent setbacks experienced by the ex-gay movement in particular. While the claim by ex-gay organizations that homosexuality can be
overcome through a combination of treatment, prayer, and counseling has
been socially controversial and scientifically contested from its origins, it
has faced increasing opposition in the opening decades of the twenty-first
century. From the admission by various prominent leaders that their same-
sex desires remain intact to the recantation of a key piece of research that
has long been used as proof for the efficacy of this approach, the ex-gay
movement has lost much of its credibility.

In the pages that follow, I make the case that such damaging revelations
have not caused anti-LGBTQ efforts in the United States to diminish; they
have merely prompted them to be reconfigured. As it has become increasingly untenable to claim that same-sex desires in adults can be eradicated,
individuals who remain committed to combating homosexuality have turned
their attention to a new and ostensibly more efficacious cause: preventing its
emergence in the first place through early intervention with young children
who exhibit gender nonconformity.

Me Tarzan, You Jane exists at the forefront of this shift in focus. The picture book offers a vivid example of how the ex-gay movement is reinventing
itself as what might be called the pre-gay movement—or, perhaps more
accurately, the *ex-pre-gay* movement. While adolescents and teenagers have
long been the target of anti-LGBTQ efforts via gender affirmation camps

and sexual "reparative" therapies, Graham's text signals the expansion of interventionist strategies even further into the realm of childhood. *Me Tarzan, You Jane* targets early elementary-aged youngsters who have not yet entered puberty but are perceived as prehomosexual. The book attempts to "cure" their proto-queer tendencies before they lead to an engagement in same-sex erotic activity and especially before they prompt the adoption of an LGBTQ identity. In so doing, Graham's narrative addresses arguably the most customized subject and engages with the most pinpoint audience of all the texts profiled in this project. *Me Tarzan, You Jane* belongs to what might be characterized as a "niche within a niche": it offers an even more specialized perspective within the already specialized subset of anti-LGBTQ narratives. Akin to all of the other niche market picture books highlighted in this study, *Me Tarzan, You Jane* is widely available via major online booksellers like Amazon and Barnes & Noble.

The confidence with which Graham's book claims that behaviors that are predictive of homosexuality can be both easily identified and quickly eliminated reenergizes the longstanding efforts by the ex-gay movement to medicalize homosexuality, while they also serve to pathologize nonconformist children and unconventional childhoods. Finally, given the text's use of characters, scenes, and settings from Edgar Rice Burroughs's politically problematic novel about a white man raised in the jungle by apes, coupled with Graham's repeated framing of same-sex attraction as "wild" and "uncivilized" behavior, *Me Tarzan, You Jane* reveals how anti-gay rhetoric is heavily imbricated with other discourses of intolerance, namely, racism, white Western imperialism, and xenophobia. As a consequence, Graham's narrative pushes niche market picture books to an even more culturally customized—as well as politically controversial—place.

On Not Getting Over the Rainbow: The Rise—and Fall—of the Ex-Gay Movement in the United States

Jean Hardisty has dubbed the ex-gay movement "the right's kinder and gentler anti-gay campaign" (116). This phenomenon was the product of various social, political, and medico-scientific events. These include the following: the 1973 decision by the American Psychiatric Association to remove homosexuality from its list of mental disorders; the increasing social presence and political power of the LGBTQ community; the ascendency of the self-help and twelve-step movements; and the steady rise along with growing cooperation of evangelical Christianity and political conservatism in the United States. Ex-gay efforts are predicated on the belief that homosexuality is the product of environmental, developmental, and/or psychological factors, not biology. Thus, proponents assert, same-sex attraction can be diminished and even eliminated in individuals who wish to change. As the website for one program asserts: "shifts in sexual desires [have] been documented over many decades" ("Change"). Meanwhile, the leader of another prominent ex-gay organization has repeatedly claimed that he knows "tens of thousands of people who have successfully changed their sexual orientation" (qtd. in Arana, par. 23).

Although the ex-gay movement is a multifaceted phenomenon that encompasses a diverse array of private therapists, religiously affiliated ministries, and secular treatment programs, the bulk of ex-gay organizations in the United States are associated with evangelical Christianity and, especially, with the Christian Right. As Tanya Erzen has pointed out, the process of becoming "born again" as a heterosexual for those in ex-gay treatment is strongly likened to being "born again" as an evangelical Christian. She writes: "Change is a conversion process that incorporates religious and sexual identity, desire, and behavior. Sexual identity is malleable and changeable because it is completely entwined with religious conversion. A person becomes ex-gay as he accepts Jesus into his life and commits to him" (Erzen 13). Furthermore, the overlap between faith and sexuality provides another crucial source of comfort for evangelical Christians who are troubled by their same-sex desires. As Erzen has remarked on this issue, "even if science were to prove that homosexuality was biological, Jesus can effect miracles, and it is ultimately with Jesus that ex-gays place their faith in change" (15).

Of all the numerous secular and faith-based organizations affiliated with the ex-gay movement, one has risen to prominence: Exodus. Founded in 1976 by Gary Cooper, Michael Bussee, Frank Worthen, Ron Dennis, and Greg Reid, the organization is, as its website explains, "the leading global outreach to churches, individuals and families offering a biblical message about same-sex attraction" ("About Us," par. 1). The mission of the group is simple: "Exodus is committed to encouraging, educating and equipping the Body of Christ to address the issue of homosexuality, gay and lesbian people and families with grace and truth" ("About Us," par. 3). To this end, the organization represents "a coalition of pastoral care ministries, churches and counselors" that collectively "provide everything from large scale national and international events to individual care for men, women and families" ("About Us," par. 4).

Exodus has enjoyed tremendous success. As Michelle Wolkomir has articulated, it has become both the largest and the most powerful ex-gay network in the United States, attaining widespread public visibility as well as palpable cultural influence (6). By the late 1990s, "Exodus had 83 chapters in 34 states" (Arana, par. 23). In addition, it had "established partnerships with prominent religious organizations like the National Association of Evangelicals" and Focus on the Family (Erzen 44). Moreover, in summer 1998, Exodus joined forces with more than a dozen other "religious-right organizations, including the Christian Coalition, the Family Research Council, and the American Family Association" in a $600,000 advertisement campaign that ran in an array of prominent national newspapers, including *The New York Times*, *USA Today*, *The Los Angeles Times*, and *The Washington Post*. "One version feature[d] Anne Paulk, her gleaming diamond ring clearly visible," Erzen reports, and "[u]nderneath her picture the caption read, 'wife, mother, former lesbian'" (183). Meanwhile, another full-page advertisement featured her husband, John Paulk: "A former drag queen named Candi, John met Anne at [the ex-gay organization] New Hope in the early 1990s while both were completing the residential program" (Erzen 183). John and Anne Paulk were thrust further into the national spotlight a few months later when *Newsweek* ran a cover story on the ex-gay movement. As the title of the feature—"Gay for Life?"—suggested, the article was "sympathetic ... [about] change therapy" (Arana, par. 19). Indeed, as Arana has noted, in the weeks and months following the *Newsweek* story, an array of "national and regional papers published ex-gays' accounts" (par. 19). Such mainstream publicity had a tremendous impact. In the words of Gabriel Arana: "There are no reliable statistics for how many patients have received ex-gay treatment or how many therapists practice it, but in the late 1990s and early 2000s, ex-gay therapy enjoyed a legitimacy it hadn't since the APA removed homosexuality from its diagnostic manual" (par. 23).

One of the reasons that ex-gay organizations like Exodus have enjoyed such mainstream success is the fact that they have their own research unit. To support their assertion that homosexuality is a choice and can be effectively treated and even cured, the ex-gay movement founded the National Association for Research and Therapy of Homosexuality (NARTH) in 1992. The organization "provides scientific validation ... and functions as a professional venue for like-minded psychiatrists. NARTH members are licensed psychotherapists, psychiatrists, and medical professionals who, by virtue of their credentials, have some influence with certain psychotherapy and medical institutions" (Erzen 143). In 1996, for example, a group of NARTH researchers "coauthored an op-ed in the *Wall Street Journal* advocating reparative therapy for gay men using a patients' rights argument" (Erzen 144). Meanwhile, Jospeh Nicolosi, one of NARTH's most visible and vocal members, has "appeared often on programs like *Oprah*, *20/20*, and *Larry King Live*" (Arana, par. 23).

While NARTH has long labored to provide scientific legitimacy to ex-gay ideology, the movement received a tremendous boost from an unexpected outside source: psychiatrist Robert Spitzer. Spitzer, "who has been justly called one of the most influential psychiatrists of the twentieth century" (Angell, par. 8), did so via the results of his highly controversial study: "Can Some Gay Men and Lesbians Change Their Sexual Orientation?: 200 Participants Reporting a Change from Homosexual to Heterosexual Orientation." Initially presented at the American Psychiatric Association Conference in 2001 and then later published in the journal *Archives of Sexual Behavior* in 2003, the study "supported the use of so-called reparative therapy to 'cure' homosexuality for people strongly motivated to change" (Carey, par. 5).

This assertion would have been controversial for any psychiatrist to make in the opening years of the twenty-first century, but it was especially astounding given Spitzer's past professional work: he had been a leading member of the committee that had successfully advocated for the removal of homosexuality from the American Psychiatric Association's *Diagnostic and Statistical Manual* in 1973. Consequently, his viewpoint gave tremendous credence to the ex-gay cause. "An Associated Press story," for example, "called [Spitzer's research] 'explosive.' In the words of one of Spitzer's gay colleagues, it was like 'throwing a grenade into the gay community'" (Arana, par. 35).

That said, Spitzer's claims were not without their criticisms. As Gabriel Arana has discussed:

> The study infuriated ... many psychiatrists, who condemned its methodology and design. Participants had been referred to Spitzer by ex-gay groups like NARTH and Exodus, which had an interest in recommending clients who would validate their work. The claims of change were self-reports, and Spitzer had not compared them with a control group that would help him judge their credibility. (par. 36)

In response, the American Psychiatric Association "conducted a review of all the literature on efforts to change sexual orientation. Judith Glassgold, the chair of the task force that produced the report, said the group found no scientific evidence that ex-gay therapy works" (qtd. in Arana, par. 50). Even more alarming, they discovered that ex-gay treatment is not simply ineffectual but harmful to many individuals. As Glassgold explained, ex-gay therapy "provided false hope, which can be devastating. ... It harmed self-esteem and self-regard by focusing on the psychopathology of homosexuality" (qtd. in Arana, par. 50). For these reasons, "[i]t runs the risk of making patients anxious, depressed, and at times suicidal" (Arana, par. 50). As a result of these findings the "APA now tells its members they should not engage in the practice" (Arana, par. 50). More than a dozen other professional organizations have issued similar denunciations of reparative therapy.[3]

Criticism about the ethics and even efficacy of the ex-gay approach has not been limited simply to sources outside of the movement. Over the decades, a number of insiders have also called into question the ability of anyone using any method to "cure" homosexuality. One of the most public and certainly most damaging admissions along these lines occurred in 1979 when one of the founding members of Exodus denounced the ex-gay ideology. "On a plane en route to speak at a church in Virginia, Michael Bussee and Gary Cooper, a volunteer with Exodus, realized that after years of working together, they were in love. They rewrote their speech, arguing that the church should come to an understanding and acceptance of gay people" (Erzen 34). Bussee's oppositional stance to the ex-gay methods only increased over time. In 1991, for example, he asserted: "After dealing with hundreds of gay people, I have never met one who went from gay to straight. Even if you manage to alter someone's sexual behavior, you cannot change his or her true sexual orientation" (qtd. in Erzen 34–35). As he went on to argue even more bluntly: "If you got them away from the Christian limelight and asked them, 'Honestly now, are you saying that you are no longer homosexual and you are now heterosexually orientated?' Not one person said, 'Yes, I am now heterosexual'" (qtd. in Erzen 35). In 2007, Bussee formally "apologized for his role in starting the [Exodus] organization" (Arana, par. 49).

More recently, John Paulk, who once served as the literal poster boy for the ex-gay movement, renounced reparative therapy. This reversal had its origins in "September of 2001, [when] two men who worked for the Human Right Campaign recognized John Paulk in a gay bar in Washington, D.C., called Mr. P's" (Erzen 213). For years, Paulk insisted that the incident was an isolated misstep. But, in April 2013, he recanted, coming out as a gay man, announcing the end of his marriage to fellow ex-gay member Anne Paulk and apologizing for his past involvement in ex-gay ministries. "'Please allow me to be clear: I do not believe that reparative therapy changes sexual orientation; in fact, it does great harm to many people,' Paulk said in a lengthy apology distributed to various gay publications" (Gibson, par. 3).[4]

Of all of these setbacks, however, by far the most surprising and certainly the most damaging came from Robert Spitzer. In early 2012, the noted psychiatrist shocked both the evangelical Christian and scientific communities when he issued a letter retracting his study that homosexuality could be cured through reparative therapy. Furthermore, he went on to admit that "failed attempts to rid oneself of homosexual attractions 'can be quite harmful'" (qtd. in Arana, par. 41). Lest any doubts remained about the psychiatrist's desire to change his position, "[Spitzer] said he spoke with the editor of the *Archives of Sexual Behavior* about writing a retraction, but the editor declined" (Arana, par. 40). The ramifications of Spitzer's shift in position could not be overstated. As Gabriel Arana remarked, the ex-gay movement "just lost its only shred of scientific support" (par. 1).

Far from denouncing or even distancing themselves from Spitzer's recantation, several prominent organizations within the ex-gay movement affirmed it. In summer 2012, "Alan Chambers, 40, the president [of Exodus International], declared that there was no cure for homosexuality and that 'reparative therapy' offered false hope to gays and lesbians and could even be harmful" (Arana, par. 3). Consequently, in June 2013, Chambers announced that the organization was closing its operations. Chambers also issued a press release, "apologizing to the lesbian, gay, bisexual and transgender community for years of undue judgment, by the organization and from the Christian Church as a whole" (Arana, par. 4).

Everything Old Is New Again: *Me Tarzan, You Jane* and the Reconfiguration of Anti-LGBTQ Efforts

The serious setbacks that ex-gay efforts have experienced over the past few years would seem to signal its death knell. However, a different phenomenon has been taking place. Rather than seeing the ex-gay movement crumble, it has merely been reconstituted. As anti-LGBTQ efforts have needed to retreat from claims about eradicating homosexual attraction in adults and adolescents, they have shifted their focus to a new and seemingly more feasible goal: preventing the emergence of same-sex desire in prepubescent young people.[5] That said, an interest in identifying and eliminating "prehomosexual" tendencies in children has been part of ex-gay research and rhetoric for decades. George Rekers's book *Growing Up Straight: What Every Family Should Know About Homosexuality*, for example, was first released in 1982. Meanwhile, Joseph Nicolosi and his wife Linda Ames Nicolosi published their similarly themed volume, *A Parent's Guide to Preventing Homosexuality*, in 2002.[6]

Although the ex-gay movement has long been involved in recognizing early manifestations of same-sex attraction in young people, these concerns have attained new ideological importance and cultural urgency in the wake of the growing awareness about the limitations of treating adults and adolescents. Confronted with mounting internal and external evidence that homosexuality cannot be altered after it has developed, anti-LGBTQ efforts have placed a new emphasis on early intervention in young children.

Me Tarzan, You Jane occupies the forefront of this new, youth-focused phase of the ex-gay movement in the United States. The narrative draws on the same theological underpinnings for justifying opposition to homosexuality as well as on the same behavioral, psychological, and familial reasons that adults develop erotic desires, but it applies these principles to preadolescent children. From the conflation of gender expression with sexual object choice, the insistence on modeling of "appropriately" masculine and feminine behavior by two parents of the opposite sex, and the religious proscription against homosexuality, *Me Tarzan, You Jane* redirects the ex-gay viewpoint, rationale, and therapeutic treatment plan onto a different target audience in a different age group.

The reconfiguration of the ex-gay movement as the pre-gay one ensures much more than merely the survival of anti-LGBTQ efforts in the United States; this new incarnation signals a bold expansion of them in many ways. *Me Tarzan, You Jane* marks the moment when efforts to identify, treat, and eliminate behavior regarded as a future index of homosexuality have moved out of the realm of materials intended for the adult parents, therapists, or counselors of potentially proto-queer children and into the venue of narratives aimed directly at these youngsters themselves.

* * *

Perhaps the most striking and certainly most central area of overlap between the ex-gay movement and the anti-pre-gay message in *Me Tarzan, You Jane* is their shared belief in the naturalness of heterosexuality and, by extension, the unnaturalness of same-sex attraction. As Tanya Erzen has discussed, for faith-based ex-gay organizations—which constitute the bulk of treatment programs in the United States—these axioms are rooted in theology. Meanwhile, for more secular forms of treatment, the "idea that all people are innately heterosexual" is a foundational premise (Erzen 130). This viewpoint, in fact, accounts for the ex-gay movement's decision to call its treatment for same-sex attractions as "reparative therapy"; their methods literally aim to "repair" an individual's innate heterosexuality.

Me Tarzan, You Jane operates under the same principle. As Graham informs her prepubescent readership in one of the opening pages: "As they grow, boys should start becoming interested in girls in a new way. Girls should start becoming interested in boys in a new way." To further emphasize the biological inevitability of such feelings, the book goes on to assert: "Right now that may sound yucky, but just you wait!" Finally, lest any doubts remain about the point or purpose of these emotions, Graham reminds them later in the narrative: "For people who have romantic feelings, there is only one right path, the one God has given us." The "right path" to which Graham alludes, of course, is monogamous heterosexual marriage and procreation: "The romantic feelings we are talking about develop as we grow up and urge us to get married and have children."

Denise I. Matulka, in *A Picture Book Primer: Understanding and Using Picture Books* (2008), discusses the possible interactions that can exist between text and image in picture books. As she explains, many printed words and visual illustrations possess what she calls a "complimentary" relationship, meaning that "the picture and/or text fill in the gaps in the other" (Matulka 117). Matulka elaborates: "In a complimentary picture book, the pictures add to or amplify the text, or vice versa, with the words adding meaning to the pictures" (118). In this way, the words and images do more than simply mirror each other, with the illustrations depicting people, objects, and actions named in the text. Instead, the pictures go further, adding detail, introducing material, and presenting information that is not contained in the text. Maurice Sendak has also commented on this dynamic in many of his narratives: "Words are left out, but the picture says it. Pictures are left out, but the word says it" (*Caldecott* 21). Maria Nikolajeva and Carole Scott argue that this feature makes picture books narratologically rich but also analytically tricky. As they explain about the unique literary phenomenon that occurs with picture books, "The reader turns from verbal to visual and back again, in an ever-expanding concatenation of understanding" (Nikolajeva and Scott 2).

The illustrations that appear throughout *Me Tarzan, You Jane* affirm this observation. The seemingly simple pencil drawings are anything but that: these images do not merely echo the message of the printed text; they augment and amplify it for the book's preadolescent and perhaps even preliterate audience. For example, on the double-page spread that discusses how "boys should start becoming interested in girls in a new way" as they get older, the drawing demystifies the remarks made in printed text. Whereas the meaning of the written passage is vague—failing to name the precise new way in which boys ought to take an interest in girls—the image makes this manner vividly apparent: the drawing shows young Tarzan giving Jane a bouquet of flowers. Lest the romantic intention of this act is not clear, Tarzan is gazing at Jane in a lovestruck way: his eyes have a dreamy look and his mouth is shaped into a sheepish half-smile. Meanwhile, Jane appears even more romantically inviting and enamored. She is wearing a beautiful, Victorian-styled dress. Moreover, she is standing with her arms folded modestly in front of her and her eyes looking coyly askance as Tarzan holds out the bouquet. Jane is also blushing noticeably. Her physical features and overall appearance have a "Disney-fied" quality. With her large oversized eyes, long flowing hair, slim waist, and nineteenth-century style dress, she looks like one of the Disney princesses. In addition to giving Jane a familiar look to child readers, this style enhances the book's emphasis on heterosexual romance. As numerous past and present critics have commented, the core concern of Disney films is the marriage plot. Moreover, the appearance of Jane in Graham's book bears a striking resemblance to the rendering of this same character from the feature-length animated film version of *Tarzan* released by Disney in 1999.

The spatial placement of Tarzan and Jane on the page reinforces the centrality of the message that the illustration conveys. The image is centered on the double-page spread. Echoing the narrative's message about restraint, however, the figures are separated by the book's spine. Even the artistic medium and drawing technique used to render Tarzan and Jane adds to the romantic mood: the illustration uses soft shading and light cross-hatching. In so doing, it transforms the pencil drawing from having an "amateurish" look to one that is intimately connected to the text's overall theme and main message.

Closely related to the ex-gay movement's view about the naturalness of heterosexuality is its equally powerful belief in the link between an individual's outward gender expression and their inner sexual identity. As Erzen explains: "the ex-gay movement is wedded to the idea of a binary system of gender roles in which heterosexuality connotes masculinity for men and femininity for women" (15). Together with positioning masculinity and femininity as mutually exclusive, the ex-gay movement also casts them as biologically determined: with boys naturally liking stereotypically "boyish" activities and girls being inherently drawn to conventionally "girlish" items. Joseph Nicolosi, for example, has made frequent reference to boys' natural proclivity for rough-and-tumble play and the color blue, while girls have an innate interest in dolls and the color pink (Nicolosi and Nicolosi 21–26).

Graham's picture book once again echoes these qualities. The text presents masculinity and femininity both as mutually exclusive forms of identity and as arising from one's biological sex. As she explains to her juvenile readers: "You can call them girls and boys, men and women, ladies and gentlemen, guys and gals, even dudes and dudettes! Tarzan figured it out pretty quickly when he said, 'Me Tarzan, You Jane.'" Echoing the book's pronouncement that there only two sexes is its assertion that gender arises naturally and even inevitably from sex. As Graham writes, "Does your reflection have anything to do with being a boy or a girl? Sure it does, and it should." She goes on to explain: "For example, if you're a boy you're wearing boy clothes. If you're a girl you're wearing girl clothes. Your hair is somewhat boyish or girlish, too. Without even thinking about it, you are being the male or female God made you." This tautology confuses cause and effect, while it also offers an unintended commentary about the performative nature of gender. First, the passage raises the question of whether an individual is a boy because he is wearing boy clothes or whether another child is a girl because she is wearing girl clothes, thereby removing the issue of biological sex entirely from consideration. Along those same lines, the remark also suggests that boys are boys because they wear clothes that are assigned to boys—rather than because they possess certain physiological qualities, genetic attributes, or biological benchmarks. Tanya Erzen has written about areas of unexpected overlap between the ideology of the ex-gay movement and that of queer theory, such as their shared distrust for biological explanations of sexual orientation and their common belief in the fluidity rather than fixity of human erotic activity over the lifespan (15). Graham's remark in *Me Tarzan, You Jane* about how wearing "boy clothes" indicates that you are a boy extends this communal territory to the performativity of gender. However unexpected and certainly unintended, this passage echoes arguments made by Judith Butler about how masculinity and femininity are not innate but rather enacted through behavior, interests, and, of course, clothing. In what has become an oft-cited passage from her book *Gender Trouble*, Butler asserts: "the performance of the gendered body in such daily activities as dress, mannerisms and behavior has no ontological relationship with what may constitute its inner reality" (136).

Such isolated passages aside, *Me Tarzan, You Jane* offers an overwhelmingly essentialist view of gender. The book makes a repeated case that an individual's biological sex dictates not simply their appearance and behavior but even their thoughts. Indeed, as Graham authoritatively informs her prepubescent child audience a few pages later: "Being a boy or a girl is more than how we look. It's how we think and act too." As before, the drawing that appears on the facing page offers a vivid demonstration of this remark in practice. The image presents Tarzan standing proudly with his hands on his hips, a self-assured smile beaming across his face. In addition, his hair is slicked back in a decidedly more grown-up fashion and he is wearing a necktie. From his body posture and facial expression to his new attire and Gordon Gecko-like hairstyle, he exudes masculine confidence.

According to ex-gay ideology, the gender expression of individuals not only arises directly from their biological sex, but so, too, does their sexual orientation. Embodying appropriate and natural forms of masculinity and femininity will lead to the embodiment of the appropriate and natural forms of sexuality, namely, monogamous, married, and procreative heterosexuality. As Joseph Nicolosi has frequently written, individuals develop erotic attractions to members of their same sex because they never learned how to be properly masculine or feminine, and thus are seeking to compensate for this gender deficit via a homosexual relationship (qtd. in "The Compassionate Answer," par. 3). Of course, neither Nicolosi nor the ex-gay movement was the first to make this claim that homosexuality arises from cross-gender identification. Such assertions can be traced back to the earliest medico-scientific discussions about homosexuality in the late nineteenth century by sexologists such as Havelock Ellis as a form of "inversion."[7] In addition, they extend in many ways to the homophobic anxieties that fueled the initial construction and ongoing clinical use of the American Psychiatric Association's "Gender Identity Disorder of Childhood" during the late 1970s and early 1980s.[8]

The ex-gay movement asserts that the cross-gender identity that results in homosexuality occurs when children are still very young, in the years before puberty. In the words of Nicolosi: "We're talking about 2 1/2 years old. This is what they call the gender-identity phase. It's the time when children begin to realize that the world is divided between males and females and that he or she is pressured into identifying with one or the other. If the father is cold, distant, aloof, detached or critical, that doesn't happen properly" (qtd. in "The Compassionate Answer," par. 4). To compensate for this lack of male approval from his father, the boy develops crushes on his same-sex classmates. For this reason, homosexuality is characterized by the ex-gay movement "as an acting-out of intrapsychic sexual forces in a symbolic attempt to resolve an identity conflict" (Nicolosi, "Homosexual Behavior," par. 4).

Once again, this phenomenon is reflected in *Me Tarzan, You Jane*. The narrative repeatedly casts heteronormative gender roles as the foundation for heterosexuality. As Graham explains, "Being a boy or a girl means more and more as we grow up. The difference between male and female are necessary to human life. Respect for this timeless truth helps people live in an orderly way." For this reason, the book goes on to inform its prepubescent readers "as you grow up you should start learning how to be the boy or girl you are." Not surprisingly, the modeling of appropriately masculine and feminine gender roles by two parents of the opposite sex plays a key part in this process. As *Me Tarzan, You Jane* explains: "You can learn a lot from your parents about the important ways to be boyish or girlish. Parents teach a lot of things without saying a word. This is one reason children have both a father and a mother, male and female."

Echoing one of the main viewpoints of the ex-gay movement once again, a key facet of boyishness in boys is developing romantic feelings for girls. In the language of *Me Tarzan, You Jane*: "Boys and girls have chances to get acquainted with one another at school, church, dances, parties, and lots of other activities. Later they go on dates." Of course, the end result of these encounters is heterosexual marriage and procreation: "There is one main purpose for romantic feelings. The purpose is mating. Mating is what can make a baby. Only a man and a woman can mate." As Graham's narrative goes on to explain, however, "mating" should only occur within a very specific relational context: "We should wait for the right person and the right time to mate. This union is called marriage. ... God gave us marriage." In the following paragraph, *Me Tarzan, You Jane* ties all of the previous discussion threads together. As it explains very clearly to its readers, "In marriage it is understood that there will be mating. Many husbands and wives become fathers and mothers. This makes a family where children can be loved and cared for." Once again, the illustration that accompanies this passage greatly enhances its message, adding a powerful personal, sentimental, and even emotional element to these matter-of-fact statements. The drawing, which appears on the facing page of these long paragraphs of text, shows a large sign tacked to a wall that says in needlepoint stitching "TREE SWEET TREE." Offering a Tarzan-friendly variation on the maxim "Home Sweet Home," the drawing's content as well as its visual style reinforces the centrality being placed on God-sanctioned marriage, heterosexual parenthood, and nuclear family in the book's written text.

By teaching young people heteronormative gender roles—and by eliminating any deviations from these identities while they are still young—the ex-gay movement asserts that later homosexual behavior can be avoided. Joseph Nicolosi, in the introduction to his co-authored book, *A Parent's Guide to Preventing Homosexuality*, laments the fact that numerous parents of homosexual young people "missed the early warning signs and waited too long to seek help for their children" (Nicolosi and Nicolosi 12). As a result, he was motivated to write this book with his wife for one simple reason: "to prevent a long and difficult therapy to change homosexuality in adulthood by encouraging early intervention in childhood" (Nicolosi and Nicolosi 25).

Me Tarzan, You Jane arises from a similar impulse and offers an analogous promise. In a passage that encourages young people to police their own actions and even thoughts, the narrative explains: "Bad ideas come from people who are against God's rule. They spread clever but false and hurtful things. You might hear some of these wrong ideas. They might even sound good at first, but God will let you know in your heart they are not good at all." While this state of constant self-evaluation and self-monitoring may seem irksome, the picture book reminds its young readership: "We didn't make these rules up. They were given to us by God. They can keep every boy and girl, every family, and every society safer and happier." As before, the illustration that appears above these remarks adds equal parts urgency and emotion to these matter-of-fact statements. The drawing, which occupies the top half of the double-page spread, shows Tarzan clinging precariously to a tree limb: his legs are crossed tightly around the bough and his arms are wrapped snugly around a branch. The intensity with which Tarzan is gripping the tree, combined with the fact that the drawing includes no background images or even ground line, suggests that the young boy is in a situation that is not simply hazardous but even life threatening: he is clearly high up in the tree and also obviously all alone. Moreover, Tarzan has a fearful look on his face. He is gazing down at the ground, suggesting that he is not only afraid of falling out of the tree but that some fierce animal or threatening enemy might also be on the ground waiting for him. Either way, the illustration injects a sense of fear, anxiety, and even danger that Graham's printed text lacks. Indeed, whereas the tone of the book's written narrative is generally flat and even staid, the illustrations take the opposite tact. The drawings routinely appeal to and even exploit the reader's emotions. In *Children's Picturebooks: The Art of Visual Storytelling* (2012), Martin Salisbury and Morag Styles assert that the words and images within this genre often do not have a symbiotic relationship but a synergistic one (7). The printed text and the visual illustrations in picture books accomplish much more together than either entity could achieve on their own (Salisbury and Styles 7). This observation certainly holds true for *Me Tarzan, You Jane*. The narrative combines the matter-of-fact tone of its written text with illustrations that are more emotionally charged to attract the attention of and ultimately persuade its audience.

The More Things Change, the More They Stay the Same: The All-Too-Familiar Pitfalls of the Ex-Gay Approach

Even though *Me Tarzan, You Jane* aims to correct or, at least, avoid the problems associated with previous attempts to eradicate homosexuality in adults, it is far from flawless. Because the narrative is based on the same ideological premise and uses much of the same treatment methods as the ex-gay movement, it contains many of the same problems while simultaneously introducing several new ones that arise from its focus on young people.

By far the most obvious and certainly the most serious problem associated with both the ex-gay movement and its pre-gay incarnation in *Me Tarzan, You Jane* is the presentation of sex and gender as not only biologically linked but historically, culturally, and regionally stable. As Jo B. Paoletti and Jeanne Maglaty have both discussed, behaviors, fashions, and colors that are coded as "girlish" or regarded as "boyish" have changed tremendously over time in the United States. As Maglaty rightly notes, "Every generation brings a new definition of masculinity and femininity." Such understandings are often powerfully evidenced in young people: how parents dress their sons and daughters, what toys they select for them, and what traits, attitudes, and behaviors they either encourage or discourage. To illustrate how greatly notions of masculine and feminine have changed in American culture during just the past two centuries, Maglaty describes a childhood photograph of the future 32nd president of the United States: "Little Delano Roosevelt sits primly on a stool, his white skirt spread out smoothly over his lap, his hands clasping a hat trimmed with a marabou feather. Shoulder-length hair and patent leather party shoes complete the outfit" (par. 1). While such attire would be regarded as atypical and even iconoclastic for boys today, it was traditional for its period: "social convention of 1884, when FDR was photographed at age 2½ dictated that boys wore dresses until age 6 or 7, also the time of their first haircut. Franklin's outfit was considered gender-neutral" (Maglaty, pars. 1–2).

Such startlingly different understandings of masculine and feminine can be found in American popular, print, and material culture throughout the twentieth century. "For example, a June 1918 article from the trade publication *Earnshaw's Infants' Department* said, 'The generally accepted rule is pink for the boys, and blue for the girls. The reason is that pink, being a more decided and stronger color, is more suitable for the boy, while blue, which is more delicate and dainty, is prettier for the girl'" (qtd. in Maglaty, par. 7). The company was not alone in this sentiment. Maglaty reports: "In 1927, *Time* magazine printed a chart showing sex-appropriate colors for girls and boys according to leading U.S. stores. In Boston, Filene's told parents to dress boys in pink. So did Best & Co. in New York City, Halle's in Cleveland and Marshall Field in Chicago" (par. 8). Jo B. Paoletti, in her book *Pink and Blue: Telling the Girls from the Boys in America* (2011), echoes these findings. As she has remarked, the current association of blue with boys and pink for girls did not emerge until the period following World War II, and "[i]t could have gone the other way" (qtd. in Maglaty, par. 9).

Me Tarzan, You Jane either ignores or is unaware of this reality. The narrative does not present "boyishness" and "girlishness" as culturally constructed and historically contingent phenomena. Instead, in passages such as "if you're a boy you're wearing boy clothes. If you're a girl you're wearing girl clothes ... Without even thinking much about it, you are being the male or female God made you," the book casts gender roles as fixed and timeless. Indeed, while Jane is always depicted in the illustrations wearing her Victorian-style dress and Tarzan is always shown adorned in his animal-skin loincloth, readers know that these highly specialized and highly gendered garments are not the only ones available to boys and girls. On the contrary, girls today routinely wear clothes—such as pants, shorts, and sneakers— that were once seen as the purview of boys, while boys have garments in pastel colors or slim-fitting tailoring that just a generation or two ago would have been deemed "too feminine" for their gender.

Closely related to the problematic presentation of gender within the ex-gay movement is its equally problematic treatment of sex and sexuality. As Tanya Erzen has discussed, one of the serious ideological shortfalls of the ex-gay movement is that it "is wedded to the idea of a binary system of gender roles in which heterosexuality connotes masculinity for men and femininity for women" (15). In reality, however, gender expression does not have a causal connection to sexual object choice and vice versa. Nontraditional gender identities may be associated with nonheteronormative sexualities, but the former is not the reason for the latter.

Me Tarzan, You Jane participates in this phenomenon, while it also builds on it. Together with conflating sex with gender, Graham's book also neglects identities that do not conform to the binary of male and female, namely, intersex. On the opening page of *Me Tarzan, You Jane*, the narrative declares: "There is no other kind of normal human being. Just those two, male and female." While the birth of infants who do not comfortably fit into the category of male or female based either on the appearance of their external sex organs or their genetic composition is not routine, it is also not statistically negligible. An article that appeared in the *American Journal of Human Biology*—and which is commonly regarded as the authority—estimated that individuals who possess anatomical and/or genetic "deviation from the ideal male and female" may be "as high as 2%" (Blackless et al. 151). Given that the current population of the United States is over 310 million, then this figure places the number of individuals who could be placed on the spectrum of intersex, at least at the time of their birth, at 6,200,000. Graham's narrative discounts the presence of these individuals; even worse, with the comment, "There is no other kind of normal human being," the narrative pathologizes them.

Finally, and most ironically, both the ex-gay movement and its pre-gay offshoot propose some decidedly (albeit unintentionally) homoerotic methods for curing same-sex attraction. For example, Joseph Nicolosi and Linda Ames Nicolosi, in their book *A Parent's Guide to Preventing Homosexuality*, stress the importance of working not simply with the gender-confused boy but also with his mother and father. Some of the recommended activities by which men can help to affirm masculinity in their sons have strong homoerotic overtones: "He can teach the toddler how to pound a wooden peg into a hole in a pegboard, or he can take his son with him into the shower, where the boy cannot help but notice that Dad has a male body, just like he has" (Nicolosi and Nicolosi 24). This final activity is far from a mere passing suggestion; Nicolosi and Nicolosi showcase it as a potentially invaluable activity in a subsequent section titled "Showering With Dad" (187). As they assert: "The experience of taking showers together has the potential to strengthen a boy's identification with his father and his father's masculinity, as well as with his own male anatomy" (Nicolosi and Nicolosi 187). In language that is undoubtedly uncomfortable for many readers, the duo goes on to explain: "The father should also be told that it is normal if his son stares at the father's sexual anatomy or if the boy spontaneously reaches up to touch him" (Nicolosi and Nicolosi 187).

While *Me Tarzan, You Jane* does not endorse any of these homoerotic means to combat homosexuality, it does ironically spotlight a literary character who has a long history as a homoerotic figure: Tarzan of the Apes. With his skimpy loincloth, rippling muscles, and tanned body, Edgar Rice

Burroughs's protagonist has long been an icon of the gay male community. Indeed, Alex Vernon has discussed how, since Tarzan's appearance in
the opening decades of the twentieth century, he has often been the subject of gay male adoration, camp routines, pinups, and even pornography
(107–138).

The illustrations to Graham's picture book can be placed on a continuum
with the longstanding eroticization of Tarzan and his physique. Throughout
the text, the eponymous male character is wearing only a small triangle of
fabric tied around his waist. The loincloth covers just his groin area; his
chest, arms, and legs are fully exposed. For a book targeting young boys
who are purportedly susceptible to same-sex attraction, the text ironically
invites and even requires them to gaze at a tanned, trim, and attractive male
body quite often.[9] Adding to the sexually suggestive overtones of Graham's
picture book, on the page where Tarzan offers Jane a bouquet, the flowers
in his hand are all inexplicably drooping. Indeed, a petal is even falling
from one of the blooms. It is difficult not to view this image of the wilting
bouquet through a Freudian lens, with Tarzan attempting to demonstrate
his sexual interest in a girl but being unable to muster or, at least, sustain
any semblance of potency. Even more ironic, this same image is repeated on
the closing page of *Me Tarzan, You Jane*. Moreover, with its placement in
the lower right corner of the page far below the few lines of dialogue, it is
presumably the last textual element that readers see. Both the fact that this
illustration is the only one other than the cover image that is repeated over
the course of the text and that it is used as the finale to the narrative suggests
that it encapsulates the book's overall message. Indeed, as the closing detail
to *Me Tarzan, You Jane*, the picture of Tarzan offering Jane the bouquet
is meant to stay with readers as a visual summary of the lesson learned.
However, far from reinforcing the picture book's message about heteronormativity, it can be read—especially by readers who are already questioning
their interest in the opposite sex—as undercutting it. The wilting or, to be
both more frank and more Freudian about their appearance, flaccid flowers
demonstrate that, just like them, Tarzan may attempt to display his interest in a girl, but he cannot feign it.[10] In so doing, the visual image actually
offers the exact opposite message as Graham's written text: it makes a case
for the immutability of sexual orientation and that same-sex desire cannot
be changed.

As Nathalie op de Beeck reminds us, no matter how seemingly clear the
political position or didactic message contained in a text for young readers
may seem, "there is no guarantee that a picture book successfully indoctri-
nates its junior readers in a given ideology" (xiv). Indeed, many children's
authors exhibit a confidence about the type of boy or girl who would be
interested in and even need their text, how he or she will interpret the story,
and what this youngster will learn from it. But, as Bruno Bettelheim and
Karen Zelan famously pointed out, children often read a text in the way

that the author—as well as a parent, teacher, librarian, and even literary critic—did not intend or likely anticipate:

> In responding to the text, the reader digests some of its meaning in an individual and sometimes idiosyncratic manner. Piaget's concept of assimilation describes well the tendency to make the text's content meaningful according to what the individual thinks he [sic] knows or what he feels. While often the content and what the reader makes of it seem far apart, upon scrutiny a connection can always be found. A misreading thus represents the person's response to the text and his attempt to communicate this response to himself [sic], to the author, or to anybody who is listening. (Bettelheim and Zelan 101)

In *The Uses of Enchantment*, Bettelheim offers a variety of examples of this phenomenon. He discusses a youngster, for example, who delights when the princess in "Rapunzel" is locked in the tower and laments when the prince rescues her at the end because he sees the dungeon as a cozy and secure "safe room" (Bettelheim 17). Such readings prompt Bettelheim to caution that "it will not do to approach the telling of fairy tales with didactic intentions" (153), because adults cannot be certain about the message that young people will glean from the story. Nathalie op de Beeck echoes this assertion, pointing out that "the site of reading is not a one-way street, transmitting adult wisdom to impressionable minds" (xi). This observation is especially true for picture books, given the complex interaction that occurs between text and image. As Perry Nodelman has said about the genre, "any given picture book contains at least three stories: the one told by the words, the one implied by the pictures, and the one that results from the combination of the first two" ("The Eye" 2). These narratives call further attention to the ways in which children's literature is always "transactional" in that "it always represents a meeting point of what texts invite from readers and what readers do in response to the invitation" (Nodelman and Reimer 24).

Me Tarzan, You Jane exemplifies this phenomenon. Echoing the critical observations made about this genre, the picture book's message is far from unified or univocal. On the contrary, the interaction between words and images in Graham's narrative—as well as between the book and its audience—leads to narrative complexity and even contradiction. For all of the emphasis on combatting homosexuality in *Me Tarzan, You Jane*, it contains a variety of elements that can paradoxically be seen as homoerotic. In this way, rather than eradiating same-sex attraction, it can be seen as sustaining it. In the words of Nodelman once again about the unique interpretive possibilities but also creative challenges of picture books: "Words can make pictures into rich narrative resources—but only because they communicate so differently from pictures that they change the meaning of pictures. For the same reason, also, pictures can change the narrative thrust of words" (*Words* 196). Maria Nikolajeva and Carole Scott elaborate about this tendency: "pictures can provide an ironic counterpoint to words, showing us something different from what the words say" (119). They go on to explain that, at worst, such disjunctions between text and image indicate that the narrator is a "deliberate liar," while, at best, they suggest that the narrative voice is uninformed, unaware, and even "naïve" (Nikolajeva and Scott 119). This observation often applies to *Me Tarzan, You Jane*, not only in relation to its written text but especially with regard to its illustrations.

Building an Empire of Intolerance: The Globalization of Anti-LGBTQ Efforts and the Exportation of Homophobia

Although homosexuality is most often cast as biblically sinful, biologically aberrant, and psychologically dysfunctional in *Me Tarzan, You Jane*, it is also framed in a different way: as "wild" and even animalistic behavior. Near the middle of the book, for example, Graham has the following to say about same-sex desires: "The feelings developing in young people that prepare them to be husband or wife, father or mother, can be hurt and get confused. They can get going in a wrong direction, like an elephant gone wild." To further underscore both the animalistic and the uncontrolled nature of such emotions, the illustration that accompanies these remarks presents an angry elephant stomping through the jungle, destroying everything in its path. On the following page, such sentiments recur, and homosexuality is once again equated with being not only uncivilized but even nonhuman: "Because of that elephant stampede of bad manners we now need God's goodness more than ever. If we didn't have God's rules for goodness, we'd be more like wild animals than people."[11]

Such passages recall the longstanding practice, dating back to the late nineteenth century in both Europe and the United States, of likening homosexuality with a stagnated state of evolutionary development and even with atavism. As both Siobhan Somerville and Neville Hoad have documented, when *fin-de-siecle* sexologists, comparative anatomists, and biologists discussed gay men and lesbians, they cast both their sexual behavior and their physical bodies in the racialized language of primitivism. In the dominant scientific discourses of the day, homosexuality was regarded as a "less evolved" state of erotic comportment than heterosexuality. Siobhan Somerville, for example, notes how in analyses of lesbian genitalia "anatomists and sexologists drew upon notions of natural selection to dismiss these bodies as anomalous 'throwbacks' within a scheme of cultural and anatomical progress" (256). Meanwhile, Neville Hoad denotes the same phenomenon in discussions about gay men. As he asserts in the opening sentence of his article: "it should not be possible to understand the initial theories of modern male homosexual identity in the west without looking at the imperial and neo-imperial contexts of such theoretical productions" (133). Hoad goes on to discuss how "the application of key tropes of Darwinian evolutionary theory permitted an imbrication of race, gender, nation and class categories in the constitution of knowledge of the body of the 'invert' and subsequent 'homosexual'" (133).

Such attitudes resurfaced in a slightly altered form during the opening decades of the twentieth century when the field of psychoanalysis framed homosexuality as a condition where an individual's psychosexual development had been stunted or halted. As Lee Walzer has discussed, although Sigmund Freud "rejected both degeneracy and third-sex theories posited by early sexologists," he nonetheless "viewed homosexuality as a form of arrested development that prevented such men and women from developing a full heterosexual identity" (26). While this viewpoint did not explicitly liken same-sex attraction with the evolutionary backsliding of atavism, it also did not connect it with appropriate levels of evolutionary progress.

Both the ex-gay movement and its newer pre-gay incarnation revive such viewpoints. As Michelle Wolkomir has discussed, when adults undergoing reparative therapy yield to same-sex desires, they are commonly described in evolutionary language as experiencing an episode of "backsliding" (105). Meanwhile, in *Me Tarzan, You Jane*, the equation of homosexuality and the racialized language of primitivism are even more apparent as same-sex desires are likened to "wildness" and "animalism." In so doing, *Me Tarzan, You Jane* makes visible the ways in which discourses of intolerance continue to overlap and interlock with one another. The book's belief in a clear sexual hierarchy—which locates monogamous, married, procreative heterosexuality at the apex—is buttressed by an equally palpable belief in a racial and ethnic hierarchy that casts certain peoples and cultures as "savage." Indeed, the opening sentence of *Me Tarzan, You Jane* denies the presence of indigenous Africans or, even more problematically, denies their humanity: "Imagine Tarzan growing up in the jungle, the only human being."

Of course, the xenophobic, imperialist, and even racist overtones to such passages are exacerbated by the narrative on which Graham chose to model her text: *Tarzan of the Apes*. In what has become a well-known plot summary, Edgar Rice Burroughs's novel tells the story of the son of British aristocrats who is orphaned as an infant and raised in the African jungle by a band of apes. As Gail Bederman has said about the narrative, "Burroughs ... constructed Africa as a place where 'the white man' could prove his superior manhood by reliving the primitive, masculine life of his most distant evolutionary forefathers" (220). In light of these details, *Tarzan of the Apes* has widely been regarded as affirming white racial hierarchy, justifying Western imperialism, and supporting Progressive era beliefs in Social Darwinism and eugenics. In the words of Mariana Torgovnick: "Tarzan always rises to the top of the hierarchies. In the first two volumes of the series, Tarzan becomes a king not once, but twice" (55–56).

Graham's decision to base *Me Tarzan, You Jane* on Burroughs's novel puts the book in dialogue with these past messages about imperialism, xenophobia, and racial hierarchy. At the same time, these details assume added significance in the present day, given both the racial composition of the ex-gay movement and the way in which its ideology and efforts have been exported to regions around the globe. As Tanya Erzen has discussed, together with being a predominantly male-dominated phenomenon, the ex-gay movement is also "predominantly white" (4). The movement does make attempts to reach out to racial and ethnic minority groups, but the fact remains that "there are very few African American, Latino, or Asian American" individuals actually involved in its programs (Erzen 43). One possible reason for this failure to attract non-white men and women is the movement's less-than-stellar record with issues of racial sensitivity and understanding. As Gabriel Arana reported, in 2005, a "member of NARTH's scientific advisory board ignited controversy by suggesting that blacks were better off having been enslaved, which allowed them to escape the 'savage' continent of Africa" (par. 47). Although his comments were quickly removed from the organization's website, the damage was done.[12]

Complicating discussions about the interaction of racial privilege, political power, and cultural hierarchy further, the ex-gay movement embodies what can be seen as an imperialistic force itself. From its origins in the 1970s, various individuals and groups have disseminated the ex-gay message to nations around the world. Tanya Erzen has documented that there are hundreds, if not thousands, of ex-gay programs in locations ranging from "Europe, South America, Canada, and Australia" to "the Philippines, Singapore, Japan, China, and Mexico" (42).

When the ex-gay movement establishes satellite organizations in countries outside of the United States, they are exporting not simply a particular theological viewpoint or purportedly scientific treatment program, but a powerful message of intolerance. The growing presence of U.S.-based ex-gay organizations in Africa—the setting for both Burroughs's *Tarzan of the Apes* and, as a result, Graham's *Me Tarzan, You Jane*—provides a poignant example. As Kapya Kaoma has written, "Pejorative attitudes towards LGBTQ in Africa has long been widespread. But the recent upsurge in politicized homophobia has been inspired by right-wing American evangelicals who have exported U.S.-style culture-war politics" (par. 2). To illustrate the prevalence as well as the perniciousness of such sentiments, Kaoma discusses Uganda's Anti-Homosexuality Bill, which was introduced in 2009. "[T]he bill imposed the death penalty for certain homosexual acts and criminalized human-rights advocacy on behalf of sexual minorities" (Kaoma, par. 3). Both the idea for the bill and the precise language that it used "grew directly out of a well-attended conference, the 'Seminar on Exposing the Truth behind Homosexuality and the Homosexual Agenda' that took place in the capital, Kampala, in March" (Kaoma, par. 2). The conference was hosted by "the Uganda-based Family Life Network, which is supported by U.S. Christian-rights groups, teamed with two leading anti-gay activists from the States, Holocaust revisionist Scott Lively and Dan Schierer of the ex-gay group Exodus International" (Kaoma, par. 3). Lively, in fact, was the keynote speaker for the event. During his speech, "Lively told his Ugandan audience that a powerful global gay movement had now set its sights on Africa. The 'gay agenda' unleashes epidemics of divorce, child abuse, and

HIV/AIDS wherever it gains a foothold, he said. If you allow homosexuality, he said, 'you can't stop someone from molesting children or stop them from having sex with animals'" (Kaoma, par. 4).

Me Tarzan, You Jane makes visible the ways in which all of these seemingly disparate geo-political threads are actually interrelated. The text demonstrates how the past medico-scientific association of homosexuality with primitivism was informed by discourses of racial hierarchy that justified white Western imperialism, which, in turn, can be placed in dialogue with current imperialist efforts by the ex-gay movement to export their message of homophobia to countries and cultures around the world.

Siobhan Somerville has written about "the various ways that late nineteenth-and early twentieth century scientific discourses around race became available to sexologists and physicians as a way to articulate emerging models of homosexuality" (264–5). *Me Tarzan, You Jane* reveals that these elements are far from simply a facet of the past; they form a key element in the way that queer identity continues to be discussed—and demonized—in the present. Moving niche market picture books, especially the ones that seem the most specialized, marginal, and fringe, from the periphery to the center of public consciousness and critical conversation makes these facets visible. *Me Tarzan, You Jane* might be targeting a very specific subset of the youth population, but its ultimate goal is to transform nothing less than mainstream American society.

Notes

1. More specifically, Tidal Wave Books is affiliated with Mormonism. As the website for the press states about its publications: "All principles presented must be in keeping with the doctrines of the Church of Jesus Christ of Latter-day Saints."
2. Janice Barrett Graham's picture book is not paginated.
3. Jallen Rix offers the following list: American Academy of Pediatrics, American Counseling Association, American Association of School Administrators, American Federation of Teachers, American Psychological Association, American School Counselor Association, American School Health Association, Interfaith Alliance Foundation, National Association of School Psychologists, National Association of Secondary School Principals, National Association of Social Workers, National Education Association, and School Social Work Association of America (53).
4. Dr. George Rekers, who has written books like *Growing Up Straight: What Every Family Should Know About Homosexuality* (1982) and has been described as "a prominent expert on gender-disturbed children" (Nicolosi and Nicolosi 187), was also involved in a scandal that seriously called into question the credibility of those who lobby against LGBTQ individuals and identity. In July 2010, "George Alan Rekers, a prominent anti-gay activist who co-founded the conservative Family Research Council, was caught returning from a 10-day trip to Europe with a male escort he found on Rentboy.com, which is exactly what it sounds like" ("George Rekers," par. 1). Rekers initially denied knowing that the twenty-year-old young man was a sex worker and likewise denied

having any intimate contact with him. "He claim[ed] he learned his 20-year-old companion was a prostitute only midway through their trip," the *Miami New Times* reported ("George Rekers," par. 5). Rekers went further, insisting that "they had no intimate contact, and [that] he hired the young man only because recent surgery meant 'I can't lift luggage'" ("George Rekers," par. 5). However, the *Miami New Times* published a photograph that called this claim into question: "*New Times* reporters spotted the retired professor pushing his baggage cart through Miami International Airport" ("George Rekers," par. 6). The article continued, even more damagingly: "It would be extremely difficult to stumble upon the Rentboy.com homepage, which features young well-muscled men rubbing each other's crotches on grainy video loops, and not figure out what the site means by 'rent boy'" ("George Rekers," par. 6). Within weeks after the story broke, the young male companion confirmed these assumptions: "The escort now says Rekers is indeed gay, and that Rekers paid him to perform daily nude body rubs during their European jaunt. 'It's a situation where he's going against homosexuality when he is a homosexual,' the young man told the *Miami New Times*, adding that Rekers—who repeatedly asked for a move he dubbed 'The Long Stroke'—ought to divorce himself from his many anti-gay associations" ("George Rekers," par. 2).

5. It should be noted that, in many ways, this change in focus is neither ideologically new nor strategically surprising. As Eve Kosofsky Sedgwick first articulated in "How to Bring Your Kids Up Gay" (1991), a similar shift occurred when the American Psychiatric Association removed homosexuality in adults from the 1973 edition of the *Diagnostic and Statistical Manual of Mental Disorders*, only to seemingly replace it with a new designation, "Gender Identity Disorder of Childhood," in its very next edition released in 1980. In the words of Sedgwick: "the *de*pathologization of an atypical object-choice [in adults] can be yoked to a *new* pathologization of an atypical gender identification [in children]" (21; emphasis in original). Akin to the transformation taking place within the ex-gay movement, the medicalization and treatment of nonheteronormativity hadn't really been eliminated, it was just redirected from adults onto children.

6. Of course, as Lee Edelman points out in *No Future: Queer Theory and the Death Drive*, children have long been used as a material argument against homosexuals and homosexuality. Not only are young people routinely co-opted by conservative forces in their portrayal of the traditional, normative, heterosexual family, but LGBTQ couples also exist outside the "cycles of reproduction" given their inability to biologically procreate (Edelman 97). Attempts to identify and "save" prehomosexual children from future same-sex erotic behavior can be viewed as an even more aggressive deployment of this practice.

7. For more on this issue, see Havelock Ellis, *Studies in the Psychology of Sex, Volume II: Sexual Inversion*, 3rd ed. (Philadelphia: F. A. Davis, 1926).

8. As Shannon Minter has written about this issue, "the introduction of GID in 1980 'followed 20 years of clinical research' on gender-atypical children. ... Much of this research was touted as a means to identify 'prehomosexual' and 'pretranssexual' children and to prevent them from growing up to be gay or transsexual" (11–12).

9. *Me Tarzan, You Jane* is not the only picture book working to steer young people away from an LGBTQ identity that paradoxically contains queerly charged content. So, too, does Christian YoungMiller's *Everybody Has Those*

Thoughts: So It Doesn't Mean You're Gay (2010). Recalling the derogatory descriptors of effeminate gay men as "fruity" or even "fruitcakes," all of the characters in the book possess heads that are different types of fruit: an apple, a bunch of grapes, etc. Moreover, the head of the protagonist, who is the one struggling with same-sex attraction, is a very phallic-looking banana.

10. This homoerotic reading of the drooping bouquet also invites the reexamination of many of the text's illustrations using this lens. In so doing, images of young Tarzan clinging to the big, firm, horizontal tree limb or holding a long, thick vine acquire a powerful queer subtext.

11. While Graham uses the term "wild" as a pejorative, this attribute can also be seen as an accolade that contradicts or, at least, undercuts her message. If same-sex attraction is characterized as being "wild" and even "uncivilized," then it is also being framed as something that comes instinctually and, thus, naturally. In this way, Graham unintentionally frames heterosexuality as something that is not innate and that must be learned.

12. These comments were made by Gerald Schoenewolf in an article titled "Gay Rights and Political Correctness: A Brief History." His exact remarks about slavery were as follows: "With all due respect, there is another way, or other ways, to look at the race issue in America. It could be pointed out, for example, that Africa at the time of slavery was still primarily a jungle, as yet uncivilized or industrialized. Life there was savage, as savage as the jungle for most people, and that it was the Africans themselves who first enslaved their own people. They sold their own people to other countries, and those brought to Europe, South America, America, and other countries, were in many ways better off than they had been in Africa. But if one even begins to say these things one is quickly shouted down as though one were a complete madman" (qtd. in Besen, par. 5).

Epilogue

Change and Continuity: Niche Market Picture Books and the Negotiation of Artistic Freedom, Iconoclastic Ideology, and Consumer Capitalism

By the start of the second decade of the twenty-first century, it had become commonplace for authors, critics, and librarians to lament the increasingly corporate nature of texts for young readers. Of course, from the origins of children's book publishing, the industry was a business designed to turn a profit. John Newbery, who is commonly credited with launching the field during the eighteenth century, not only printed and sold books for young readers as a moneymaking venture, but he routinely promoted them with merchandise. "Most famously," Lissa Paul reminds us, "Newbery offered a ball for boys and pincushion for girls as the toy tie-ins for *A Little Pretty Pocket-Book*" (*Children's* 29). Such practices are even more common today, making the profit motive that fuels the children's book business even more visible. As one author quipped anonymously on this subject: "I'm not naïve enough to think that publishing houses are in the charity business or that the goal of the conglomerate is to serve the needs of children. First and foremost, they are in the business to make money'" (qtd. in Taxel, "Children's" 146).

During the late twentieth century, however, the attention that publishers paid to profits dramatically increased. As Tom Engelhardt observed: "past commercial book ventures for children—even those of a few decades ago—seem quaint and limited matters of momentary opportunism, when set against the ongoing rhythms of the present entertainment environment" (58). Starting in the 1970s and accelerating rapidly during the 1980s and 1990s children's book publishing underwent catastrophic change. For generations, the industry had been primarily comprised of relatively small, often family-owned, and independently operated presses (Taxel, "Children's" 158). According to John B. Thompson, "these houses were run by individuals who either owned the company outright or had a substantial stake in it, and other members of the family were commonly involved in the business" (102). He goes on to provide some examples: "In the 1950s and before there were dozens of independent publishing houses in New York, Boston and London. Among the better-known American houses were Random House, Simon & Schuster, Scribner, Doubleday, Harcourt, Harper, Boni and Liverlight, Henry Holt, Dutton, Putnam, Viking, Alfred Knopf, Farrar, Straus & Giroux, William Morrow, W. W. Norton, Houghton Mifflin and Little, Brown, to name just a few" (102). Many of these publishers released books for children. Houghton, for example, had issued Esther Forbes's *Johnny Tremain*, which won the Newbery Award in 1944. Meanwhile, Viking was the publisher of Kate Seredy's *The Good Master* (1935), while Doubleday had released Caroline Snedeker's *Downright Dencey* (1927); both were Newbery honor titles. Finally, Harper was the publisher for E. B. White's now-classic story *Charlotte's Web* (1952).

During the closing decades of the twentieth century, though, this situation shifted. Independent, family-owned firms rapidly disappeared, bought out by big corporations for whom publishing was only one branch of their operations. As Thompson explains: "By the 1990s the shape of the industry had changed dramatically: in a field where there had once been dozens of independent publishing houses, each reflecting the idiosyncratic tastes and styles of their owners and editors, there were now five or six large corporations, each operating as an umbrella organization for numerous imprints, many of which still bore the names of previously independent houses that were now part of a larger organization" (103). This flurry of corporate mergers and company buy-outs brought "all the major book publishers into the hands of large transnational communication conglomerates with holdings and interests with many other, usually more profitable, areas of mass media" (Moran 441).[1] Joel Taxel delineates the construction of one such media conglomerate: "Viacom, for example, owns Paramount movie studios, the MTV and VH1 cable television networks, the Blockbuster music and video rental stores, radio and television stations, and Simon and Schuster. The latter is among the largest publishers of children's books" ("Children's" 158). This scenario was far from anomalous; by the dawn of the twenty-first century, it applied to every other major publisher of children's books. For example, "Rupert Murdoch's News Corporation owns the Los Angeles Dodgers, newspapers and magazines published throughout the world, television networks (including Fox), Twentieth Century Fox movie producers, and HarperCollins, another of the largest, most influential publishers of books for young people" (Taxel, "Children's" 158). The new multinational corporate pedigree of children's publishers becomes even more alarming when it is viewed in the context of the market share that they hold. André Schiffrin estimated that, by 2000, a mere five major media conglomerates controlled around 80% of children's book sales (2).

The new corporate ownership of children's book publishing brought with it new fiscal goals and financial models: "In previous decades the profit expectation on books was about 4% after taxes" (Taxel, "Children's" 160). As Taxel goes on to explain, this very modest rate of return "meant that many people were not in publishing for the money itself" ("Children's" 160). Instead, editors were driven by their love for great storytelling, their commitment to the creation of literary art, and their desire to add to collective cultural accomplishments. While individuals working in publishing drew salaries and the companies that they worked for made money, the book business was historically not conceived as a place for anyone—editor, publisher, or author—to proverbially strike it rich (Taxel, "Children's" 154–60). On the contrary, presses routinely released narratives that they believed were socially, artistically, or intellectually important even though they knew that these titles would never become big commercial successes.

The large companies who bought these small presses, however, had vastly different economic expectations. As Taxel explains, "While publishers such as Alfred Knopf were wealthy, the emphasis was less on annual profit than on the steady growth of the firm. ... This emphasis on earnings meant that instead of a novel's generating 4%, it was expected to make profits anywhere from 10%–20%" ("Children's" 160). These new financial goals meant that editors needed to pay more attention to how a potential title would enhance company profits, not just enhance society. Now, "every book [had] to be put through tedious profit and loss statements to justify its publication" (Taxel, "Children's" 161). In the words of Schiffrin, this shift by corporate-owned publishers to "rationalize profits on a title-by-title basis" meant that every book now had "to pay its own way" (116).

This increased emphasis on profitability precipitated alterations to the editorial selection process. According to Schiffrin: "Publishers have always prided themselves on their ability to balance the imperative of making money with that of issuing worthwhile books" (5). In the past, titles that had mass appeal and sold well were used to financially underwrite the ones that were more unusual, eclectic, or experimental. Consequently, for generations, "even small houses would 'publish one or two well-written, beautiful books a year (knowing that they would not make money), simply because the book was special and it deserved to be out there'" (Taxel, "Children's" 162). The new corporate business model that was focused on expanding profits, however, steadily eradicated this practice. For publishers that were now under corporate control, "[i]t is increasingly the case that the owner's *only* interest is in making money and as much of it as possible" (Schiffrin 5; emphasis in original). Children's narratives were now primarily seen as means to yield profits—instead of as a venue to transmit ideas, convey culture, or create art.

Of course, as Joel Taxel reminds us, "it is an error to examine cultural phenomena without reference to human agency" ("Economics" 490). He goes on to explain: "It is easy ... to reduce the women and men work-ing in publishing to helpless pawns in the face of changes wrought when transnational conglomerates assume control of the companies in which they work" ("Economics" 483–4). Many editors at children's publishing houses owned by multinational media conglomerates either actively resist corporate-driven models or work to strike a balance between generating quality literature with generating profits. As John B. Thompson has written, "Within most publishing corporations there are some houses or imprints that have established reputations for publishing works of quality, both liter-ary fiction and serious non-fiction, and it is acknowledged, even by the most number-crunching of senior corporate managers, that publishing works of quality is and should remain an important part of what a publishing company does" (396).

That said, even the most optimistic of assessments concedes that the ability to meet both goals is becoming increasingly more difficult. Thompson goes on to add, for example, "Does this mean that those publishers and editors in the large corporations who care about quality literature and serious non-fiction are not under pressure? No, it does not" (396). Even in publishing houses that remain the most committed to producing quality literature "[t]here are limits to the extent to which editors can follow their hunches and experiment with new books that don't bear the obvious signs of success" (Thompson 395).

Transformations in the publishing industry were the product not only of the new corporate ownership, but another equally powerful force: shifts in the children's book market. As Tom Engelhardt has discussed, prior to the 1970s, librarians and elementary teachers were the primary customers for children's books. Buoyed by generous federal funding to use for the purchase of reading materials—such as the National Defense Education Act in 1957 and the Elementary and Secondary School Education Act in 1965 (Taxel, "Economics" 480)—they were the ones who reviewed book catalogs, selected texts, and placed orders. "This relationship changed," Taxel relays, "when the economic downturn during the Vietnam War years led to the slashing of federal funds for libraries and the concomitant erosion of book sales" ("Children's" 154). With elementary teachers and public librarians no longer in a position to purchase books for young people (or, at least, to purchase as many titles as they had in the past), publishers needed to find a new customer base for their products. As Engelhardt has written, they did not have to wait long or look far: "help was on the way in the form of the fast-growing chain bookstores then staking its claim in the suburban mall" (57). In these venues, along with discount stores, supermarkets, and drug stores, publishers would market books directly to children—and their parents. In the words of Engelhardt once again: "Thus was established the basis for a second boom in children's publishing, and a quite different form of children's book was born—the book designed for the consumer child" (57). This new mode of business operations gave rise to a whole slate of narratives that were "inconceivable when a librarian stood between the child and the book" (Engelhardt 58). If publishers wanted children to buy their titles, then they had to provide the kind of narratives that these customers wanted—which was a far different type of text than what many teachers and librarians desired. Whereas adult educators made their selections based on literary substance, young people were often seduced by superficial style: with books that were flashy and fun.

This new need to appeal directly to child consumers, coupled with the firm corporate mandate to increase profits, precipitated massive changes in the way books for young readers were conceptualized, packaged, and marketed. As author Jane Kurtz has explained:

> The Rupert Murdochs and other money-spinners of the world own the big publishing companies, and those companies are supposed to be profitable. If your job was to buy clothes for K-Mart, you wouldn't choose to stock quirky clothes that only a few people wear—you'd stock clothes that masses of people buy. So if a money-spinner owns a publishing company and gives its employees the mandate to make money, of course the huge temptation is going to be to publish only books that masses of people buy. (qtd. in Taxel, "Children's" 161)

Corporate-owned children's publishers do not wish to take risks on experimental or unconventional books. In light of the pressures they face concerning profitability, coupled with their need to catch the attention of young consumers, they seek to offer ones that have the greatest chance for commercial success. As Carol Lynch-Brown and Carl M. Tomlinson explained about this new modus operandi: "To increase profits, the corporate publishers downsized backlists, causing good titles to go out of print more quickly; published fewer unusual or 'risky' books; and favored mass appeal over literary excellence" (241).

The most visible and certainly most lucrative example of this ethos is the rise of licensed or branded fiction. In examples ranging from chapter books like American Girl, Hannah Montana, and The 39 Clues to picture books such as Olivia, Curious George, and Clifford, the corporate-fueled world of children's publishing has moved away from a primary interest in generating literary classics and toward the goal of producing lucrative corporate franchises. Given that presses are now parts of large, multifaceted media conglomerates who also own newspapers, magazines, movie studios, television stations, and Internet sites, books are not considered discrete, self-contained products; rather, they are viewed as one installment on a long and multiplatform chain of product synergism. As Diane Carver Sekeres has explained about this phenomenon: "the reader constructs the imaginary characters of the fiction through the multiple experiences of buying and living with the multiple products of the brand" (399). For example, the American Girl series is a sequence of historical novels. But, the content and characters also appear in a myriad of other material forms. Catalogs from the publisher of the American Girl collection, feature "clothes, furniture, tea sets, needlework kits, music boxes, trading cards, sweet potato pudding kits, dress patterns, stationary sets, skin care kits, starter collections," and, of course, dolls (Lynch-Brown and Tomlinson 242).

This phenomenon is especially prevalent among picture books. In comments that echo those of many children's book critics, Daniel Hade has lamented the growing commercialization of these texts: "The corporate owners of children's book publishing really aren't interested in the business of publishing books anymore. ... The business of corporate owners is developing brands" (512). As he goes on to explain, if you examine the annual reports from children's publishers,

> you may be surprised to learn that these brands and media assets are Madeline, Curious George, Peter Rabbit, Clifford, and the Magic School Bus. In other words, these corporations are hoping that children are attracted not to books so much as to *any* product that carries the brand's name. To the corporation, a Clifford key ring is no different from a Clifford book. Each is a "container" for the idea of "Clifford." Each "container" is simply a means for a child to experience "Cliffordness." In this world there is no difference between a book and a video or a CD or a T-shirt or a backpack. (Hade 512; italics in original)

Operating with this new marketing ethos, "[t]he corporation, then, seeks to expand its brand to as many aspects of a consumer's life as possible. ... The goal isn't to see as many copies of *Madeline* as possible (though that is still desirable) but to extend Madeline into as many aspects of a child's life as possible" (Hade 512–3). Hade draws primarily on the Curious George series to illustrate this phenomenon: listing the numerous toys, clothes, games, household goods, electronic items, food products, dolls, videos, and school supplies available that are based on the narratives. But, a myriad of other popular picture books—such as those featuring the characters Olivia, Clifford, Madeline, and Peter Rabbit—would serve just as well. In this way, the licensing, branding, and merchandizing of corporate-issued children's books is not an isolated incident but a widespread industry practice. Indeed, Philip Nel asked in an article concerning the merchandizing bonanza that has emerged from, and undoubtedly helped to fuel, the tremendous success of J. K. Rowling's *Harry Potter* series: "Is There a Text in this Advertising Campaign?" (236).

As the line separating laissez-faire commerce from literary creativity continues to blur in the children's publishing industry, it erodes what Scott Stossel has termed the formerly "sacred status" (43) that texts have held as important ideological entities. Instead, it recasts them as simply one more material commodity—items that are, from a business standpoint, no different from toothpaste, plastic storage tubs, or paper towels. Books are viewed as merely another revenue stream; to paraphrase Hade's remarks, they are interchangeable with toys, lunchboxes, or backpacks featuring this same branded figure. As a result, Curious George, Clifford, or Madeline cease to be regarded primarily as literary characters and instead become identified as lucrative licensed properties. Patricia Lee Gauch, a longtime industry insider, decried the cumulative impact of these changes via the following blunt comments: "What has this meant? It has turned publishing into a fast-food process!" (qtd. in Taxel, "Children's" 156).

Natasha Cane, the juvenile specialist for the Brooklyn Heights branch of the Brooklyn Public Library, has commented on the impact of this phenomenon on children's relationship with books. Cane began her position in 2003 and, consistently over this period, "has found it difficult to get young children interested in titles that are not based on licensed characters" (qtd. in Thomas 65). She reports: "The kids come in and say, 'Look Mommy, Clifford!' And go right to [that book] and get instant gratification" (qtd. in Thomas 65). Journalist Tom Engelhardt predicted this event back in 1991. In an article that appeared in *Harper's Magazine*, he made the provocative claim that "reading may be harmful to your kids" (qtd. in Thomas 169). Given the way in which major corporate publishers were increasingly using literary characters for merchandising, "reading children's books, he maintained, was just another way of shopping" (qtd. in Thomas 169). The increasing output of series books, sequel narratives, and licensed properties by corporate-owned children's book publishers over the past few decades is making visible how a "world built upon respect for the written word has been replaced by one dominated by a bottom-line sensibility" (Simon 25).

Only time will tell how this new business ethos will affect arenas like children's literacy, youth consumerism, and cultural conceptions about the place and purpose of art for young people. However, this practice does have immediate significance for an array of equally pressing socio-political issues. As Lauren Wohl, who is the former director of School and Library Marketing for Hyperion Books for Children, asserts: "the concentration of ownership of book publishing in the hands of a handful of giant corporations poses an ominous threat to democracy" (qtd. in Taxel, "Children's" 160). Discussing this subject during an interview, she expressed concern that with "fewer and fewer people making decisions, the free flow of ideas is limited or diminished and there are fewer and fewer points of view available" (qtd. in Taxel, "Children's" 160).

This telescoping of ideas is already well documented in the realm of books for adults. Not only do corporate-owned publishers seek out texts that appeal to, rather than challenge, the status quo, but they also routinely decline to publish books that criticize corporate capitalism, engage with controversial socio-political issues that might offend or, at least, alienate some of their potential customers, or shine a negative light on the company's other economic interests and business affiliations. Daniel Simon provides a few specific examples: "Remember how lightly HarperCollins let go of former Governor of Hong Kong Chris Patten's book because, up the corporate ladder, Rupert Murdoch wanted to protect his satellite TV deal with China ... or how St. Martin's turned against its author (the imprint's editor resigned in the controversy) when it canceled its biography of George W. [Bush]" (par. 15). With all of the major children's publishers now under the control of these same multinational conglomerates, an identical editorial policy—and restriction to First Amendment freedoms—applies.

Given these serious social, economic, and intellectual implications, the new corporate ownership of children's publishing has precipitated a situation that, to quote Daniel Simon, "has not been good for readers or writers" (par. 8). Award-winning children's author Jane Yolen agrees. She has decried how "a bottom-line sensibility [is] running most major companies" (qtd. in Taxel, "Children's" 161). As Yolen goes on to assert, the industry's new obsession with "saleable products [is] not what literature is about" (qtd. in Taxel, "Children's" 161). Longtime children's literature critic Jack Zipes echoes such sentiments. Zipes has written that at corporate-controlled children's presses "decisions to design and publish books are more often than not made by the marketing people in the firm" and not the editors, who are simply instructed to "acquire and shape products in keeping with corporate guidelines" (7). As a result, the past few decades have given rise to "a growing apprehension both inside and outside of the industry that the obsession with finding the next blockbuster is causing the artistic worth of many authors to be 'slighted, ignored, and their minimum means of livelihood rendered more precarious than ever'" (Taxel, "Children's" 162). For this reason, Taxel laments how "[t]he time when the realm of ideas that historically were 'exempted from the usual expectations of profit' [has] passed" ("Children's" 161).

Niche market picture books embody an important counterpoint to this trend. These narratives exist outside of corporate-driven business practices concerned with maximizing profits, extending brand synergy, and appealing to the greatest common denominator. In light of the nonmainstream means by which these texts are made and marketed, as well as the unconventional and often iconoclastic subject matters that they address, narratives like *It's Just a Plant* and *Maggie Goes on a Diet* embody a potent site of resistance to the growing commercialization and commoditization of literature for young readers. These works constitute a vital refuge for or, at least, much-needed alternative to the growing number of corporate-produced books with safe, generic, and sometimes even vapid themes. While niche market picture books are not without their problems and shortcomings—as my discussions in the previous chapters attest—they serve an important cultural, intellectual, and artistic purpose. Even at their most flawed and faulty, books like *Little Zizi* and *My Beautiful Mommy* give voice and visibility to a range of social, cultural, and political issues that their corporate counterparts are unable or unwilling to present. In so doing, niche market picture books embody crucial arenas for the preservation of artistic freedom, the protection of free speech, and the expression of cultural dissent that are essential for a healthy democracy. In a powerful affirmation of this viewpoint, Daniel Simon notes that all of the adult-audience books that were dropped by major corporate publishers because their messages conflicted with company interests were picked up by small independent houses (par. 16). While none of the niche market books profiled in the previous chapters were ever, to my knowledge, under contract with a major press, it would be difficult to imagine a multinational corporation being comfortable with topics like legalizing marijuana or fretting over penis size. Indeed, Ricardo Cortés did initially seek a mainstream publisher for his book but to no avail. As Susan Avery documents, "He sent it out to a dozen publishers, 80 percent of whom just said no. The rest liked the idea but thought bookstores might not. So, he self-published" (par. 2).

Giving further credence to this contention, while the corporatization of children's publishing has received the bulk of media attention, independent presses have not simply continued to survive but to thrive in many cases by adhering to a distinct social, cultural, aesthetic, or political niche. As the trade magazine *Publisher's Weekly*, which features a yearly column on the state of independent publishing, observed: "Finding a niche and sticking to it is considered the golden rule for an independent publisher to have long-term success" ("Go Your Own Way," par. 1). Blue Apple Books in Maplewood, New Jersey, forms a poignant example. Founded in 2003 by Harriet Ziefert, the company specializes in what might be called a niche-within-a-niche: Blue Apple Books publishes texts not simply for youngsters from birth through age ten, but what Ziefert calls "modern books for modern kids" (qtd. in Milliot, "Carpe," par. 7). Their titles spotlight issues such as "separation, loss, and reunion; the emotional bond between parents and children; the development of empathy" (Kennedy, par. 2). This editorial plan has served them well. As *Publishers Weekly* has documented, from 2007 to 2009, when many corporate publishers were witnessing their sales remaining flat or even dipping, Blue Apple Books saw theirs grow by an impressive 117% (Milliot, "Carpe," par. 24). In the years since, the niche publisher has continued to experience a boom. In 2011, Blue Apple Books posted a further 87% growth in sales from their levels three years earlier ("Go Your Own Way," par. 12).

Such statistics are not atypical. Many other small independent presses have experienced tremendous success even in the face of the near oligarchy that multinational media corporations hold in the children's literature market. Once again, the key in each of these instances is that the publisher has identified a particular niche. The UK-based Barefoot Books, for example, which was founded in 1993 by Tessa Strickland and Nancy Traversy, and specializes in "cross-cultural board books," began releasing titles in the United States only in 1998 (Milliot, "Finding," par. 9). By 2002, as Jim Milliot has documented, "the American market accounted for approximately 54% of the children's book publisher's total revenue" and played a major role in the company's 22% increase in sales from 2000 to 2002 ("Finding," pars. 9, 11). Likewise, Sleeping Bear Press in Chelsea, Michigan, was founded in 1998 and publishes books that address regional Michigan events, spotlight local state figures, and relay indigenous tribal tales. This niche has yielded both commercial success and critical acclaim. In the three years directly following its founding, the company's sales increased by an impressive 58.5% (Milliot, "Independently," par. 10). In addition, *The Legend of Sleeping Bear*—which was the press's first book as well as the inspiration for its moniker—was named an "officially recognized" title for the state of Michigan via a special House Resolution in June 1998 (Michigan).

Finally, and just as significantly, Groundwood Books, located in Canada, forms another important success story in the realm of independent, niche publishing. Founded in 1978, the press operates according to the following specialty-market mandate: "Many of our books tell the stories of people whose voices are not always heard. Books by the First Peoples of this hemisphere have always been a special interest, as have those of others who through circumstance have been marginalized and whose contribution to our society is not always visible" ("About Us"). Over the years, Groundwood has become known around the world for releasing artistically innovative, materially experimental, and culturally iconoclastic narratives. Among its recent titles, for instance, is Menena Cottin and Rosana Faria's picture book *The Black Book of Colors* (2008), a pioneering narrative whose text is printed both in words and in Braille, and whose illustrations are tactile as well as visual, thus engaging both sighted and blind child readers. The book was included among the Best Illustrated Children's Book Awards by *The New York Times*' Book Review. Additionally, Groundwood's offerings have included such corporate-unfriendly texts as Thomas King and Gary Clement's *A Coyote Solstice Tale* (2009), which, as Julia L. Mickenberg and Philip Nel have aptly summarized, "uses the native figure of the coyote trickster to mock holiday spending and greed" ("Radical" 461). In so doing, the press demonstrates that there still is a place for daring, unconventional, and even radical books in the industry. While these titles may lamentably be unable to secure a contract at corporate-controlled presses, a bevy of small and successful niche market publishers are eager to sign them. In the words of Mickenberg and Nel once again: "Groundwood's acquisitions are not driven solely by market potential, as is the case for most US trade publishers; ... the press can publish more controversial books, and it has made a niche for itself by doing so" ("Radical" 446–7).

All this said, it is important to be cautious about framing either niche market publishers like Groundwood or niche market books like those profiled in the previous chapters as a panacea that will fix all of the problems arising from the increasing influence of big business on children's literature. After all, rather than existing outside of the forces of Western consumer capitalism, these enterprises operate firmly from within them. The starting point for this economic system is identifying what the consumer wants (or, in some cases, artificially creating and then persuasively convincing consumers about what they want) and then giving it to them. By locating overlooked markets and then tailoring their subject matter to target these exact customers, niche market products arguably engage in this core capitalistic principle even more effectively than mass-produced ones. As a result, books like *Little Zizi* and *It's Just a Plant* can be seen not so much as representing an off-ramp to consumer capitalism, but simply embodying a new form of on-ramp. They do not reject hegemonic economic practices; they merely return them to their origins.[2]

A similar observation could be made about one of the central facets to the niche market ethos: that of "democratizing the tools of production" (C. Anderson 54). While the rise of the Internet, the proliferation of the personal computer, and the accessibility of desktop publishing have leveled the economic playing field and provided countless individuals with an unprecedented ability to participate in the open marketplace, they have also made it easier for new economic entrants to control every facet of the supply chain from the ground up. The bulk of the books profiled in the previous chapters were written, edited, published, marketed, sold, and distributed by the same person. While figures like Seth Godin, Chris Anderson, and Susan Friedmann praise this phenomenon as a victory for independent producers being able to retain control over their own output, it can also interpreted in a more pessimistic way: as a vertical monopoly, however small-scale and innocuous.

Additionally, but far from insignificantly, sometimes media that is produced independently does not offer a true alternative to the offerings from large corporations. Instead, it ends up functioning as their unofficial research-and-development division. In this scenario, the web-based release of a certain book, movie, or song is not an end product. Rather, it embodies a stepping-stone designed to garner publicity, generate buzz, and build a fan base in service of striking a deal with a major media conglomerate. Bill Osgerby has discussed the prevalence of this phenomenon—whether by personal choice or by capitalistic force—in the music industry. As he explains, there is a "long tradition in which small, independent companies have pioneered new musical genres and talent, only to be 'co-opted' by large corporations through processes of amalgamation, joint venture or buy-out" (49). For this reason, Osgerby questions the notion of any truly "independent" media. He writes: "More flexible and dynamic than the majors, independent companies are able to develop and 'road test' new products and genres—the bigger corporations subsequently picking up the most successful ideas and exploiting them more systematically" (Osgerby 50).

Finally, and of equal significance with regard to the democratizing socio-political potential of niche market books, is the question of audience: who is actually buying and reading these narratives? While this question most immediately applies to the issue of whether these books are being chosen by young people who are interested in the subjects that they discuss or by adults who think that that children *should* be interested in them, it has another implication that applies to the highly divisive nature of American social, political, and cultural life in the twenty-first century. Given both the specialized subject matter and equally specialized cultural viewpoint contained in books like *It's Just a Plant* and *Me Tarzan, You Jane*, the question of audience also encompasses whether individuals from a broad range of socio-political perspectives are examining these narratives or whether they are only reaching a tiny segment of the population—namely, the one who likely already agrees with the messages that they contain.

This observation certainly characterizes the proliferation of socio-political viewpoints on the Internet. As figures like Eli Pariser, Cass Sunstein, and Peter James Saalfield have discussed, the World Wide Web has not enhanced national discussion about contentious cultural subjects; rather, it has given rise to increasing political polarity and social insularity. In the words of Saalfield: "Instead of searching out new perspectives, all too many users flock to websites that support their views, pop out occasionally to post an angry comment somewhere else, and then flee back to the comfort of Red State or Paul Krugman" (par. 2). Cass Sunstein, who serves as the administrator of the White House Office of Information and Regulatory Affairs, affirms this observation. He has commented how "the Internet creates 'echo chambers' where users surround themselves only with the like-minded. This not only preserves partisanship—it exacerbates it" (Saalfield, par. 4). For this reason, Saalfield asserts: "The niche driven nature of the Internet is pushing us further and further apart" (par. 4). It is accelerating the fragmentation of American social, cultural, and political life, not serving as a force for amalgamation or, at least, understanding.

Many of the picture books profiled in the previous chapters pose a similar conundrum. By definition, these narratives address niche issues that target an equally niche audience. But, do these texts serve a democratizing socio-cultural purpose by encouraging thoughtful and informed discussion about difficult subjects, or do they merely further the entrenchment of their readers' existing socio-political position? Phrased in a different way, all of these books take up a clear battle station in the U.S. culture wars, but are they striving to broker a truce or to perpetuate and possibly even escalate hostilities? Viewed from this perspective, the way in which many of these narratives spotlight a new and even formerly taboo subject in books for young readers—marijuana regulation, penis size, plastic surgery, etc.—brings one longstanding literary silence to a close while it simultaneously may precipitate a new skirmish in another arena.

These alternative and less laudatory ways of viewing niche market products engages with ongoing discussions about the hazards of believing that capitalism will fix the problems within capitalism and capitalistic societies. As Phil Buchanan, in an article that appeared in the online version of the *Harvard Business Review* in January 2013, observed: "Increasingly, I see people looking starry-eyed to business and markets to solve social problems" (par. 1). From disparities in health care coverage to inequities in economic opportunity, there are a variety of issues that fall under the umbrella category of what Buchanan flatly deems "What Capitalism Can't Fix." "I'm a huge believer in free-market capitalism," he asserts, "But I think we're better off being sober about what markets can and can't accomplish" (Buchanan, par. 9). As Buchanan goes on to articulate, a variety of factors give rise to this condition, but many of the most serious and immutable arise from the inherent nature of how capitalism is structured and functions. Oftentimes, the goal of maximizing profits for company stockholders is at odds with a concern for the good of the larger populace (Buchanan, pars. 9–10). In examples ranging from companies polluting the environment because doing so is cheaper than abiding by guidelines for responsible disposal of waste materials to local news outlets failing to criticize—or even call attention to—dubious business practices by their corporate owners, capitalism has historically proven to be a poor regulator of, and corrective to, itself. As Barry C. Lynn argues in *Cornered: The New Monopoly Capitalism and the Economics of Destruction* (2009), in its pure laissez-faire form, this economic system is not interested in correcting disparities in economic power, but establishing, maintaining, and exploiting them to maximize profit (xii–xiv). Market monopolies and the financial oligarchies to which they give rise are both the ideal conditions for and the natural result of unregulated capitalistic enterprise (Lynn xiv–xvi). Lynn joins others in asserting that these systems, whether appearing in the realm of book publishing or consumer manufacturing, "threaten independent businesses, squelch innovation, degrade the quality and safety of basic products, destabilize our most vital industrial and financial systems, and destroy the very fabric of democracy" (publisher's summary).

While these points are certainly valid, they engage in their own form of oversimplification: they collapse the massive distinctions between and among economic players. Not all capitalists are multinational corporate conglomerates, nor do they aspire to be. Similarly, not all commercial products, even those tailored to meet the needs of specific markets, have profit motive as their raison d'être. Furthermore, not all consumer goods are on the same inevitable commercial pathway. Narratives like *My Beautiful Mommy* and *It's Just a Plant* were not created with the intent of generating sequels, being picked up by a major publisher, establishing branding, selling licensing, and spawning merchandising. Furthermore, their success has also not ineluctably lead to these outcomes. In fact, at the time of this writing, only two of the authors profiled in this project—Ricardo Cortés and Paul M. Kramer—have released any additional narratives for young people. Moreover, unlike their counterparts in the corporate world who strive to create a brand and then reproduce it across a wide array of media platforms, their subsequent texts do not engage with the same characters, themes, or even subject matters. On the contrary, Cortés and Kramer have moved on to other, albeit equally specialized, topics. Cortés has written books for young readers about the New York City blackout; the Jamaican bobsled team; and the racial, ethnic, and religious stereotyping that has emerged in the wake of the terrorist attacks of September 11, 2001. Meanwhile, Kramer has penned stories about subjects ranging from bullying and bedwetting to divorce and nose-picking. Finally, and perhaps most important, all of the subsequent narratives by Cortés and Kramer have been written, marketed, sold, and distributed using the same niche methods.

For this reason, while it might be overstating the case to tout niche market books as salvific, it would also be understating the situation to refrain from pointing out how they are offering a much-needed commercial, material, and ideological alternative to corporate-produced children's literature. It is certainly wise for us to remain mindful of the ways in which niche market products have the potential to replicate the same problems and pitfalls of corporate consumer capitalism, but lumping them in with the products of multinational media conglomerates—either in whole or in part—is equally misguided. Niche market picture books may be operating within the same basic economic system as their mainstream counterparts, but they are doing so with different aims and outcomes.

The same observation applies to the investment that these books have within the U.S. culture wars. Although these texts can be seen as furthering the polarization of American social and political life—given their niche subjects, messages, and audience—they also give voice and visibility to new ideological issues and alternative societal perspectives. Books like *It's Just a Plant* add to the range of subjects and subjectivities represented in books for young people. Thus, while the concern that these narratives may only further entrench the attitudes that their readers already hold is valid, narrowing the range of issues available or limiting the opinions being expressed about them will certainly not help to foster democratic debate or increase cross-cultural understanding.

In the closing sections of *Sticks and Stones: The Troublesome Success of Children's Literature from Slovenly Peter to Harry Potter*, Jack Zipes bemoans how the growing corporate control of the children's book industry has been steadily altering the intellectual content of narratives for young readers. This new emphasis on commercialism and consumerism, he argues, has been causing multinational companies to increasingly conceive, commission, and release narratives not on the basis of their artistic merit or cultural worth, but "according to market needs and calculations" (Zipes 181).

In many regards, Zipes's assessment is correct. The landscape of the children's publishing industry along with the books that it produces has changed radically over the past few decades and the bulk of these alterations has been precipitated by the growing presence of big business in the lives of young readers. However, when niche market picture books are folded into this portrait rather than kept separate from it, the topography of children's publishing changes. Instead of a flat and uniform world, it becomes one containing peaks, valleys, and variations. While niche narratives, of course, are not panaceas that will right all of the wrongs within the industry, they do make its future seem less ominous—and, possibly, even somewhat hopeful.

Joel Taxel, in the closing remarks to his 2011 essay, "The Economics of Children's Book Publishing in the 21st Century," asserted about independent writers, books, and publishers: "Whether these smaller companies can compete in the U.S. and elsewhere over the long haul ... is a question crucial to the future of children's literature" (485). I could not agree more.

The Small Bang Theory: American Children's Literature in a Brave New Niche World

While this project has focused on the niche market influence in the realm of picture books, the move toward increasingly specialized subjects for an equally specialized audience has permeated many other facets of children's literature. During the past several decades, for instance, the genre broadly known as "Baby Books" has increasingly atomized. In previous generations, children from birth through age four were a relatively neglected demographic in the juvenile publishing industry. Seen as too young to enjoy or even focus on a book, infants, toddlers and preschoolers were not regarded as a lucrative market. Thus, both the number and the variety of reading materials designed for them were limited (Dwyer and Neuman 489–90). For decades, books for early readers were comprised of the standard slate of alphabet books, counting texts, and narratives teaching various forms of identification—be it colors, shapes, animals, or textures.

However, as Julie Dwyer and Susan B. Neuman have discussed, this trend began to change during the final years of the twentieth-century. Fueled in part by new scientific evidence affirming that "it is never too early to read to young children" (Dwyer and Neuman 489) and in part by the advent of new media technologies that gave rise to a whole new arena of interactive learning possibilities, a paradigm shift occurred. Whereas the literary choices of very young children had previously been restricted to a relatively small repertoire of concept texts, "[t]oday a superabundance of wonderful books awaits them due to the virtual explosion in publishing for the very young" (Dwyer and Neuman 489). Moreover, these already specialized texts are divided into even-more customized niches. Dwyer and Neuman, for example, sort this new outpouring of Baby Books by a myriad of classifying characteristics, from subject, theme, and format to age, authorial tone, and developmental skills both needed and taught (489–94).

Meanwhile, the entire genre of young adult (YA) literature has not simply become increasingly "nichified" over time; it has its origins in this ethos of specialization. As figures like Michael Cart, Jay Daly, and Sheila Egoff have discussed, this new facet of children's literature emerged in the years following the Second World War. These books were written in a new gritty style that came to be known as the "New Realism" (Cart 39; Daly 15), and they were also dedicated to specific and formerly taboo topics. S. E. Hinton's landmark novel *The Outsiders* (1967), for example, addressed the pressing topic of juvenile delinquency and gang violence. Meanwhile, the faux nonfiction text *Go Ask Alice* (1971) discussed the controversial issue of teen drug use. Finally, Judy Blume's groundbreaking narrative *Forever* (1975) tackled the sensitive subject of a young girl's first sexual experience. Given the way in which each of these books spotlighted a particular social, cultural, or personal difficulty that young people faced, they quickly became known as "problem novels" (Cart 24, 64–68). While this development greatly expanded the range of issues addressed in children's literature, it simultaneously narrowed the potential readership for any specific book. No longer were narratives for adolescents seeking to appeal to the broadest possible audience by engaging with universal experiences; instead, with their focus on a particular socio-cultural problem, they targeted a specific subset who were personally facing—or, at least, intellectually interested in—that particular issue.

This shift toward increasingly specialized books for young readers has prompted a shift in the advice that authors, editors, and publishers give to aspiring writers. Previously, in handbooks like May Emery Hall's *Writing the Juvenile Story* (1939) and Jean Poindexter Colby's *The Children's Book Field* (1952), budding authors were urged to choose common subjects that would have a wide appeal. In a chapter titled "What Makes a Good Book Good," for example, Colby stresses the importance of a story having "definite appeal" to a juvenile audience and then provides the example of *Walter, the Lazy Mouse* (7–8). May Emery Hall makes analogous suggestions throughout her text. In the opening chapter of *Writing the Juvenile Story*, Hall stresses to her readers how countless current children's writers "have made profitable use" of "modest, everyday material" and "[y]ou can, too, if you will form the habit" (11). Later, when listing tips for composing picture books, she recommends finding "a simple plot" and offers the example of a story where a child mistakes tulip bulbs for onions (Hall 16).

By contrast, more recent guides offer vastly different advice. Instead of urging budding writers to select subjects that will appeal to the largest possible audience, they offer the opposite suggestion. As *Writing for Children: Understanding the Needs of Young Readers* (2011) makes clear in its opening pages, the days of regarding the United States as a demographically homogenous nation are over: "Children live in a multicultural society and attend school with children from a wide range of other cultures and religions" (7). Given that American society has changed, so too must its literature. As *Writing for Children* informs aspiring authors, "young readers may be drawn from a wide range of cultures and religions, and stories should reflect this" (7).

Such messages are repeated in numerous other author blogs, how-to books, and informational websites. In a discussion about the current strengths of children's publishing on the Children's Literature Network, for instance, established author April Halprin Wayland remarks: "What's good is that children's literature, like cable TV, seems to be actively looking for niche audiences" ("There's," par. 3). Consequently, she informs aspiring writers that, no matter how seemingly unusual or obscure their narratives, "as the song in West Side Story says, 'There's a place for us'" ("There's," par. 3; emphasis in original). Meanwhile, Friesen Press offers "Niche Market Starter Publishing Packages" on its website ("Niche Market"). Moreover, these items are further customized. For example, there is one specifically designed for "Children's Publishing" ("Niche Market"). As the description explains, its "Children's Niche Market Starter package is best suited for titles that are created for a specific audience" ("Niche Market"). Finally, the most recent edition of *The Complete Idiot's Guide to Publishing Children's Books* (2008), by Harold D. Underdown, proudly proclaims that it "includes new chapters on self-publishing" ("Overview," par. 1).

As even this brief overview suggests, children's literature publishing in the twenty-first century is increasingly characterized by what Joseph Turrow has termed "niche envy." As he observes about the move away from mass appeal and toward specialized products: "Optimistic executives insist that such customization will 'satisfy [the] difference and diversity' of the American population" (Turrow 20). In the wake of the growing success of small-market, small-press books, children's writers, editors, and publishers are increasingly making the same argument. Max Rivlin-Nadler, writing about current trends in YA literature, remarked: "Publishers now follow the independent authors, not the other way around" (par. 5).

Chris Anderson, near the conclusion of *The Long Tail*, speculates on the impact that the niche market boom will have on the larger consumer climate:

> This shift from the generic to the specific doesn't mean the end of the existing power structure or a wholesale shift to an all-amateur, laptop culture. Instead, it's simply a rebalancing of the equation, an evolution from an 'Or' era of hits *or* niches (mainstream culture vs. subcultures) to an 'And' era. Today, our culture is increasingly a mix of head *and* tail, hits *and* niches, institutions *and* individuals, professionals *and* amateurs. Mass culture will not fall, it will simply get less mass. And niche culture will get less obscure. (182; italics in original)

While Anderson was not commenting on the growing number of specialty narratives for young readers, the picture books profiled in the previous chapters affirm this claim. Narratives like *It's Just a Plant* and *My Beautiful Mommy* do not signal the end of more conventional texts written by professionally trained authors and released by mainstream publishers; rather, they mark the advent of a parallel or companion commercial arena. To be sure, the sales tracking information on websites like Amazon and Barnes & Noble indicates that individuals who bought texts like *Little Zizi, Maggie Goes on a Diet*, and *My Beautiful Mommy* also purchased more canonical titles like *The Cat in the Hat, The Secret Garden*, and *Where the Wild Things Are*.

For this reason, Anderson sees the growth of niche products as largely complementing rather than competing with the conventional marketplace. In the wake of the increasing number of specialized services, he asserts: "we can now treat culture not as one big blanket, but as the supposition of many interwoven threads, each of which is individually addressable and connects different groups of people simultaneously" (Anderson 183–4). With both mainstream products and niche items enjoying strong sales, he advises that it is more instructive to "[t]hink 'and,' not 'or'" (Anderson 222). Previous business models cast the marketplace as a zero-sum game: if one product sells, then another does not. But, the new niche environment has room for both. As Virginia Postrel has written, "there are lots of bell curves, and pretty much everyone is on a tail of at least one of them. We may collect strange memorabilia or read esoteric books, hold unusual religious beliefs or wear odd-sized shoes, suffer rare diseases or enjoy obscure movies" (par. 7). Even if our unconventional interests are shared with only fraction of a percent of the population, "being unusual is not the same as being alone. In a country whose population tops a quarter billion, 1% of 1% is still tens of thousands of people" (Postrel, par. 3). Moreover, the Internet makes it exponentially easier for individuals with even the most obscure hobbies to locate, connect, and interact with others who share their interests.

Niche market picture books like *My Beautiful Mommy*, *Maggie Goes on a Diet*, and *It's Just a Plant* put this theory into action. Their unconventional subjects and viral advertising campaigns suggest that children's literature in the coming decades will be made, marketed, and managed far differently than it has been in previous generations. While this industry has historically been dominated by broadly themed books released by major publishing houses, the ongoing nichification of the marketplace portends that it will become increasingly receptive to work about specialized topics by amateur authors from small presses. As a consequence, this "brave new niche world" of children's literature has the potential to reinvent while it reinvigorates the genre.

Astrophysicists have long postulated "the big bang theory" as a means to account for the origins of the universe. In the wake of the growing presence of niche marketing in the realm children's literature, literary critics may soon be discussing "the small bang theory" with regard to books for young readers. In a millennial marketplace dominated by massive multinational corporations, bigger has long been seen as better. However, as the considerable commercial success of niche market picture books like *It's Just a Plant* and *Maggie Goes on a Diet* attest, a new and contrasting mantra is emerging in children's literature: think small. Chris Anderson has commented about the thrilling potential of a marketplace that is not restricted by the limits of available shelf space: "On the infinite aisle, everything is possible" (226). The same observation applies to the increasingly nichified world of books for young readers.

Seth Godin, in his book *Small Is the New Big*, commences his discussion of the new niche phenomenon with the following wake-up call and even battle cry: "How Dare You? How can you squander even one more day not taking advantage of the greatest shifts of our generation?" (xi). The picture books profiled in the previous chapters heed this advice. And, if this project has accomplished its purpose, then enthusiasts of children's literature will likewise realize the need to recognize and embrace, rather than underestimate or even ignore, this phenomenon. Niche products and promotions are changing not simply the isolated ways that books for young readers are being made and marketed; they are challenging the manner in which children's literature is being conceptualized and consumed. In this way, the bigness of this new smallness may be both more far-reaching and more multifaceted than previously imagined.

John B. Thompson, in *Merchants of Culture: The Publishing Business in the Twenty-First Century*, commented about the difficulty of making any lasting, concrete observations about a field as dynamic as contemporary publishing: "Writing about a present-day industry is always going to be like shooting at a moving target: no sooner have you finished the text than your subject matter has changed—things happen, events move on and the industry you had captured at a particular point in time now looks slightly different" (xi). This observation also applies to the realm of children's books. Only time will tell the full impact that the new trend in niche marketing has on the creation, construction, and consumption of books for young readers in the United States. That said, niche market picture books do not appear to be going away any time soon. From their widespread commercial success to their powerful cultural influence, these texts have been a growing presence in children's book publishing during the opening decades of the twenty-first century. Indeed, nearly every few months in the United States, another amateur-authored, independently published picture book about a controversial subject appears that becomes a sensation on social media and makes headlines around the nation. From past examples like *Help! Mom! There Are Liberals Under My Bed!* (2005) and *Why Mommy is a Democrat* (2006) to more recent ones like *My Parents Open Carry* (2011) and *Melanie's Marvelous Measles* (2012), these books have become recurring features of American popular culture, while they also embody potent sites of collection about a variety of social, political, and literary issues.

Anita Silvey, in an article from the early 1990s that commented on innovations in literature for young readers, remarked that "when I look at the last fifty years of children's book history, inevitably, almost always, the books that changed the industry were published contrary to all trends. By going against the current wisdom, creators and publishers set new standards and directions and gave children and young adults some of their finest books" (par. 2). While children's literature is commonly cast as a conservative genre—one whose primary aim is to acculturate boys and girls in the conventional manners and mores of society—she detected a contrary strain. "The ultimate irony about children's books," Silvey asserted, "is that, over time, the greatest successes come from those who defy the trends" (par. 8). Niche market picture books are poised to reaffirm the veracity of this observation. As a product of the powerful confluence of changing consumer tastes, socio-political conditions, and production modes, these narratives embody one of the most dynamic developments in children's publishing in the early twenty-first century. Whatever ultimate place the five specific texts that I profiled assume in literary history, one feature about the larger narrative category to which they belong seems clear: niche market picture books are not anomalies in the present; they are forerunners of the future.

Notes

1. It should be noted that a similar phenomenon has been occurring with the journals that review children's books. As sites like Media Source Incorporated reveal, many of the major publications that critique newly published narratives for young readers are owned by the same corporation. For example, both *The Horn Book Magazine* and *School Library Journal*—two of the arguably most influential publications about children's literature—belong to the same communications conglomerate. Their common ownership calls into question whether readers encounter a true diversity of perspectives when they examine reviews from these publications. Even more serious than this issue of a possible horizontal monopoly is that of a potential vertical one. If the parent company for various children's journals also has holdings in children's publishing, then their reviews possess a powerful conflict of interest at best and can be seen as mere cross-promotional puff pieces at worst. For more on this subject, see Media Source Incorporated.
2. I would like to thank an anonymous outside reader of an earlier version of this manuscript for first suggesting this implication of the niche market model.

Works Cited

Abate, Michelle Ann. *Raising Your Kids Right: Children's Literature and American Political Conservatism*. New Brunswick, NJ: Rutgers UP, 2010. Print.

———. *Tomboys: A Literary and Cultural History*. Philadelphia, PA: Temple UP, 2008. Print.

Abel, Ernest. "Prohibition. Marijuana—First Twelve Thousand Years." *Schaffer Library of Drug Policy*. Schaffer Library of Drug Policy. Web. 11 July 2011. http://www.druglibrary.org/Schaffer/hemp/history/first12000/10.htm.

"About the Author." Page for *My Beautiful Mommy*. BarnesandNoble.com. Web. 21 July 2009. http://search.barnesandnoble.com/My-Beautiful-Mommy/Michael Salzhauer/e/9781601310323/?itm=1.

"About the Author: Nathan Nephew." *My Parents Open Carry*. Amazon.com. Web. 24 October 2014. http://www.amazon.com/Parents-Open-Carry-Brian-Jeffs/dp/1618081012/ref=sr_1_1?s=books&ie=UTF8&qid=1413999341&sr=1-1&keywords=%22nathan+nephew%22.

"About the Book." *It's Just a Plant*. Web. 20 June 2011. http://www.justaplant.com/info/index.html.

"About Us." *Exodus International*. Exodus International. Web. 31 March 2013. http://exodusinternational.org/about-us/.

"About Us." *Groundwood Books*. Groundwood Books. Web. 8 January 2012. http://www.houseofanansi.com/aboutGroundwood.aspx.

Agovino, Theresa. "More Men Having Plastic Surgery." *CBS News*. CBS News, 5 December 2007. Web. 14 January 2012. http://www.cbsnews.com/stories/2004/06/14/health/main623083.shtml.

Alagna, Magdalena. *Everything You Need to Know about the Dangers of Cosmetic Surgery*. New York: Rosen, 2002. Print.

Alexie, Sherman. "Why the Best Kids Books Are Written in Blood." *The Wall Street Journal*. The Wall Street Journal, 9 June 2011. Web.

Aloha Publishers. Web. 18 January 2012. http://www.alohapublishers.com/.

American Psychological Association. *Report on the APA Task Force on the Sexualization of Girls*. Washington, D.C.: APA, 2010. Available full-text here: http://www.apa.org/pi/women/programs/girls/report-full.pdf.

American Society for Aesthetic Plastic Surgery. "Statistics." Press Center. Web. 14 January 2012. http://www.surgery.org/media/statistics.

Anderson, Chris. *The Long Tail: Why the Future of Business Is Selling Less of More*. New York: Hyperion, 2006. Print.

Anderson, Hans Christian. *The Ugly Duckling*. 1843. New York: North-South Books, 2008. Print.

Angell, Marcia. "The Illusions of Psychiatry." *The New York Review of Books*, July 14, 2011. Print.

Anonymous. *Go Ask Alice*. 1971. New York: Simon Pulse, 2005. Print.

Anslinger, Harry J. "Marijuana: Assassin of Youth." *The History of Drugs: Marijuana*. Ed. Jordan McMullin. Detroit: Thomson Gale, 2005. 62–71. Print.

Arana, Gabriel. "My So-Called Ex-Gay Life." *The American Prospect*. The American Prospect, 11 April 2012. Web. 10 March 2013. http://prospect.org/article/my-so-called-ex-gay-life.

Armentano, Paul. "Marijuana is Rarely Harmful to Your Health." *Marijuana*. Ed. Christine Van Tuyl. Detroit: Thomson Gale, 2007. 21–27. Print.

Avery, Susan. "Junior High: A New Pot-Friendly Book—for Kids." *New York*. NYMag.com, 10 January 2005. Web.

Bader, Barbara. *American Picture Books from Noah's Ark to The Beast Within*. New York: Macmillan, 1976. Print.

Banks, Amanda Carson. *Birth Chairs, Midwives, and Medicine*. Jackson: UP of Mississippi, 1999.

Barlow, Tom. "10 Toys that Likely Won't Be on Holiday Wish Lists." *NBC News*. NBC News.com, 22 November 2010. Web. 31 October 2014. http://www.nbcnews.com/id/40257937/ns/business-holiday_retail/t/toys-likely-wont-be-holiday-wish-lists/#.VFOunRYtHXI.

Barrell, Doris, and Mark Nash. *Reaching Out: The Financial Power of Niche Marketing*. La Crosse: Dearborn Real Estate, 2003. Print.

Beckett, Sandra L. *Crossover Picturebooks: A Genre for All Ages*. New York: Routledge, 2012. Print.

Bederman, Gail. *Manliness and Civilization: A Cultural History of Gender and Race in the United States, 1880–1917*. Chicago: U of Chicago P, 1995. Print.

Besen, Wayne. "TWO Calls on Focus on the Family to Drop Therapist as Conference Speaker After His Group Justifies Slavery." *Truth Wins Out*. Truth Wins Out, 24 September 2006. Web. 15 November 2015. https://www.truthwinsout.org/pressrelease/2006/09/7/.

Bettelheim, Bruno. *The Uses of Enchantment: The Meaning and Importance of Fairy Tales*. 1976. New York: Random House, 2010. Print.

Bettelheim, Bruno, and Karen Zelan. *On Learning to Read: The Child's Fascination with Meaning*. New York: Doubleday, 1982. Print.

Bianco, Anthony. "The Vanishing Mass Market." *Business Week*. Business Week, 12 July 2004. Web. 2 January 2012. www.businessweek.com.

Bingham, Jane. *Marijuana: What's the Deal?* Chicago: Heinemann Library, 2006. Print.

Bishop, Bill. *The Big Sort: Why the Clustering of Like-Minded Americans Is Tearing Us Apart*. New York: Mariner Books, 2009. Print.

Bishop, Rudine Sims. *Free Within Ourselves: The Development of African American Children's Literature*. Portsmouth: Heinemann, 2007. Print.

Blackless, Melanie, Anthony Charuvastra, Amanda Derryck, Anne Fausto-Sterling, Karl Lauzanne, and Ellen Lee. "How Sexually Dimorphic Are We?: Review and Synthesis." *American Journal of Human Biology* 12 (2000): 151–166. Print.

Blum, Virginia L. *Flesh Wounds: The Culture of Cosmetic Surgery*. Berkeley: U of California, 2003.

Blume, Judy. *Forever*. 1975. New York: Simon Pulse, 2005. Print.

Boodman, Sandra G. "Taking a Kid's-Eye View of Cosmetic Surgery." *The Washington Post*. 22 April 2008: HE05. Print.

Borst, Charlotte G. *Catching Babies: The Professionalization of Childbirth, 1870–1920*. Cambridge, MA: Harvard University Press, 1995.

Branford, Nathan. "In Defense of Dead/Absent Parents in Children's Literature." *The Huffington Post*. The Huffington Post, 23 September 2010. Web. 5 February 2014. http://www.huffingtonpost.com/nathan-bransford/in-defense-of-deadabsent_b_736998.html.

Brantz, Loryn. "If Disney Princesses Had More Realistic Waists." *BuzzFeed*. BuzzFeed, 29 October 2014. Web. 26 November 2014. http://www.buzzfeed.com/lorynbrantz/if-disney-princesses-had-realistic-waistlines.

"Brian Jeffs." Author Profile. *Amazon.com*. Amazon, Web. 24 October 2014. http://www.amazon.com/Brian-Jeffs/e/B00MKDV09K/ref=sr_ntt_srch_lnk_1?qid=1413999270&sr=8-1.

Brodsky, Phyllis L. *The Control of Childbirth: Women versus Medicine through the Ages*. Jefferson: McFarland, 2008.

Brooke, Lindsay. *The Ford Model T: The Car that Put the World on Wheels*. Norwalk: MBI Publishing, 2008. Print.

Brown, Margaret Wise. *Goodnight Moon*. Illus. Clement Hurd. 1947. New York: Harper Collins, 1991. Print.

Bruhm, Steven, and Natasha Hurley. "Curioser: On the Queerness of Children." *Curiouser: On the Queerness of Children*. Eds. Steven Bruhm and Natasha Hurley. Minneapolis: U of Minnesota P, 2004. ix–xxxviii. Print.

Buchanan, Phil. "What Capitalism Can't Fix." HBR Blog Network. *Harvard Business Review*, 23 January 2013. Web.

Burnett, Francis Hodgson. *The Secret Garden*. 1911. New York: HarperCollins, 2011. Print.

Burroughs, Edgar Rice. *Tarzan of the Apes*. 1914. New York: Ballantine, 1963. Print.

Butryn, Meghan L., and Thomas A. Wadden. "Treatment of Overweight in Children and Adolescents." *International Journal of Eating Disorders* 37.4 (2005): 285–93. Print.

Butler, Judith. *Gender Trouble: Feminism and the Subversion of Identity*. 1990. London: Routledge, 2006. Print.

———. *The Psychic Life of Power: Theories in Subjection*. Stanford, CA: Stanford UP, 1997. Print.

Butt, Sheila K. *Does God Love Michael's Two Daddies?* Illus. Ken Perkins. Montgomery, AL: Apologetics Press, 2006. Print.

Cameron, Joan, and Karen Rawlings Anderson. "'Circumcision,' Culture and Health-Care Provision in Tower Hamlets, London." *Violence Against Women*. Ed. Caroline Sweetman. London: Oxfam, 1999. 48–54.

Capshaw, Katharine. *Civil Rights Childhood: Picturing Liberation in African American Photobooks*. Minneapolis, MN: University of Minnesota Press, 2014. Print.

Carey, Benedict. "Psychiatry Giant Sorry for Backing Gay 'Cure.'" *The New York Times*. The New York Times, 18 May 2012. Web. 31 March 2013.

Carroll, Lewis. *Alice's Adventures in Wonderland and Through the Looking Glass*. New York: Penguin, 2003. Print.

Cart, Michael. *From Romance to Realism: 50 Years of Growth and Change in Young Adult Literature*. New York: Harper Collins, 1996. Print.

Centers for Disease Control. "Overweight Children and Adolescents: Screen, Assess and Manage." Web. 29 January 2012. http://www.cdc.gov/nccdphp/dnpa/ growthcharts/training/modules/module3/text/page5a.htm.

"Change." Center for Gender Wholeness. Web. 31 March 2013. http://gender-wholeness.com/main-cgw-page/change/.

Chapman, Steve. "Barack Obama on Weed." *Reason.com*. Reason.com, 4 February 2008. Web. 5 April 2013. http://reason.com/archives/2008/02/04/barack-obama-on-weed.

Coats, Karen. "Power, Voice and Subjectivity in Literature for Young Readers [Review]." *Children's Literature Association Quarterly* 36.3 (Fall 2011): 338–41.

Codey, Richard J. "Should States Ban Junk Food in Schools?" *The New York Times Upfront: The Newsmagazine for Teens*. Scholastic. Web. 15 November 2015. http://teacher.scholastic.com/scholasticnews/indepth/upfront/debate/index. asp?article=d0919.

Cohen, Richard. *Alfie's Home*. Illus. Elizabeth Sherman. Washington, DC: International Healing Foundation, 1993. Print.

Colby, Jean Poindexter. *The Children's Book Field*. New York: Pellegrini and Cudahy, 1952. Print.

Colomer, Teresa, Bettina Kümmerling-Meibauer, and Cecilia Silva-Díaz, eds. *New Directions in Picturebook Research*. London: Routledge, 2010. Print.

"The Compassionate Answer: Homosexuality Avoidable, Doctor Tells Parents." *San Francisco Faith: The Bay Area's Lay Catholic Newspaper* 2.7 July–August 1998. Web. 5 February 2013. Available full text at: *Lambert Dolphin's Library*, http://www.ldolphin.org/narth2.html.

Connolly, Sean. *Straight Talking: Marijuana*. Collingwood, Ontario: Saunders, 2007. Print.

"A Conversation with Brian Jeffs & Nate Nephew, Hosts of 'At Odds.'" *Red State Talk Radio*. Red State Talk Radio, 31 December 2013. Web. 22 October 2014. http://redstatetalkradio.com/redstatewp/?p=7060.

Cooney, Elizabeth. "Half of Boys Blame Victims for Bullying." *Boston.com*. The Boston Globe, 22 November 2010. Web. 2 October 2011. http://articles.boston. com/2010-11-22/news/29301964_1_color-victims-pill.

Cortés, Ricardo. *It's Just a Plant: A Children's Story about Marijuana*. Brooklyn: Magic Propaganda Mill, 2006. Print.

———. "Personal Story: Interview with Ricardo Cortés." *The O'Reilly Factor*. Fox News Network, 7 March 2005. *LexisNexis*. Web. 10 July 2011.

Cottin, Menena, and Rosana Faria. *The Black Book of Colors*. Toronto: Groundwood, 2008. Print.

Crampton, Gertrude. *Scuffy the Tugboat*. Illus. Tibor Gergely. New York: Golden Books, 1946.

"Creating a Book for a Niche." *Children's Book Creation*. Children's Book Creation, 5 April 2011. Web. 10 December 2013. http://childrensbookcreation.blogspot. com/2011/04/creating-book-for-niche-market.html.

Daly, Jay. *Presenting S. E. Hinton*. Rev. ed. Boston: Twayne, 1989. Print.

Davis, Kathy. *Reshaping the Female Body: The Dilemma of Cosmetic Surgery*. New York: Routledge, 1995.

Deardoff, Julie. "My Beautiful Mommy's Plastic Surgery." *Julie's Health Club*. Chicago Tribune, 18 April 2008. Web. 16 June 2009. http://featuresblogs. chicagotribune.com.

Desjardins, Patricia N. "In Defiance of Childhood?: An Exploration of Children's Activism." M.A thesis, Carleton University, 2007.

Donelson, Kenneth L., and Alleen Pace Nilsen. *Literature for Today's Young Adults.* 7th ed. Boston: Pearson, 2005. Print.

"'Don't Make Me Go Back Mommy': A Creepy Children's Book About Satanic Ritual Abuse." *Before It's News.* Before It's News, 13 August 2015. Web. 15 November 2015. http://beforeitsnews.com/power-elite/2015/08/dont-make-me-go-back-mommy-a-creepy-childrens-book-about-satanic-ritual-abuse-2449686.html.

Douglas, Susan J., and Meredith Michaels. *The Mommy Myth: The Idealization of Motherhood and How It Has Undermined All Women.* New York: Free Press, 2004. Print.

Dresang, Eliza. *Radical Change: Books for Youth in a Digital Age.* New York: H. W. Wilson, 1999. Print.

Duncan, Neil. *Sexual Bullying: Gender Conflict and Pupil Culture in Secondary Schools.* London: Routledge, 1999. Print.

Durham, M. Gigi. *The Lolita Effect: The Media Sexualization of Young Girls and What We Can Do About It.* New York: Overlook, 2008. Print.

Dwyer, Julie, and Susan B. Neuman. "Selecting Books for Children Birth Through Age Four: A Developmental Approach." *Early Childhood Education Journal* 35.6 (2008): 489–94. Print.

Edelman, Lee. *No Future: Queer Theory and the Death Drive.* Durham, NC: Duke UP, 2004 Print.

Edwards, Sue Bradford. "Children's Nonfiction: A Niche Worth Pursuing." *WOW!: Women On Writing.* WOW!: Women On Writing, 2011. Web. 5 May 2012. http://www.wow-womenonwriting.com/47-FE4-ChildrensNonfiction.html.

Egoff, Sheila. *Thursday's Child: Trends and Patterns in Contemporary Children's Literature.* New York: American Library Association, 1981. Print.

Elliott, Anthony. *Making the Cut: How Cosmetic Surgery Is Transforming our Lives.* London: Reaktion, 2008.

Engelhardt, Tom. "Reading May Be Harmful to Your Kids: In the Nadirland of Children's Books." *Harper's Magazine* 282.1693 (1991): 55–62. Print.

English, Bella. "'Snowplow Parents' Overly Involved in College Students' Lives." *The Boston Globe.* The Boston Globe, 9 November 2013. Web. 5 November 2014. http://www.bostonglobe.com/arts/2013/11/09/parents-overly-involved-college-students-lives/mfYvA5R9IhRpJytEbFpxUP/story.html.

Erzen, Tanya. *Straight to Jesus: Sexual and Christian Conversions in the Ex-Gay Movement.* Berkeley, CA: U of California P, 2006. Print.

"Exploit this Hot Kindle Niche; Easiest Kindle Niche to Tap Into." *Warrior Forum.* Warrior Forum, 22 October 2012. Web. 12 December 2013. http://www.warriorforum.com/warrior-special-offers-forum/699356-exploit-hot-kindle-niche-easiest-kindle-niche-tap-into.html.

"FAQs." *It's Just a Plant.* Web. 20 June 2011. http://www.justaplant.com/info/index.html.

Favaro, Avis. "'Maggie' Is Not on a Diet Anymore." CTV,14 October 2011. Web. 20 November 2014. http://ambulatorily2.rssing.com/chan-1594330/all_p1.html.

Fishberger, Jeffrey. "When Teenagers Question Their Sexuality." *Consults: New York Times Blog.* The New York Times, 29 September 2009. Web. 26 December 2013. http://consults.blogs.nytimes.com/2009/09/29/when-teenagers-question-their-sexuality/?_r=0.

Ford, Henry. With Samuel Crowther. *My Life and Work*. Garden City, NY: Garden City Publishers, 1922. Web.

Foucault, Michel. *Discipline and Punish: The Birth of the Prison*. 1975. Trans. Alan Sheridan. New York: Vintage, 1995. Print.

Frank, Thomas. *The Conquest of Cool: Business Culture, Counterculture, and the Rise of Hip Consumerism*. Chicago: U of Chicago, 1998. Print.

Freeman, Don. *Corduroy*. 1968. New York: Penguin, 1976. Print.

Friedman, Emily. "Kids' Book About Tummy Tucks, Nose Jobs." *ABC News*. ABC News, 18 April 2008. Web. 16 May 2009. http://abcnews.go.com/Health/BeautySecrets/story?id=4675368.

Friedmann, Susan. *Riches in Niches: How to Make it BIG in a Small Market*. Franklin Lakes: Career Press, 2007. Print.

"Fulfillment Service Agreement between 'Publisher' and Big Tent Books." Dragonpencil. com. Web. 22 October 2014. http://www.dragonpencil.com/HTML/sample_fulfillment.pdf.

Garofoli, Joe. "Parenting through the Haze." *SFGate*. San Francisco Chronicle, 22 April 2007. Web. 7 July 2011. www.sfgate.com.

Garrett, Anne G. *Bullying in American Schools*. Jefferson: McFarland, 2002. Print.

"George Rekers, Anti-Gay Activist, Caught with Male Escort 'Rentboy.'" *The Huffington Post*. The Huffington Post, 5 July 2010; updated 25 May 2011. Web. 19 February 2013. http://www.huffingtonpost.com/2010/05/05/george-rekers-anti-gay-ac_n_565142.html.

Gerber, Rudolph J. *Legalizing Marijuana: Drug Policy Reform and Prohibition Politics*. Westport: Praeger, 2004. Print.

Gibson, David. "John Paulk, Former Christian Ex-Gay Spokesman, Recants and Apologizes." *The Washington Post*. The Washington Post, 26 April 2013. Web.

Gilman, Sander L. *Making the Body Beautiful: A Cultural History of Aesthetic Surgery*. Princeton: Princeton UP, 1999.

"Go Your Own Way." *Publisher's Weekly*. Publisher's Weekly, 7 March 2011. Web. 18 December 2011. www.publishersweekly.com.

Godin, Seth. *Purple Cow: Transform Your Business by Being Remarkable*. New York: Portfolio, 2002. Print.

———. *Small Is the New Big, and 183 Other Riffs, Rants, and Remarkable Business Ideas*. New York: Portfolio, 2006. Print.

———. *Unleashing the Ideavirus*. New York: Hyperion, 2001. Print.

Goldstein, Patrick. "Oscars Foundering in Era of Niches." *Los Angeles Times*. Los Angeles Times, 5 March 2006. Web.

Gomi, Taro. *Everyone Poops*. La Jolla, CA: Kane/Miller, 1993. Print.

Gottfried, Ted. With Lisa Harkrader. *Drug Facts: Marijuana*. New York: Marshall Cavendish, 2010. Print.

Graham, Janice Barrett. *Me Tarzan, You Jane*. Illus. Andrew S. Graham and Lili Ribeira. Pleasant Grove: Tidal Wave Books, 2011. Print.

Gravelle, Karen. With Nick and Chava Castro. *What's Going on Down There?: Answers to Questions Boys Find Difficult to Ask*. Illus. Robert Leighton. New York: Walker and Company, 1998. Print.

Green, Richard. *The "Sissy Boy Syndrome" and the Development of Homosexuality*. New Haven: Yale UP, 1987. Print.

Green, Shari. "The Myth of Supermom." *Suite101*. Suite101, 1 September 2001. Web. 16 July 2009. http://www.suite101.com/article.cfm/post_partum/78872.

Greene, Jim. "Liposuction Recovery Time—What is Liposuction Recovery Period Like?" *EzineArticles.com*. EzineArticles.com, 20 March 2008. Web. 20 July 2009. http://ezinearticles.com/?Liposuction-Recovery-Time---What-is-Liposuction-Recovery-Period-Like?&id=1059524.

Gruner, Libby. "Blog U: On Children's Literature and Academic Administration." *Mama PhD*. Inside Higher Education, 5 October 2009. Web. 20 March 2011. http://www.insidehighered.com/blogs/mama_phd/on_children_s_literature_and_academic_administration.

Gubar, Marah. *Artful Dodgers: Reconceiving the Golden Age of Children's Literature*. New York: Oxford UP, 2009. Print.

Hade, Daniel. "Storyselling: Are Publishers Changing the Way Children Read?" *The Horn Book Magazine*. (September/October 2002). 509–17. Print.

Haiken, Elizabeth. *Venus Envy: A History of Cosmetic Surgery*. Baltimore: Johns Hopkins UP, 1997.

Halberstam, Judith. *The Queer Art of Failure*. Durham: Duke UP, 2011. Print.

Hall, May Emery. *Writing the Juvenile Story*. Boston: The Writer, Inc., 1939. Print.

Hardisty, Jean. *Mobilizing Resentment: Conservative Resurgence from the John Birch Society to the Promise Keepers*. Boston: Beacon, 1999. Print.

Harris, Sandra, and Garth F. Petrie. *Bullying: The Bullies, the Victims, the Bystanders*. Lanham: Scarecrow, 2003. Print.

Harrop, Amy. "This Kindle Niche Has Seen Over a 400% Increase Since Last Year." *Amy Harrop's Blog*. Amy Harrop's Blog, 14 September 2012. Web. 14 December 2013. http://amyharrop.com/this-kindle-niche-has-seen-over-a-400-increase-since-last-year/#.

Hatfield, Charles. "Comic Art, Children's Literature and the New Comics Studies." *The Lion and the Unicorn* 30.3 (September 2006): 360–82. Print.

Herron, Carolivia. *Nappy Hair*. New York: Random House, 1997. Print.

Hoad, Neville. "Arrested Development or The Queerness of Savages: Resisting Evolutionary Narratives of Difference." *Postcolonial Studies* 3.2 (2000): 133–58. *Humanities International Complete*. Web. 26 March 2013.

Hoffman, Heinrich. *Struwwelpeter*. 1845. Web. Available full-text via Project Gutenberg: http://www.gutenberg.org/files/12116/12116-h/12116-h.htm.

Hopper, Jessica, and Jane E. Allen. "'Maggie Goes on a Diet' Author Defends Controversial Teen Dieting Book." *ABC News*. ABC News. Web. 9 October 2011. http://abcnews.go.com/Health.

Hounshell, David. *From the American System to Mass Production, 1800–1932: The Development of Manufacturing Technology in the United States*. Baltimore: Johns Hopkins UP, 1984. Print.

Hurley, Robert. "Liberation through Story: Children's Literature and the Spirit of the Child." *International Handbook of Education for Spirituality, Care and Wellbeing*. International Handbooks of Religion and Education. Vol. 3 (2009): 1173–88. Print.

"I Can't Recognize Mommy Anymore!" Customer review of *My Beautiful Mommy*. Posted by "The Mystic Eye of the Hipster." *Amazon.com*. Amazon, 23 June 2008. Web. 31 October 2014.

"If the Dr.'s Plastic Work is as Bad as His Writing, I Would be Very Worried!" Customer review of *My Beautiful Mommy*. Posted by "jerseygirl_librarian." *Amazon.com*. Amazon, 22 July 2008. Web. 31 October 2014.

Ingram, W. Scott. *Junior Drug Awareness: Marijuana.* New York: Chelsea House, 2008. Print.

Italie, Leanne. "'Maggie Goes on a Diet' Upsetting Some." *Charlottesville Woman.* The Daily Progress (Charlottesville, NC), 7 September 2011. Web. 9 October 2011. http://www.cvillewoman.com/index.php/moms/article/maggie-goes-on-a-diet-upsetting-some/203207/.

Jackson, Kathryn. *The Saggy Baggy Elephant.* 1947. New York: Random House, 1999. Print.

Jefferson, Whitney. "*Maggie Goes on a Diet* Author Was 'Amazed' By Backlash." *Jezebel.* Jezebel, 23 August 2011. Web. 5 November 2014. http://jezebel.com/5833529/maggie-goes-on-a-diet-author-was-amazed-by-backlash.

Jeffs, Brian, and Nathan Nephew. *My Parents Open Carry.* Illus. Lorna Bergman. 2011. White Feather Press, 2014. Print.

Jenkins, Henry. "Introduction: Childhood Innocence and Other Modern Myths." *The Children's Culture Reader.* Ed. Henry Jenkins. New York: NYU Press, 1998. 1–37. Print.

Johnson, Crockett. *Harold and the Purple Crayon.* 1955. New York: Harper Collins, 1998. Print.

Jones, Abigail. "The Mother of Perfection." Boston.com. The Boston Globe, 15 May 2008. Web. 15 May 2008. http://www.boston.com/bostonglobe/editorial_opinion/oped/articles/2008/05/15/the_mother_of_perfection.html.

Jones, Laura. "Douching Is Bad for You." *TheBody.com.* TheBody.com, September/October 2000. Web. 20 July 2009. http://www.thebody.com/content/treat/art941.html.

Juniper J. "You Have GOT To Be Kidding Me." Customer review of *My Beautiful Mommy. Amazon.com.* Amazon, 1 August 2008. Web. 16 November 2014.

Kaoma, Kapya. "Exporting the Anti-Gay Movement." *The American Prospect.* The American Prospect, 24 April 2012. Web. 19 February 2013. http://prospect.org/article/exporting-anti-gay-movement.

Kaplan, Karen. "'Maggie Goes on a Diet' the Sensible Way in Children's Book." *Los Angeles Times.* Los Angeles Times, 23 August 2011. Web. 25 October 2011. http://articles.latimes.com/2011/aug/23/news.

Keats, Ezra Jack. *The Snowy Day.* 1962. New York: Penguin, 1976. Print.

Kennedy, Elizabeth. "Blue Apple Books." *Children's Book Publishers.* About.com. Web. 19 February 2014. http://childrensbooks.about.com/od/publishers/a/Blue-Apple-Books.htm.

Kiefer, Barbara Z. *The Potential of Picturebooks: From Visual Literacy to Aesthetic Understanding.* Englewood Cliffs: Prentice Hall, 1995. Print.

Kincaid, James. *Child-Loving: The Erotic Child and Victorian Culture.* New York: Routledge, 1992. Print.

King, Thomas, and Gary Clement. *A Coyote Solstice Tale.* Toronto: Groundwood, 2009. Print.

Kotzwinkle, William. *Walter, the Farting Dog.* Berkeley: North Atlantic Books, 2001. Print.

Kramer, Paul M. *Maggie Goes on a Diet.* Illus. Mari Kuwayama. Maui: Aloha Publishers, 2011. Print.

———. "Maggie Goes on a Diet." Message to Michelle A. Abate. 11 January 2012. E-mail.

Kuczynski, Alex. *Beauty Junkies: In Search of the Thinnest Thighs, Perkiest Breasts, Smoothest Faces, Whitest Teeth, and Skinniest, Most Perfect Toes in America.* New York: Broadway Books, 2006.

"Learn the Facts." *Let's Move!* Web. 18 January 2012. http://www.letsmove.gov/learn-facts/epidemic-childhood-obesity.

Lenain, Thierry. *Little Zizi.* Trans. Daniel Zolinsky. Illus. Stéphane Poulin. El Paso: Cinco Punto, 2008. Print.

Levin, Diane E., and Jean Kilbourne. *So Sexy So Soon: The New Sexualized Childhood and What Parents Can Do To Protect Their Kids.* New York: Ballantine, 2008. Print.

Lewis, C. S. *The Lion, the Witch and the Wardrobe.* 1950. New York: HarperCollins, 2000. Print.

Libal, Autumn. *Can I Change the Way I Look: A Teen's Guide to the Health Implications of Cosmetic Surgery, Makeovers and Beyond.* Philadelphia: Mason Crest, 2005.

Linneman, Robert E., and John L. Stanton, Jr. *Making Niche Marketing Work: How to Grow Bigger by Acting Smaller.* New York: McGraw, 1991. Print.

Lissim, Susan. "It's Just a Plant [Review]." *School Library Journal* 52.9 (September 2006): 164.

"Little Zizi." *Kirkus Reviews,* 28 March 2008. *LexisNexis.* Web. 2 October 2011.

"Little Zizi." *Midwest Book Review,* 2008. *The Free Library.* Web. 1 November 2014 http://www.thefreelibrary.com/Little+Zizi.-a0180100831.

Lowen, Linda. "Plastic Surgery Picture Book My Beautiful Mommy All About 'Pretty.'" *Women's Issues.*About.com, 18 April 2008. Web. 16 June 2009. http://womensissues.about.com/b/2008/04/18/plastic-surgery-picture-book-my-beautiful-mommy.

Lowrey, Janette Sebring. *The Poky Little Puppy.* 1942. New York: Random House, 2001. Print.

Lundin, Anne. "Little 'Pilgrim's Progress': Literary Horizons for Children's Literature. *Libraries & Culture* 41.1 (Winter 2006): 133–52. Print.

Lynch-Brown, Carol, and Carl M. Tomlinson. "Children's Literature, Past and Present: Is There a Future?" *Peabody Journal of Education* 73.3/4 (1998): 228–52. Print.

Lynn, Barry C. *Cornered: The New Monopoly Capitalism and the Economics of Destruction.* Hoboken: John Wiley & Sons, 2009. Print.

Madaras, Linda, and Area Madaras. *My Body, My Self for Boys.* New York: Newmarket, 2007. Print.

Maglaty, Jeanne. "When Did Girls Start Wearing Pink?" *Smithsonian.com.* Smithsonian, 8 April 2011. Web. 19 February 2013.

Mahoney, Sarah. "Keeping Amazon in Check: Consumers Keep Plucking up the Fruits of Bezos' Labor, But Privacy Crusaders Are on the Prowl." *Advertising Age* 1 June 2005: 13.

Mar, Jonathan, and Grace Norwich. *The Body Book for Boys: Everything You Need to Know About Growing Up.* New York: Scholastic, 2010. Print.

Marano, Hara Estroff. *A Nation of Wimps: The High Cost of Invasive Parenting.* New York: Broadway Books, 2008. Print.

"The Marihuana Tax Act of 1937." *Schaffer Library of Drug Policy.* Schaffer Library of Drug Policy. Web. 1 July 2011. http://www.druglibrary.org/schaffer/hemp/taxact/mjtaxact.htm.

"Marijuana for Kids." *Media Assassin.* Media Assassin, 10 April 2009. Web. 19 July 2011. http://harryallen.info/?p=3102.

Martin, Michelle. *Brown Gold: Milestones of African American Children's Picture Books, 1845–2002*. New York: Routledge, 2004. Print.

Mattern, Joanne. *Bullying: The Real Deal*. Chicago: Hinemann Library, 2009. Print.

Matulka, Denise I. *A Picture Book Primer: Understanding and Using Picture Books*. Santa Barbara: Libraries Unlimited, 2008. Print.

McGillis, Roderick. "Learning to Read, Reading to Learn; or, Engaging in Critical Pedagogy." *Children's Literature Association Quarterly* 22.3 (1997): 126–132. Print.

McKay, Hollie. "Bill Maher's Mockery of 'My Parents Open Carry' Book Spurs Sales." *Fox News*. Fox News, 14 August 2014. Web. 22 October 2014. http://www.foxnews.com/entertainment/2014/08/14/bill-mahers-mocking-my-parents-open-carry-book-spurs-sales/.

McMullin, Jordan. Foreword. *The History of Drugs: Marijuana*. Ed. Jordan McMullin. Detroit: Thomson Gale, 2005. 9–11. Print.

McNeal, Laura, and Tom McNeal. *Crooked*. New York: Random House/Dell Laurel-Leaf, 1999.

Media Source Incorporated. "Our Companies." Web. 22 November 2014. http://mediasourceinc.net.

Medical Marijuana Policy Project. "Medical Marijuana Helps Sick Patients." *Marijuana*. Ed. Christine Van Tuyl. Detroit: Thomson Gale, 2007. 41–49. Print.

Messenger, Stephanie. *Melanie's Marvelous Measles*. Bloomington: Trafford Books, 2012.

Michigan. House of Representatives. H. Res. 286. 89th Legislature (1998). Web. 5 January 2012. http://legislature.mi.gov/doc.aspx?1998-HR-0286.

Mehling, Randi. *Maijuana*. Philadelphia: Chelsea House, 2003. Print.

Mickenberg, Julia, and Philip Nel. "Introduction: What's Left?" *Children's Literature Association Quarterly* 30.4 (Winter 2005): 349–53. Print.

———. "Radical Children's Literature Now!" *Children's Literature Association Quarterly* 36.4 (Winter 2011): 445–73. Print.

———, eds. *Tales for Little Rebels: A Collection of Radical Children's Literature*. New York: NYU Press, 2010. Print.

Middleton-Moz, Jane, and Mary Lee Zawadski. *Bullies: From the Playground to the Boardroom*. Deerfield Beach: Health Communications, 2002. Print.

Milliot, Jim. "Carpe Diem." *Publisher's Weekly*. Publisher's Weekly, 1 March 2010. Web. 18 December 2011. www.publishersweekly.com.

———. "Finding Their Way." *Publisher's Weekly*. Publisher's Weekly, 3 March 2003. Web. 18 December 2011. www.publishersweekly.com.

———. "Independently Growing." *Publisher's Weekly*. Publisher's Weekly, 4 March 2002. Web. 18 December 2011. www.publishersweekly.com.

Minter, Shannon. "Diagnosis and Treatment of Gender Identity Disorder in Children." *Sissies and Tomboys: Gender Nonconformity and Homosexual Childhood*. Ed. Matthew Rottnek. New York: NYU, 1999. 9–33. Print.

Mintz, Steven. *Huck's Raft: A History of American Childhood*. Cambridge: Belknap/Harvard UP, 2004. Print.

"Mommy's Makeover: Book Explains Plastic Surgery to Kids" *Today*. NBC, 23 April 2008. Web. http://www.msnbc.msn.com/id/21134540/vp/24272192#24272192.

Moran, Joe. "The Role of Multimedia Conglomerates in American Trade Book Publishing." *Media, Culture and Society* 19 (1997): 441–55. Print.

Munsch, Robert. *Love You Forever*. 1986. Illus. Sheila McGraw. Tonawanda: Firefly, 1995.

"My Parents Open Carry." Web. 23 October 2014. www.myparentsopencarry.com.

National Society for the Prevention of Cruelty to Children. "The NSPCC Working Definition of Sexual Bullying." NSPCC. Web. 2 October 2011. http://www.nspcc.org. uk/Inform/resourcesforteachers/classroomresources/sexual_bullying_definition_ wdf68769.pdf.

Nel, Philip. "Is There a Text in This Advertising Campaign?: Literature, Marketing and Harry Potter." *The Lion and the Unicorn* 29 (2005): 236–67.

Newman, Lesléa. *Heather Has Two Mommies*. 1989. Illus. Diana Souza. Los Angeles: Alyson, 2000. Print.

"Niche." *Oxford English Dictionary*. 2nd ed. 1989. Print.

"Niche Market Starter Publishing Packages." *Friesen Press*. Friesen Press. Web. 28 November 2012. http://friesenpress.com/packages/niche.

Nicolosi, Joseph. "Homosexual Behavior as Reparative Theatre." *NARTH*. NARTH Institute, 29 January 2013. Web. 3 February 2013. http://narth.com/2013/02/ homosexual-behavior-as-reparative-theatre/.

Nicolosi, Joseph, and Linda Ames Nicolosi. *A Parent's Guide to Preventing Homosexuality*. Downers Grove: IntervarsityPress, 2002. Print.

Nikolajeva, Maria. *Power, Voice and Subjectivity in Literature for Young Readers*. New York: Routledge, 2009. Print.

Nikolajeva, Maria, and Carole Scott. *How Picturebooks Work*. New York: Garland, 2001. Print.

Nodelman, Perry. "The Eye and the I: Identification and First-Person Narratives in PictureBooks." *Children's Literature* 19 (1991): 1–30. Print.

———. *The Hidden Adult: Defining Children's Literature*. Baltimore: Johns Hopkins UP, 2008. Print.

———. "The Other: Orientalism, Colonialism and Children's Literature." *Children's Literature Association Quarterly* 17.1 (Spring 1992): 29–35. Print.

———. *Words about Pictures: The Narrative Art of Children's Picture Books*. Athens: U of Georgia P, 1988. Print.

———. "Words Claimed: Picturebook Narratives and the Project of Children's Literature." *New Directions in Picturebook Research*. Eds. Teresa Colomer, Bettina Kümmerling-Meibauer, and Cecilia Silva-Díaz. New York: Routledge, 2010. 11–26. Print.

Nodelman, Perry, and Mavis Reimer. *The Pleasures of Children's Literature*. 3rd ed. Boston: Allyn & Bacon, 2003. Print.

O'Donoghue, Jennifer L., and Karen R. Strobel. "Directivity and Freedom: Adult Support of Activism among Urban Youth." *American Behavioral Scientist* 51.3 (November 2007): 465–85. Print.

Office of National Drug Control Policy. "Marijuana Resource Center: State Laws Related to Marijuana." The White House. Web. 22 October 2014. http://www. whitehouse.gov/ondcp/state-laws-related-to-marijuana.

———. "The National Drug Control Budget: FY 2013 Funding Highlights." The White House. Web. 22 October 2014. http://www.whitehouse.gov/ondcp/ the-national-drug-control-budget-fy-2013-funding-highlights.

Oliver, Christine, and Mano Candappa. "Bullying and the Politics of 'Telling.'" *Oxford Review of Education* 33.1 (February 2007): 71–86. Print.

Op de Beeck, Nathalie. *Suspended Animation: Children's Picture Books and the Fairy Tale of Modernity*. Minneapolis: U of Minnesota P, 2010. Print.

Osgerby, Bill. *Youth Media*. London: Routledge, 2004. Print.

"Outrage of the Week." *Entertainment Weekly* 14 January 2005: 91. Print.

"Overview: *The Complete Idiot's Guide to Publishing Children's Books.*" *Barnes & Noble.* Barnes & Noble. Web. 22 October 2014. http://www.barnesandnoble.com/ w/complete-idiots-guide-to-publishing-childrens-books-3rd-edition-harold-d-und erdown/1100624920?ean=9781592577507.

Paley, Maggie. *The Book of the Penis.* New York: Grove, 1999. Print.

Paoletti, Jo B. *Pink and Blue: Telling the Girls from the Boys in America.* Bloomington: Indiana UP, 2011. Print.

Parker, Amber Dee. *God Made Mom and Dad.* Illus. Hannah Segura. Bridge Logos, 2013. Print.

Paul, Lissa. *The Children's Book Business: Lessons from the Long Eighteenth Century.* New York: Taylor & Francis, 2010. Print.

——. "Niche Marketing and the (Shallow) World of Crabtree." *Jeunesse: Young People, Texts, Cultures* 1.1 (Summer 2009): 169–83. Print.

Petri, Alexandra. "A Children's Book for Gun Rights? *My Parents Open Carry*—and Beyond." *The Washington Post* 6 August 2014. Print.

Pfister, Marcus. *The Rainbow Fish.* 1992. New York: North-South, 1999. Print.

Piehl, Norah. Headnote. "Teasing and Bullying Start Early." By Jane Katch. *Bullying.* Ed. Norah Piehl. Detroit: Gale, 2009. Print. 17.

Pietras, Jamie. "It's Just a Book." *The Village Voice.* The Village Voice, 22 February 2005. Web. 20 November 2013. http://www.villagevoice.com/2005-02-22/news/ it-s-just-a-book/.

Pitts-Taylor, Victoria. *Surgery Junkies: Wellness and Pathology in Cosmetic Culture.* New Brunswick: Rutgers UP, 2007.

"Plastic Surgery." ABC 7 Morning News San Francisco, 28 April 2008. *YouTube.* Web. 22 October 2014. https://www.youtube.com/watch?v=3OwNer7YqNQ.

Pont, Simon. *Digital State: How the Internet Is Changing Everything.* London: Kogan Page, 2013. Print.

Pope, Harrison G., Katherine A. Phillips, and Roberto Olivardia. *The Adonis Complex: How to Identify, Treat, and Prevent Body Obsession in Men and Boys.* New York: Simon & Schuster, 2002. Print.

"Post-Fordism." *The Sage Dictionary of Cultural Studies.* London: Sage UK, 2004. *Credo Reference.* Web. 14 December 2011.

Postrel, Virginia. "Alone But Not Lonely." *Forbes ASAP* 163.4, 22 February 1999. *Business Source Complete.* Web. 8 December 2011.

Potter, Beatrix. *The Tale of Peter Rabbit.* 1902. St. Louis: Turtleback Books, 1987. Print.

Price, Catherine. "My Beautiful Mommy." *Salon.com.* Salon, 17 April 2008. Web. 16 May 2009. http://www.salon.com/mwt/broadsheet/2008/04/17/beautiful_ mommy/print.html.

Prihoda, Deborah. *Mommy, Why Are They Holding Hands?* Hartline Marketing, 1996. Print.

Pugh, Allison J. *Longing and Belonging: Parents, Children, and Consumer Culture.* Berkeley: U of California P, 2009. Print.

Purcell, Andrew. "American Losing the War on Drugs on the Home Front." *Sunday Herald.* 19 June 2011: 30. Print.

Rekers, George. *Growing Up Straight: What Every Family Should Know About Homosexuality.* Chicago: Moody Press, 1982. Print.

Rivers, Ian, Neil Duncan, and Valerie E. Besag. *Bullying: A Handbook for Educators and Parents.* Lanham: Rowman & Littlefield, 2007. Print.

Rivlin-Nadler, Max. "The Rise of 'New Adult' Fiction." *Lulu Blog*. Lulu Blog, 28 December 2012. Web. 19 February 2013. www.lulu.com/blog/2012/12/the-rise-of-new-adult-fiction/.

Rix, Jallen. *Ex-Gay No Way: Survival and Recovery from Religious Abuse*. Scotland: Findhorn Press, 2010. Print.

Rochman, Bonnie. "'Maggie Goes on a Diet': A Kids' Book About Dieting? Not Without Controversy." *Healthland*. Time. Web. 25 October 2011. http://healthland.time.com/2011/08/25/will-fat-kids-become-popular-if-they-go-on-a-diet-maggie-goes-on-a-diet-makes-the-case/.

Rogers, Steve. "ABC's 'Extreme Makeover' Ratings Increase Sharply Versus Previous Week." *Reality TV World*. Reality TV World, 10 October 2003. Web. 21 July 2009. http://www.realitytvworld.com/news/abc-extreme-makeover-ratings-increase-sharply-versus-previous-week-1848.php.

Rose, Jacqueline. *The Case of Peter Pan; Or, the Impossibility of Children's Literature*. Philadelphia: U of Pennsylvania P, 1984. Print.

Rosenbaum, Marsha. "An Epilogue." *It's Just a Plant: A Children's Story about Marijuana*. By Ricardo Cortés. Brooklyn: Magic Propaganda Mill, 2006. n. pag. Print.

Rosenthal, Ed, and Steve Kubby. *Why Marijuana Should Be Legal*. 1996. Philadelphia: Running Press, 2003. Print.

Ruschmann, Paul. *Legalizing Marijuana*. 2nd ed. New York: Chelsea House, 2011. Print.

Saalfield, Peter James. "Is the Internet Polarizing Politics?" *Big Think*. Big Think, 2 January 2012. Web. 22 October 2014. http://bigthink.com/think-tank/is-the-internet-polarizing-politics.

Salisbury, Martin, and Morag Styles. *Children's Picturebooks: The Art of Visual Storytelling*. London: Laurence King Publishing, 2013. Print.

Salzhauer, Michael. *My Beautiful Mommy*. Illus. Victor Guiza. Georgia: Big Tent Books, 2008. Print.

Schafer, Alyson. *Breaking the Good Mom Myth: Every Modern Mom's Guide to Getting Past Perfection, Regaining Sanity, and Raising Great Kids*. Mississauga: John Wiley & Sons, 2007. Print.

Schiffrin, André. *The Business of Books: How International Conglomerates Took Over Publishing and Changed the Way We Read*. New York: Verso, 2000. Print.

Schmidt, Caitlin. "Open Carry Kid's Book a Sensation." *CNN*. CNN, 6 August 2014. Web. 22 October 2014. http://www.cnn.com/2014/08/06/living/open-carry-book/.

Sedgwick, Eve Kosofsky. *Between Men: English Literature and Male Homosocial Desire*. New York: Columbia UP, 1985. Print.

———. "How to Bring Your Kids Up Gay." *Social Text* 29 (1991): 18–27. Print.

Sekeres, Diane Carver. "The Market Child and Branded Fiction: A Synergism of Children's Literature, Consumer Culture, and New Literacies." *Reading Research Quarterly* 44.4 (Oct/Nov/Dec 2009): 399–414. Print.

Sendak, Maurice. *Caldecott and Co.: Notes on Books and Pictures*. New York: Farrar, Straus & Giroux, 1988. Print.

———. *Where the Wild Things Are*. 1963. New York: Harper Collins, 1988. Print.

Seuss, Dr. *The Cat in the Hat*. New York: Random House, 1957. Print.

———. *One Fish, Two Fish, Red Fish, Blue Fish*. New York: Random House, 1960. Print.

Shinn, Annys. "Building Apps for Children A Profitable Niche." *The Washington Post*. The Washington Post, 19 July 2010. Web. 14 December 2013. http://www.

washingtonpost.com/wp-dyn/content/article/2010/07/16/AR2010071605573. html.

Silvey, Anita. "The Problem with Trends." *Horn Book Magazine* 70.5 (1994): 516–17.

Simon, Daniel. "Keepers of the Word." *The Nation*. The Nation, 7 December 2000. Web. http://www.thenation.com/article/keepers-word.

Singer, Natasha. "Is the 'Mom Job' Really Necessary?" *The New York Times*. The New York Times, 4 October 2007. Web. 16 May 2009. http://www.nytimes. com/2007/10/04/fashion/04skin.html?pagewanted=print.

Sipe, Lawrence R., and Sylvia Pantaleo. "Introduction: Postmodernism and Picture-books." *Postmodern Picturebooks: Play, Parody and Self-Referentiality*. Eds. Lawrence R. Sipe and Sylvia Pantaleo. London: Routledge, 2008. 1–8. Print.

Sircar, Sanjay. "The Sense of the Nineties: Current Assumptions about Children's Liter-ature." *Children's Literature Association Quarterly* 24.1 (Spring 1999): 47–49. Print.

SIRIUS XM. Channel Lineup. Effective from July 1, 2011. Web. http://www.siriusxm. com/sxm/pdf/sirius/channelguide.pdf.

Smith, Katharine Capshaw. *Children's Literature of the Harlem Renaissance*. Bloomington: Indiana UP, 2004. Print.

Snyder, Solomon H. Foreword. *The Science of Marijuana*. 2nd ed. Ed. Leslie L. Iverson. Oxford: Oxford UP, 2008. v–vii. Print.

Solomon, David. Introduction. "The Marihuana Tax Act of 1937." *Schaffer Library of Drug Policy*. Schaffer Library of Drug Policy. Web. 1 July 2011. http://www. druglibrary.org/schaffer/hemp/taxact/mjtaxact.htm.

Somerville, Siobhan. "Scientific Racism and the Emergence of the Homosexual Body." *Journal of the History of Sexuality* 5.2 (1994): 243–66. Print.

Specter, Michael, and James R. Dickenson. "Politicians Line Up To Admit or Deny Past Marijuana Use." *The Washington Post* 8 November 1987: A1. Print.

Springen, Karen. "Mommy 2.0." *Newsweek*. Newsweek, 15 April 2008. Web. 15 May 2009. http://www.newsweek.com/id/132240/output/print.

Sreenivasan, Jyotsna. "Funny, Touching, Important." Customer Review of *Little Zizi*. *Amazon.com*. Amazon, 19 September 2009. Web. 22 November 2014.

Stallcup, Jackie E. "Power, Fear, and Children's Picture Books." *Children's Literature* 30 (2002): 125–58. Print.

Stanek, Linda. "Corporate Publishing and the Need for the Niche Publisher." *Ari's Garden*. Ari's Garden, 10 November 2011. Web.

———. "Organizations as Publishers—What New POD Capabilities Mean to You." *Ari's Garden*. Ari's Garden, 7 September 2011. Web. 19 September 2013. http://www.arisgarden.com/organizations-as-publishers—what-new-pod-capabilities-mean-to-you/.

Stephens, John. *Language and Ideologies in Children's Fiction*. London: Longman, 1992. Print.

Stockton, Kathryn Bond. *The Queer Child: Or Growing Sideways in the Twentieth Century*. Durham: Duke UP, 2009. Print.

Stossel, Scott. "Bibliosophy." *American Prospect* 12.2 (2001): 40–43. Print.

Subramaniam, Aarti, and Fe Moncloa. "Young People's Perspectives on Creating a 'Participation-Friendly' Culture." *Children, Youth and Environments* 20.2 (2010): 25–45. Print.

Sullivan, Deborah A. *Cosmetic Surgery: The Cutting Edge of Commercial Medicine in America*. New Brunswick: Rutgers UP, 2001.

Sutherland, Robert D. "Hidden Persuaders: Political Ideologies in Literature for Children." *Children's Literature in Education* 16.3 (1985): 143–57. Print.

Swearer, Susan M., Amie E. Grills, Kisha M. Haye, and Paulette Tam Cary. "Internalizing Problems in Students Involved in Bullying and Victimization: Implications for Intervention." *Bullying in American Schools: A Social-Ecological Perspective on Prevention and Intervention.* Eds. Dorothy L. Espelage and Susan M. Swearer. London: Taylor & Francis, 2004. 63–83. E-Book.

Sweetman, Caroline, ed. *Violence Against Women.* London: Oxfam, 1999.

Szalavitz, Maia. "The Dangers of Marijuana Are Exaggerated." *Marijuana.* Ed. Louise I. Gerdes. Detroit: Thomson Gale, 2007. 22–29. Print.

Taxel, Joel. "Children's Literature at the Turn of the Century: Toward a Political Economy of the Publishing Industry." *Research in the Teaching of English* 37.2 (November 2002): 145–97. Print.

———. "The Economics of Children's Book Publishing in the 21st Century." *Handbook of Research on Children's and Young Adult Literature.* Eds. Shelby A. Wolf, Karent Coats, Patricia Enciso, and Christine A. Jenkins. New York: Routledge, 2011. 479–94. Print.

"There's a place for us." *Children's Literature Network.* Children's Literature Network, 10 October 2011. Web. 8 December 2011. http://www.childrensliterature-network.org/magazine/whats-right/2011/10/10/theres-a-place-for-us/.

Thomas, Susan Gregory. *Buy Buy Baby: How Consumer Culture Manipulates Parents and Harms Young Minds.* New York: Houghton Mifflin, 2007. Print.

Thompson, John B. *Merchants of Culture: The Publishing Business in the Twenty-First Century.* 2nd ed. New York: Plume/Penguin, 2012. Print.

Torgovnick, Marianna. *Gone Primitive: Savage Intellects, Modern Lives.* Chicago: U of Chicago, 1990. Print.

Trites, Roberta Seelinger. *Disturbing the Universe: Power and Repression in Adolescent Literature.* Iowa City: University of Iowa, 2000. Print.

"Tummy Tuck Recovery." *DocShop.com.* Einstein Industries, Inc., 2008. Web. 20 July 2009. http://www.docshop.com/education/cosmetic/body/tummy-tuck/recovery/.

Turner Corporation. "Company History." *Funding Universe.* Funding Universe. Web. 14 June 2011. www.fundinguniverse.com/company-histories.

Turrow, Joseph. *Niche Envy: Marketing Discrimination in the Digital Age.* Cambridge: MIT Press, 2006. Print.

"Ugh." Customer review of *My Beautiful Mommy.* Posted by "M." *Amazon.com.* Amazon, 13 August 2014. Web. 31 October 2014.

Underdown, Harold D. *The Complete Idiot's Guide to Publishing Children's Books.* London: DK Publishing, 2008. Print.

United States. Executive Office of the President of the United States. FY 2013 Budget and Performance Summary: Companion to the National Drug Control Strategy. April 2012. Web. 5 April 2013.

Van Allsburg, Chris. *Jumanji.* Boston: Houghton Mifflin, 1981. Print.

Van Tuyl, Christine. "Facts About Marijuana." Ed. Christine Van Tuyl. Detroit: Thomson Gale, 2007. 111–2. Print.

———. Foreword. *Marijuana.* Ed. Christine Van Tuyl. Detroit: Thomson Gale, 2007. 9–12. Print.

Vernon, Alex. *On Tarzan.* Athens: U of Georgia, 2008. Web.

Vigna, Judith. *I Wish Daddy Didn't Drink So Much.* Morton Grove: Albert Whitman, 1988. Print.

———. *Mommy and Me by Ourselves Again*. Morton Grove: Albert Whitman, 1987. Print.

———. *My Big Sister Takes Drugs*. Morton Grove: Albert Whitman, 1990. Print.

Viorst, Judith. *Alexander and the Terrible, Horrible, No Good, Very Bad Day*. 1972. New York: Simon & Schuster, 1987. Print.

Walker, Leslie. "Looking Beyond Books: Amazon's Bezos Sees Personalization as Key to Cyber-Stores' Future." *The Washington Post*. 8 November 1998: H01. Print.

Walzer, Lee. *Gay Rights on Trial: A Reference Handbook*. Santa Barbara: ABC-CLIO, 2002. Print.

Warner, Judith. *Perfect Madness: Motherhood in the Age of Anxiety*. 2005. New York: Riverhead Books, 2006.

White Feather Press. *White Feather Press*. Web. 15 November 2015. http://www.whitefeatherpress.com.

Wilhoite, Michael. *Daddy's Roommate*. Los Angeles: Alyson, 1991. Print.

Willems, Mo. *Knuffle Bunny*. New York: Hyperion, 2004. Print.

Winkler, Kathleen. *Cosmetic Surgery for Teens: Choices and Consequences*. Berkeley Heights: Enslow, 2003. Print.

Wolkomir, Michelle. *Be Not Deceived: The Sacred and Sexual Struggles of Gay Men and Ex-Gay Christian Men*. New Brunswick: Rutgers UP, 2006. Print.

Writing for Children: Understanding the Needs of Young Readers. Launchpoint, 2011. E-Book.

Young, Iris Marion. "Pregnant Embodied: Subjectivity and Alienation." *Feminism and Philosophy: Essential Readings in Theory, Interpretation, and Application*. Eds. Nancy Tuana and Rosemarie Tong. Boulder: Westview, 1995. 407–19. Print.

YoungMiller, Christian. *Everybody Has Those Thoughts: So It Doesn't Mean You're Gay*. RateABull Books, 2010. Print.

Zipes, Jack. *Sticks and Stones: The Troublesome Success of Children's Literature from Slovenly Peter to Harry Potter*. New York: Routledge, 2001. Print.

Zuckerman, Diana. "Teenagers and Cosmetic Surgery." Commentary. *Virtual Monitor*, March 2005. National Center for Health Research. Web. 19 July 2009. http://www.breastimplantinfo.org/what_know/teencosurgery.html.

Index